When Love Gives You Lemons...

When Love Gives You Lemons...

~∞~

THE CURIOUS DATING LIFE OF COURTNEY SCHELLIN

Courtney Schellin

Courtney Schellin

Legal Disclaimer

This work depicts real events and moments in my life based on my memories. The stories I am sharing are as truthful as my recollection permits and/or can be verified. Good thing I don't delete text messages and photos.

However, this is a book of memories, and memories have a story to tell. Some are in much more vivid detail than others. In some instances, dialogue consistent with the nature of the person speaking has been filled in. However, all the people within these pages are actual human beings and there are no fictional characters. Though, I have changed the identities of many of them to protect their privacy.

If I'm being honest though, there are quite a few chapters in here who I probably should've just let wear their shame. Still, I'm not in the mood to get sued. So you're welcome, I suppose.

THE HOLY BIBLE, NEW INTERNATIONAL VERSION®,
NIV® Copyright © 1973, 1978, 1984, 2011 by Biblica, Inc.™
Used by permission. All rights reserved worldwide.

Copyright © 2023 by Courtney Schellin

All rights reserved. No part of this book may be reproduced in any manner whatsoever without written permission except in the case of brief quotations embodied in critical articles and reviews.

First Printing, 2023

FOR MY SISTER, HAILEY

No matter how many lemons are thrown our way, I know I can always count on you to turn them into cocktails we can sip. I know God has someone perfect picked out for us.

We're not late to the party, we're right on time.

"God is light; in him there is no darkness at all."
1 John 1:5

Contents

1	Introduction	1
2	Jared	14
3	Dirty Don	21
4	Tyler	35
5	Anthony	48
6	Keagan	58
7	Matt	80
8	Bradley... and Josh	119
9	Kenzo	151
10	Alex	174
11	Kyle	186
12	Marco	201
13	Jesse	221
14	Tanner	244
15	Rob	279

Acknowledgements	339
About The Author	345
Let's Connect	347

1

Introduction

I'm one month and two days away from my twenty-ninth birthday and I haven't had an orgasm from a guy in two years. Wait—no. That's an aggressive way to start. Let me try this again.

I'm in my green, fuzzy robe, typing in my iPhone notes about what could be the subject of the next Great American Novel and that's how I decide to start?

LOL, yeah right. Good going, slick.

Actually, I finally decided I'm going to write about something that has been sadly comical since I was a teenager—my dating life. Was this decision brought upon by the fact I went on a mediocre date last week on which I ended up getting wasted by the end? Perhaps. Why did I even let him come into my place? Not to mention that sketchy pill with the markings PLIVA that I stepped on and cracked this morning wasn't promising. Google shows it's a medication for depression, anxiety, or eating disorders. After that discovery and nearly having a panic attack that my German Shepherd, Boone, was about to sniff aka snort the white powder, I wiped up the pill and retreated back to my bed. And by bed, I mean mattress.

I step over no less than three takeout bags on my way there and plop into bed, being sure not to knock over a large Harry Potter coffee mug inscribed with "I solemnly swear I'm up to no good" and has two pieces of pizza crust and remains of white wine in it from when I had to mask my drink of choice for a Zoom class call. I reach for the Coors Light can next to my bed and take a sip. There's actually just water inside—it's my repurposed water cup I refilled in the sink since I'm too hungover to go downstairs and get a glass. I spy four books stacked next to my bed, too. *See, there is some evidence I'm a scholar! Well, MFA student. Let's not get episodic.*

I'm not even this dirty usually! It's just the hangover, I swear.

And my mattress is still sitting on the damn hardwood for the last six months thanks to the ridiculous number of wrong items—none of them being my actual bed slats—sent to my house by Birch Lane. Now the headboard, still in plastic wrap, and the canopy kit just awkwardly stare at me across the room. Thankfully we've become accustomed to each other after months of neglect.

Wait—am I talking about the bed or me now? Who knows anymore.

I'm now on the phone with my best friend Kassidy talking about the different houses on Zillow she's looking to buy. I'm eating hard pizza crust that I forgot to refrigerate while simultaneously trying to create a poster print of Damon and Elena kissing in the rain from *The Vampire Diaries*. The stupid website won't let me make it as big as I want. Are there still twenty-eight-year-olds out there who watch *TVD* as obsessively as I do? There must be. Right? Meanwhile, Kassidy is bitching about not being engaged yet to her boyfriend of nearly six years, but little does she know, I already helped Tom design the 3-carat knockout of a ring. She says she deserves a big ring for waiting so long. I'm doing this in between swiping on the dating apps Bumble and Hinge. I just came across one guy whose profile read: "Usually a dealbreaker: I used to do porn."

Hey, maybe he's good in bed. I swipe right.

"It's a match!" The screen violently streams yellow and confetti my way.

Great. Now I'm matching with porn stars.

"Whatever," I say out loud to my blaring thoughts, now off the phone with Kassidy. I look over my iPhone screen at Boone, laying by my feet tucked into my green and orange bass-shaped fish flops at the end of my bed.

An Instagram notification pops up for an incoming video call from one of my random followers on my @courtdoessports account. I ignore the call to read some incoming DMs from the day. There must be something in the water: five marriage proposals, a sugar daddy offer, someone wants to be on a nude beach with me, another wants to smoke cigars in bed with me, and another sends me pictures of heart-shaped engagement rings and houses they want to buy me. Oh, and that one fuck boy I matched with a few months ago texted me today. I should've checked if it was a full moon that night. There probably was. At least there weren't any more messages from the guy who kept photoshopping me into photos with him. They started out with innocent scenes of us photoshopped on a park bench but then quickly transitioned to X-rated photoshop hack jobs with arrows pointing to where things were supposed to be going... as if the Pornhub screengrabs weren't self-explanatory enough.

"I deserve to get laid at this point," I say to Boone, looking for a response, petting him with my fish flop. His eyebrows are less than reassuring. *Ok, judgey.*

Apparently, I'm not the only woman in this dry spell. Well, "dry spell" meaning no orgasm from sexual interaction, I guess. I had sex last month, so you can't exactly call this a dry spell. But besides him having a really big dick, the sex wasn't much to write home about since I was worried my period cup was still in and if he could feel it. I didn't want to leave to take it out, but I also didn't want it to dislodge and risk my all-white bedspread looking like a small massacre. Needless to say, my mind was in other places. Still, the show must go on. And it did that night, for him anyway. The next morning I borderline forgot about him in my bed. That's because when I woke up, he wasn't in the bed, and so I kind of reminisced on it until I suddenly heard a toilet flush. He came back into bed and we laughed about the night and then did it again, but no grand finale from either party. I found out that morning he was in the middle of a nasty divorce and that he and his son had actually trick-or-treated past my apartment last Halloween. "Wouldn't that have been funny if we met that way," the 6'6" man said in a thick Boston accent, sounding and looking very much like Rob Gronkowski, New England Patriots tight end and party boy.

The sex wasn't bad—I'm not complaining. But I think it's just the fact that I'm having sex and not getting off that's more irritating. There's no priority given to the woman by the men. Or, at least, not by the men I'm sleeping with. Apparently, I'm sleeping with the wrong men, I've been told. I mean you'd think this is 2021 and guys should know where the clit is. Don't we deserve to be treated like queens by now? Is an orgasm too much to ask for? What happened to equal rights?

Woah, simmer down, Court. *You were on your period.* But *still.*

Regardless, back to the dry spell fact. People don't have sex with a lot of people, I guess. While drowning in thoughts of my own "number" I googled an average number or "body count," as the new kiddos call it, and an article published in 2019 said, on average, a person sleeps with seven partners in their lifetime. SEVEN. In their LIFETIME.

Is that a fucking joke? That can't be right.

I thought people were hoes, respectfully speaking of course. And by hoes, I mean normal. And by normal I mean, well, actually what the fuck does normal mean? I guess I just thought people liked sex as much as I do. And seven just won't do. Seven is like the number you used when lying in college so you sounded experienced enough, but not like too much of a slut. My college girlfriends and I used to joke about it while getting ready for our club nights out, usually on Thursdays, while gluing on fake eyelashes and putting on lipstick and three layers of bronzer.

SEVEN?

I mean, hell, I was on the light end of my friends' body counts, with my number tipping the scales at twenty-four bodies. I really don't know who came up with this "body count" reference, but saying it like this makes me feel really creepy-crawly, like I'm some serial killer like the guy from *Jeepers Creepers*. Anyways, I still don't think that twenty-four is *bad*, to be honest. And don't hit me with any of that "as a girl it should be lower" double standard bullshit.

Seriously, if you feel like that's raunchy, one of my past boyfriends by the age of twenty-four had eclipsed seventy-five partners and another had surpassed one hundred by the age of twenty-eight! One hundred people. One hundred bodies. *One hundred vaginas.* Can you imagine? Borderline impressive if you really think about it. Three were in one night at a Halloween frat party. He brought one Catwoman back to his room and when he left he was descended upon by another kitty cat. Like rapid fire. And to think, he was probably just wearing a Hawaiian shirt and a lei. Must've been those blue eyes and that Adam's apple. Or were the girls dressed as angels? Oh, the irony.

Unfortunately, I have been on the other side of a night like that and I had no idea I was body number two. It was Big-Little night for my sorority, and I was wearing this little red dress and massive platform wedges. I looked hot. If only I'd known I was number two; never in that dress, baby, could I be a number two. But I digress.

Maybe Californians like me and my exes are just more freaky than the rest of the population. I don't know. After all, I, as well as both of those previous boyfriends mentioned, hail from the good old Golden State. Certainly Arizona ranks up there too. Shout-out to the University of Arizona Wild Kitties and the Arizona State Sun Devils. The numbers coming out of those schools are like HOT DAMN. I knew this one girl who had hooked up with an athlete from every single pro sport. Probably even curling. She's what we might call a "cleat chaser," or, in her case, a "cleat collector."

Then again, maybe it's a Catholic school thing? How come whenever you're told not to do something you always want to do it more? I remember when we got "the talk" at school in our Family Life classes (similar to sex ed classes), and for homework we had to go home and ask our parents a series of questions. I sat in the kitchen digging my fingernail into our mahogany table, carving out my initials and a smiley face and heart, which would go unnoticed for years by my parents until it was too late to actually get mad at me. I went through the questions without looking up, mortified, asking them as my mom did the dishes and my dad likely searched the cabinets for popcorn.

"Did you and dad save yourself for marriage?" I asked.

"Well, —" my mom started.

I heard a spurt of laughter from my dad.

"Jay!" my mom yelled back at him.

"Psh, college cheerleader," he laughed, side-eyeing her.

She splashed water from the sink at him.

"Yeah, whatever college baseball player!" my mom said.

I slammed my workbook shut with so much force it might have been a thesaurus, just to make a point to these infidels, and stood up defiantly.

"I'm going to my room. And now I can't finish my homework because of, because of, because you... I'm just going," and I turned on my heels and left, mortified, with their chuckles still in the kitchen. *The sinners!*

In hindsight, this story always makes me laugh. My mom and I are close and can talk about almost anything. I try to keep the gruesome details to a minimum, but sometimes the moment is too good to pass up. For instance, the first time my mom and I road tripped to Boston seven years ago when I was living in Connecticut at the time, we were listening to the song "Truffle Butter" by Nicki Minaj and I couldn't resist.

"Mom, do you know what *truffle butter* is?" I asked, smirking, knowing damn well what I was doing.

She just kept smiling at the road driving, blissfully ignorant. "No! What is it?"

I then went into full detail trying to stay as monotone as possible.

"It's when a guy has sex with a girl in her butthole and then her vagina—"

"OK, stop."

"—and the mixture of poop and vaginal fluids..."

"I don't want to know."

"...creates this kind of butter-like substance—," me motioning with hand gestures now.

"Stop."

"So when Lil Wayne says "you don't have to tell her that I eat it in the morning," he's basically referring to—"

She started gagging. "COURTNEY, JESUS CHRIST I WILL PULL THIS FUCKING CAR OFF THE ROAD AND WE WON'T GO TO BOSTON. I DON'T WANT TO KNOW. I DON'T WANT TO KNOW."

At this I buckled over with laughter and responded, "Geez, just trying to keep you hip with the times, Mom!" winking at her.

She was less than thrilled in the moment and death-stared me longer than was probably safe to look away from the road. Now she laughs at the story and still tells it today. Honestly, I don't think my mom's number is below seven either. Seven. Psh, a joke.

Despite my higher-than-average count, tsk-tsk, I've never had an STD or accidentally wound up pregnant, so I guess there's that. I'm not saying that the sex ed teachers were wrong when they said we would get pregnant and die of an STD if we had sex one time, but let's just say I'm beating their odds 24-0, and that's just in bodies. I remember when my undergrad friends would turn twenty they would always say, "Congrats! You beat teen pregnancy" as if it were something that happened so regularly to our friends. Well, let's just say in Orange County it didn't. Not openly anyway.

It's not like I was going crazy sleeping around by the age of twenty either. Racking up my number. Racking up bodies. *Ugh*, I can barely even type it without gagging—why did you make this a thing, Gen Z?

I do think it's funny that someone like me—outgoing, fun-loving, sex-driven, confident (eh, bordering on cocky), a smack-talker, a little reckless (scratch the little, actually), and a booze hound—used to be a tomboy who was so shy when it came to boys, that I couldn't even talk to them. Well, romantically speaking, anyhow.

Do we have any *Sex and The City* fans in the house? I'm like a perfect combination of Samantha and Carrie, probably like 60% Samantha, 40% Carrie. Although, I'd say it's leaning back to 50/50 because here I am, now officially moved to the big city of Boston at age twenty-eight and I'm writing about my dating life. Doesn't get much more Carrie than that. All the women on the show are boss babes, just with totally different personalities. But at the end of the day, they all have needs in the bedroom just like any woman. I'm like the one who can't seem to find the right guy, so she decides to grab a cheeseburger and a cosmopolitan and write an article to mull things over while drunk-sexting an ex (Carrie), while also being the same girl who decides to do a striptease on Valentine's Day covering my naked body in a sushi buffet for some guy I just met that's way younger but totally adorable (Samantha). So how did *this* woman emerge from the same girl who in seventh grade at the handball courts ran away from the boy who asked her to be his "girlfriend"?

Maybe I hit my head one day and decided I was going to be a bad bitch. Nah, who am I kidding? I've always been a spitfire, as my mother likes to call me.

After I split my lip in half at the age of five at our Lake Tahoe cabin, my parents brought me to the hospital where the doctors said they needed to wrap me tightly in a blanket to keep me from flailing while they sewed my lip back together. They started forcing me into a blanket and I said I didn't want it, to take it off of me. I would sit still. My mom told the doctor to let me free.

"But, ma'am, she hasn't had pain medication yet and she's a child. She's going to throw her arms at us when it starts to hurt," the doctor said, or something like this at least.

"She won't." My mom looked at me way too confidently.

The doctor looked back to me, hesitant, and told the other doctors to unwrap me. With that, I shook off the blanket and according to my mother, stuck my split-in-half lip out by protruding my lower jaw at him and muttered two words out defiantly.

"Do it."

Some of my thick skin definitely can be credited to middle school boys. I knew at a young age I was going to work in sports broadcast or journalism, a male-dominated industry, so when it came to getting into classroom arguments of who the Green Bay Packers should draft or telling Brett Steed that quarterback Doug Flutie was not, in fact, the

GOAT, I was always well-equipped with confidence, facts, and stats. I read articles on ESPN.com on our shared family desktop when I could, until my sister would beg me off to play doll-dressing games with her best friend and read sad poetry and love poems about boys so they could cry. *Weirdos.* My older sister and her friends and I were not on the same wavelength, despite being just sixteen months apart. One time they made me dance in her bedroom to Chingy and the Ying Yang Twins by myself to see if I knew how to "freak dance" (aka grind) for the upcoming dance. Do you know what grinding alone looks like? It's not great. Especially from a lanky, seventh-grade girl with braces, highlights, acne, and low-rise bleached jeans. IT'S NOT GREAT.

On the braces topic: Fun fact, I had them for seven years. It was so long that my orthodontist actually felt bad for me and took them off just so I could have one class picture without braces. Actually, come to think of it, it was probably right around that time of freedom, fresh teeth and all, I caught a boy's eye. I'll never forget the first time a boy started showing interest in me in *that way*. Jake Adams. Fifth grade. Mrs. Persey's class. He would always stare at me in class and try and whisper across the room that he liked me. *Gross.* Funny enough, some men clearly haven't evolved much even today based on my recent Instagram DMs. But back to Jake. Finally, one day this bold little fifth-grade boy decided he was going to buck up and make sure I was his partner for when we had to dance with boys for Colonial Day. I was horrified to have to do so in my little bonnet and brown brigade of fabrics and hooped skirts, but there I was, waiting in line and going to have to dance with a boy and Jake wouldn't let anyone cut him no matter how many times I traded places with other girls in line. Finally his moment came, and he went to put his hand on my back and looked me in the eyes when I barely glanced at him and he told me straight to my face, "I really like you" with this big, cute grin. I immediately took his hands off of me and told the teacher he said something mean and he made me upset.

I LIED. I *never* lied. Shit, I still hardly ever lie.

He looked shocked and full of broken heart syndrome and as punishment he had to sit the next few hours of Colonial Day out. And I watched him receive his punishment. *Heartless, little colonial looking bitch.* Shit, maybe I needed a pitchfork, or a broom and pointed hat even. He just *liked you.* It's not like he loved you and broke your heart. Or ghosted you. Or fucked you over. Or fucked you second in one night without telling you. Damn, there were worse things.

Despite my propensity for pushing these odd feelings away, I did manage to snag a few of these so-called "boyfriends" in middle school and early high school, though I continued to run from them. And to think, now I can't get any of them to stay. Oh, how the tables have turned. Karma, you little slut, you. Colonial Day is going to haunt me forever, isn't it? Needless to say, when it came to feelings, I was (am?) a runner. But, when it came to insults and shit-talking back in the day, your girl could take the heat, especially if it was about me.

Like in seventh grade when Cam Grames called me an "acne-faced, thunder-thighed freak," because I liked Jake Adams better. Big mistake in hindsight. Trust me when I say Jake was no longer the sweet innocent boy from Colonial Day. Pretty sure he used to do whippets in our Spanish class and he and his friend would always laugh after they huffed and say "Waa, Waa, Wee, Waa!"

Or in sixth grade when those little shits, aka Jake and his friends, would chase me across the yard at recess to slap my ass the days I wore Dickies because I had a bubble butt in them. *This is a family establishment, damn it!* But their antics never really bugged me too badly. Maybe an occasional lash out or some typical teenage suicidal thoughts, but hey, we've all been there, serotonin be damned. But mess with my friends or my family? It's game over.

I remember one time walking up the stairs after lunch, this boy Jamie was making fun of my friend Sylvie's red hair and said it was ugly and I straight up, no hesitation, swung my metal SpongeBob lunch box and smacked him across the face with it. He immediately grabbed his face and started crying and said he was going to tell on me. I was scared but I held my ground, "If you do, I'll tell them what you said." He looked back at me shook.

Maybe that was the moment I changed. Or maybe it was in sixth grade when the boys were saying girls aren't as good as boys in sports. I decided if I could play softball, I was good enough to play baseball with the boys. I made my dad take me to the ballpark down the street in my pink converse and baseball bat in hand. And he taught me how to pitch a baseball. But before you get *Field of Dreams* or *A League of Their Own* going in your head, I really wasn't that great at softball so the baseball dream was really like a month-long pipe dream. I could either hit a triple or strike out looking. There really wasn't any in-between.

Once my dad had to step in to umpire a game because the ump didn't show up. My dad used to play in the minors for the Oakland A's and was an assistant coach, so they probably thought, *for sure bring in that guy*. I was up to bat and I let a strike go by. He called it. The next pitch went so high over the catcher's head and slammed into the back wall.

"Strike!" he yelled out.

Everyone gasped and I turned around to face my new nemesis.

"What the? That wasn't even close to a strike," I said, throwing my hands up.

"Better start swinging," he replied with a smirk.

Lesson learned. Even though I still wasn't a slugger. Just fast. Jesus—did I mention I have raging ADD? Like, actually. I'm sure it'll come up a few more times. Just a couple.

Something that might add to making sense of my decision-making skills is that I was plagued an optimist at birth—literally. After having autoimmune issues my whole life, one of my doctors found a new thing that wasn't necessarily a bad thing. Apparently my body doesn't break down serotonin well. Normally when people get happy and their brain produces serotonin, there's an enzyme that then breaks it down. My brain isn't producing this enzyme (or whatever he called it). In other words, once I'm happy and serotonin-juiced, I'm just on this happy high with it just bouncing back and forth in my brain.

So maybe I've made some mistakes, or questionable decisions to say the least, courtesy of my leveled-up serotonin ass. But no regrets. It's through these experiences I've become who I am today and I'm happy to report: I do still think the majority of people are good. That said, I do still believe there are people who are Satan out there. I don't think all men are trash, though at times I do seem to be stuck rummaging through the dump. Most importantly, I do believe Mr. Right is out there. And I do believe I'll find him. And I don't even care if that sounds corny or overly optimistic. You should know, despite these horrible dates, I still have hope and so should you.

If we're being honest, half these stories are one-time dates, half of them "just friends with benefits" kind of stories (HAH, like that ever works), some one night stands, some undefinable relationships, some actual boyfriends, some—er—"boyfriends?," and even some loves.

My dad always told my sister and me, "I want you to date it all, the assholes, the nice guys, the dickheads, the losers—I want this for you both so that when a good one comes along, you recognize him. And when you meet the right one, you'll know." To that standard, let's just say I'm killing it on Jay's requests.

Although, recently my Dad overheard me reading my dating profile out loud to my sister in the car and his response was "Jesus, Court! How are we ever going to get you married!" I guess he wasn't thrilled with my prompt and answers to questions on my profile being...

Dating me is like: Babes. Booze. Ball Games.

The key to my heart is: An ice cold 30 rack of Keystone Light or a bottle of Cakebread Chardonnay #getyouagirlwhodoesboth

Typical Sunday: Football. Beer. Football. Beer. FOOTBALL.

What! At least I was being honest.

Look, if you're going to get anything out of this book, I hope it's authentic. I hope it brings you back. I hope it makes you laugh. I hope it takes you away, like all good books do. I hope it teaches you something (likely, what not to do in many cases). I hope it's relatable. And I hope, in some ways, that it's not relatable, too. Because—fair warning—things will get dark at points. And I often push through the dark sides with a whole lot of sarcasm and a couple tablespoons of humor. I'm not a person who likes to hang out in the dark for too long. If you get stuck in parts where I'm being a bit reckless or juvenile or pounding wine or diving from bars into crowds and you're worried about me and wondering how the hell

I'm still alive or why I make the decisions I make, just know, you don't have to worry. The dark times don't define me, and sure, I've probably obliterated a few brain cells from binge drinking in college and maybe broken a toe or a tailbone here or there. Or taken a ride home from some nice, random trucker guy because my phone died. Or booked a flight to see a guy I haven't seen in seven years because he texted me, *"I'd die to be on a beach with you right now."*

Without further ado, let's take a trip down memory lane. The ghosts of Courtney's past dating life, one might say.

Welcome to my ridiculous, unrealistic, hilarious, pathetic, sad, amazing, human experience of the dating world.

Shall we?

2

Jared

The Tinder nightmare from hell. This one is an oldie, but a goodie. My sorority used to make me tell this story to incoming freshman girls because it always made people laugh.

This was my first dating app-generated date ever courtesy of Tinder. And this was when Tinder was brand new. Like it wasn't the hookup app it is now. You matched, barely talked, and met up. I actually kind of miss when it was like that. I remember when the spokespeople came to my sorority house and had us all download the app and I opened it up only to see my friends from Beta Beta Beta and the other frats on there, clearly having just gotten the talk we had. After a couple months, I got more into it. I would mass match and throw out the same opening line: "Cats or dogs?" They would always say dogs, and if they didn't, then I didn't respond. As soon as they would say "Dogs" I would respond back with, "Oh, so you don't like a good pussycat?"

Like I said, Tinder was the Wild West in 2013.

I matched with this guy Jared and did my same antics. Right off the bat, he wanted to go on a date. I hadn't actually gone on any dates using the app, I merely used it as an entertainment function to message and text guys. So when he was persistent about going on a date, I let the messages go by until one day he told me he had tickets to the next Dallas Mavericks game a few rows back and did I want to go?

Asking a sports girl to any sporting event is really like giving a twelve-pack of White Claws to a college freshman now. And a few rows back, too? Did I want to go? *Uhm, duh.*

I was nervous and decided to go to my friend's apartment building so when Jared picked me up, he wouldn't know where I lived. You know, just in case he was a serial killer or something. He showed up in an Uber to take us to the arena and he was in a white Henley tee and jeans. He looked good. I can't remember what I was wearing, but probably jeans, heeled boots, and some variation of a blue blouse in honor of the Mavericks.

We walked in and got beers together, and proceeded to head down to our seats, which were, as promised, a few rows back.

"Need another beer? I'm going to go grab one," he asked.

I thought he was joking since we had just come from the concession stand with beers, but I noticed the empty cup in his hand. He apparently had already crushed his. Odd—because I'm usually the drinker and the one who keeps up.

"No thanks! I'm still working on mine," I said smiling, looking down at my nearly full beer. *When the hell did he chug that?*

I started getting to work on mine, and he came down with his new beer. He sat down and we had some brief conversation about who was playing, and I mentioned some stats I had looked up prior to tip-off. He smiled at me, raising his eyebrows and taking a big swig of his beer, impressed. I told him it was just out of habit. I noticed he was going to town on beer number two, so I got back to taking a few big sips of mine. He crushed his second beer before the game had even started and asked if I wanted another. I said yes, and he arrived back to our seats just as tip-off was happening with my second and his third beer.

To balance the new beer cup and my almost-finished other beer, I tried to adjust my purse to the floor without it spilling out. I did this unsuccessfully as ChapStick, my Adderall prescription bottle, and an alligator hair clip fell to the floor below my feet and thankfully didn't roll down the cement to the chairs in front of us. He reached to help me and picked up the prescription bottle, naturally.

"Adderall, huh? I love Adderall. Do you mind if I take one?" he asked.

An odd question, but I didn't really care so I said sure.

"It's 25 milligram extended release though, just so you know. Sometimes that can throw people off," I warned him as he popped one in his mouth and swigged it back with beer.

I reminisced on the time I gave my good friend and total frat bro Perry one in the college library, and he ended up snorting it off the tables (classy) and running to me thirty minutes later saying he thought he was dying and *what the fuck* had I given him. I had to remind him it's extended.

"You're going to be fine, Perry! Maybe you shouldn't have snorted it, though." I said.

Jared and I kept drinking our beers and hooting and hollering at the game, but every time there was a break he was all over me. Like kissing me and then trying to make out with me, tongue in mouth, saliva swap AT A BASKETBALL GAME IN PUBLIC. Like bro, do you realize how close these people sitting next to us are? Let's just relax.

Still, I was loving the seats and getting free beer, so I held strong and probably added an inch to my neck in that night alone by keeping my face out of tongue's reach.

At halftime, I suggested we go up to the club bar, where at least, hopefully, he wouldn't try to mount me on the seats while people break for popcorn. He disappeared into the abyss of people leaning up to the bar, waving and flagging down the mere two bartenders serving the horde of humans. While waiting back, I met an adorable, much older couple and we started up conversation. Naturally, we talked basketball and Dirk and what was next for the Mavs. Suddenly, I heard behind me a slurred, "Yo, you trying to talk to my girlfriend or what?"

I turned, appalled and embarrassed, to see Jared coming over with what looked like whiskey-somethings. I blurted out laughing.

"Someone's getting a little ahead of himself!" I said looking to the older man. "We just met and we're on our first date."

I gritted my teeth to the old man and then to Jared. At this point, he didn't apologize or say anything and the older couple left us and said to have a good night. So awkward.

As if the Jack and Cokes were necessary, Jared continued crushing beers at the game, and since I was getting the likely twenty-two dollar beers for free, I said why not and had a couple more myself. Plus, it was the only thing I could use as a blocking device from his clingy mouth.

The game ended and we flooded out with the sea of people. He dropped a pin for us to get an Uber. I immediately texted my friend Ashley who was out and lying in wait in case I needed saving.

"Code Red."

She responded back something like, "Haha ok we are going to Standard Pour, meet there." Once in our Uber, I told Jared I wanted to go to The Standard Pour because it's one of my favorites—which wasn't a lie. He agreed and told the Uber driver to head to the bar. We walked in the door and Ashley wasn't there yet with the guy she was kind of dating, so that meant I was stuck with Jared until she came to the rescue. Great.

"Let's take shots!" he slurred out, flagging down a bartender and ordering dark liquor shots.

Upon delivery, he slid one to me in a large shot glass. "No, I have to work early tomorrow and I really don't think you need any either," I said.

"Fine. I'll do them both," he said, slamming back the first one and then throwing the empty shot glass over his head. *Yes, you read that right*—I said he threw the empty shot glass over his head into the people behind us. I looked behind him, shocked, wondering if it hit anyone or landed on some dinner goers table, only to watch him take the second shot and do the exact same thing again.

"What are you doing! They're going to kick you out," I said, hoping they actually would, but the bar was packed so I didn't know if anyone witnessed it.

From there, he began to tell me his name is not Jared but "Jinx," his drunk alter ego. It comes out when he's sloshed and being crazy. He let me know Jinx was out and about and ready to play. *No shit.*

Finally, Ashley and her man-friend walked in and pretended to run into us. But Ashley wasn't much of a savior, as she was all over her guy. The only time she came up for air is when she decided the guy I'm on the date with is really cute. She liked him.

"Literally, have him, dude. I will give you his number right now," I said, waving my phone at her.

Naturally, Ashley went up to say hi and introduced herself to him while her arm candy was likely in the bathroom. Jared had gone to pay for the shots he tossed into the oncoming traffic of people with a hundred dollar bill from his pocket. But rather than just pay the bill, he kept waving the hundred dollar bill around and then started taking photos of the Benjamin on the bar next to his bill. Then he tried to start climbing up on the bar. At this point, I was acting like I didn't know him.

Thankfully, I see one of the bartenders pointing him out and two people rush over to escort him out. Finally, a miracle!

"Courtney, they're kicking me out! Come with me," Jared said, arms flailing.

I just smiled and waved goodbye like the bitch I was allowed to be.

After I waved my goodbye, sayonara, hell-to-the-no, buh-bye, I hung with Ashley and her flavor of the month for a little, before grabbing a cab home since I had to be at the Dallas Cowboys Stadium at 6 a.m. for work. I walked out the door and all of a sudden someone grabbed my arm as I was waving to a cabbie.

"I've been waiting for you! People kept coming out but it was never you. Let's go home." The slurred words came from a half-alive Jared.

Shocked he had waited this whole time and a little freaked out, I basically yelled with wide eyes at him, "What? No! I'm going home."

"No, I want to come with you. I'm coming with you," he continued. He kept begging as I was getting in the cab repeatedly saying,

"*NoNoNoNoNoA ThousandFuckingTimesNo.*"

Finally the cabbie, irritated, put it in park. He pulled Jared's hand off my leg and started yelling at him.

"The woman says no! She mean no! Get out of here! Get!" The cabbie pulled Jared away from the cab door and shooed him away like some feral animal. He slid the minivan door shut. And I don't even know why, but I started to cry. My cabbie noticed I was crying and reassured me that I was better than that guy. He felt so bad for me he gave me the cab ride for free.

The next day my alarm went off at 4:30 a.m. and was likely snoozed multiple times before it was time to get ready and head to work. We always had to be on site six hours before game time. That said, I think it was probably about 9 a.m. when, at the stadium, my phone started getting berated with calls from Jared. 87 missed calls, 114 text messages, and 30-some voicemails. Impressive, I know. I was running around for work and didn't have time for this so I finally whipped out my phone to text him back.

"You have got to stop. I'm at work and I can't have my phone keep going off," I responded, not even reading his millions of messages.

"Oh, I'm sorry… I didn't realize you're working… Sorry… What happened last night???" he kept buzzing in.

He continued his berating of questions about what happened last night. I did the best I could responding to some of his messages, but frankly he must have started to understand the idea of what his antics included after I keyed him into his slamming fifty drinks and just throwing back an Adderall on top of it all. He tried to keep talking to me a couple times after that, but really, I think he had to have realized there was no way after date number one that I was up for a second.

Funny enough, I did run into him again in Dallas. At The Standard Pour.

My mom was in town visiting and I wanted to show her one of my favorite places. She, Ashley, and I had just walked in and went up to the bar to order when I saw Jared at the outdoor patio section talking to people.

"Oh shit!" I ducked down below the bar.

"What? What do you see?" my mom asked.

"That guy I went on the bad date with is here," I said, peering up at her from below the bar top.

Ashley looked around and spotted him and showed my mom. I popped up for air to peek again and, of course, just then he caught eye contact with me and his eyes lit up.

"Yup, that's it for me. We gotta go." I grabbed my mom's arm while ducking below the hordes of people trying to blend in and hide in the crowd.

We narrowly escaped without having to have a conversation with him. Still, after getting his number previously, Ashley ended up texting him for a little while after.

3

Dirty Don

When it comes to dating apps, I have this weird problem with either power-swiping or being really picky until I come across one person I can't decide on. And from there: terrible domino effect. I get all emotional about it. *Well, he does have a dog. But in this photo he looks cute. Aw, that's a sweet answer.* And then people I would never match with pop up and I just start feeling bad and I have to chuck my phone across the room. So I pop open a bottle of wine to ease this inner turmoil and, hello, Oprah.

You get a car! And you get a like! And you get a match!

At this point, I had just moved to Boston to go to grad school. I really didn't think I would go to school up North considering the majority of the schools I applied to were in the South. I had planned to get back to Texas or at least nearby where I could chase my dreams and hopefully find a good southern man to share them with. My mom saw the list of schools I was applying to and tears welled in her eyes.

"I don't know why you have to go so far away from me."

"Mom, we've talked about this. I want to move somewhere I can put roots down. I want to chase my writing dream and meet my future husband, hopefully, while I'm in school. The life I see for myself is me living in a home with a lot of land, where my husband can teach our kids to hunt and fish, and bring home some meat and we can cook it up. Do you honestly see that happening for me in California?"

I did appease her sadness by applying to five schools on her side of the Mississippi: Chapman (quite literally up the street), Boise State, Boulder, Texas, and LSU. The other side of the Mississippi included the bulk though.

When it came down to final schools, rejections, acceptances, and waitlists, Emerson was the final one standing. So off to Boston this Southern California girl went! My hunting and fishing southern man be damned. I'd just have to find him there. Maybe a transplant.

So when I moved to Boston I was fresh on the dating scene, but of course, there was a pandemic going on, so that wasn't exactly making things easy. To clarify where in the pandemic we were and ground you in this date, it was September 2020. In other words, we had passed the original frightful phase and moved into "Please, let this be over with" phase and had not moved into full blown "You must be wearing a mask" phase.

I had downloaded Bumble and Hinge and set my parameters thirty miles outside of Boston and was looking for someone who was at least six feet tall. Yep, that was the only standard set at the beginning of this fun. Six feet tall.

Before I was getting my Oprah on swiping, Don was actually one of my first matches. I had been in Boston for about a month and I had not met anyone. I had two friends in Boston, but we'd been too busy to see each other. I was taking three classes, but only two in person and it was all "mask on, six feet apart, don't even look at each other or you'll get the virus" kind of activity so making new friends wasn't exactly encouraged.

So, if anything I thought I could use dating apps to meet people and maybe make some friends. Yes, I'm that naïve.

Don popped up: 6'3" brunette guy, blue eyes, scruffy, went to Clemson, from South Carolina.

Southern guy? *Yes, honey.* Sign me up!

I swiped right. It's a match! YES.

We began talking and naturally it went to sports. I asked where he was watching the games that weekend. He said his parents were in town Saturday so he would be having a boozy day with them until the Clemson game that night. But would I want to Sunday Funday the next day? Absolutely, I would.

We would be going out in Southie, a bar haven in Boston. Sweet, sounds fun. He said it was the best place to go day drinking on the weekend. Needless to say, I was stoked. I was going to get to Sunday Funday with a living human being finally, so if the date sucked, who cared! He said we should add each other on Snapchat because he could send me funny drunk snaps with his dad that night. Sure, why not.

That night he sent me a couple snaps that said "taking shots," "chugging with dad," "go Tigers," that kind of thing, which consisted of close-up videos of his face chugging drinks and beers. I decided to creep on this guy's social media, but I couldn't find him on Instagram or Twitter.

Then he moved from the snaps to texting me.

So at first I was like, 9:30 a.m.? Yeah, that's totally normal for Sunday Funday since games start at 10 a.m. But then I remembered, this is the East Coast, not West Coast. Games don't start until 1 p.m.! Why the hell do we have to get there that early? And what am I going to do about my dog Boone? Do I want to drink all day with this guy I've never met?

I woke up the next morning prepared to do the damn thing, but weirded out by the urgency in us being there so damn early.

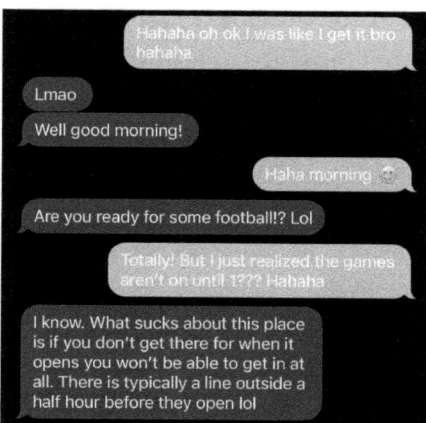

My Uber pulled up to the bar and I hesitated to get out because I wasn't sure this could be right. There was no line. Hell, there were no people inside even. The bar's sign said "Stats" up top though. I walked in and was seated immediately as I was their only customer. Despite being minutes late to Don's strict itinerary, he was not there. Fifteen minutes later, a typical frat-looking guy, sporting a red flannel, Patagonia vest, scruff, and Ray Bans nonchalantly approached my high top.

"Sup," he said without making eye contact, pulling out a seat.

I had to double-take because was this the guy I was meeting? 6'3" was about four inches too generous, and this man's face looked much rounder. But it was him. And who was I to judge a face being a little plumper than expected? We'd all put on weight during quarantine. Still, after that intro, I knew immediately this date was probably not going to be it.

I ordered a Coors Light and he got a pumpkin beer and a shot. I asked him if he wanted to get something to eat and he said he had to start out with liquids because he was struggling from last night and this was actually the scene of the crime.

"My mom went home before my dad because he wanted to stay out. He was like throwing around his black card and—you know what a black card is right?" he asked.

"HAH, yeah." *Douche.*

"So he kept throwing it down on the table going 'You hear that ting, boys? We drinking tonight.'"

I sipped my beer. "How long are they visiting?"

"Not long, they're looking to buy a vacation home on one of those islands."

"Islands? Oh... Nantucket?" I asked.

"Yeah, yeah, *Nantucket*," he said, nodding and sipping his beer.

He proceeded to tell me how poppin' Stats usually was. It was probably not today because it was the Patriots' bye week, he explained. Suddenly, I realized I needed to check my fantasy football lineup.

"Sorry, gotta check my fantasy," I said, scrolling on my phone.

"Fantasy football? Who you starting?" he asked.

I smiled.

We started talking football and odds and he realized I knew what I was talking about. I explained I had been a sports writer all my life working at ESPN and now I was going back to school to get my MFA in Creative

Writing at Emerson. I asked him what he does for work and he said very easily he worked for Barstool.

"Barstool Sports?" I tried not to sound too enthusiastic. "That's freaking awesome. What do you do for them?"

He went on to tell me he hosts one of the podcasts with a name I didn't recognize which was odd.

"I'm actually the one who broke the news about Cam Newton getting COVID, I got a tip so I got on Twitter," Don said.

"No way! So when you're getting breaking news, do you have to break it on Barstool or are you allowed to on your own account? At ESPN, we would have to break it through our stories or through the company profile," I said, showing him I was still in the know of how these things worked.

"No, we get to do it from our own."

But then things started clicking for me... *I already looked this guy up on social media last night. I couldn't find him. Surely someone who works for Barstool would be findable? Unless he had a nickname like KFC or Big Cat. Hmm.*

"So how did you get that job at Barstool?"

"I actually used to call into their show all the time and would mess with the hosts and back talk with them and then eventually they got to know my name and reached out about a job."

"That's so funny. That's seriously how it works nowadays in the sports world I feel like."

"Yeah, Portnoy was actually just texting me. He wants me to do a show tonight on the NFL games. I texted him I'm out because I'm out with you, but he said suck it up and don't be too hammered. But I'm going to ask some people to cover for me. I bet Kayce will. Do you know Kayce Smith?"

First off, Portnoy was just texting *this guy*? Could that really be true... and second off, do I know Kayce Smith? Uh, I don't know. Do I live under a rock? I didn't just like Kayce's Instagram post or anything. She's like one of the coolest chicks at Barstool. I decided to ignore the Portnoy comment and stick with Kayce.

"Yeah, Kayce is hilarious! Super hot, too. We actually have very similar vibes and target demographic I feel like." I pulled out my phone. "Here's some snippets of the sexy kind of sports shows I do on my Instagram, Court Does Sports, and on my Only Fans account."

His eyebrows lifted at the mention of Only Fans.

"Relax. Contrary to popular belief, Only Fans isn't just used for porn. The subscribers who pay and join mine looking for that are quickly disappointed."

He laughed as I showed him some quick sports video hits with my picks, odds, and bets for games and fantasy. He seemed impressed and not scared by the Only Fans thing and pulled out his phone and said he was texting Kayce.

"I should text her about you. I heard we're trying to do a new show that's more female sports focused and that would be right up your alley with the shows you do."

But was he *really* texting her? I mean, if he was, great! If not, what did I really have to lose at this point?

I went to the bathroom and texted my best friend Grant, who also worked in sports, about what was occurring on my date.

"I don't know him. Kinda weird we don't?" Grant replied.

Yeah, it is weird that we don't know this guy or his Barstool podcast.

"What did you do before Barstool?" I asked Don back at the table.

"I was actually working on a campaign in New Hampshire for the GOP and Republican Party before, so this is totally different."

"Woah, Trump supporter in Mass? That's rare, right?"

"Yeah, definitely. But I'm from the South—Charleston, South Carolina."

Uh, Charleston, too? Love that for me.

"In high school, I played baseball and got recruited right out to the local community college," he said but then quickly corrected himself nearly choking on his beer. "I mean, well—uh—actually the community college wanted me but then Clemson called and gave me a full ride scholarship as a pitcher."

Hold the phone.

Now he wasn't recruited by a community college, but rather, he got a FULL RIDE to a well-established SEC baseball program as a PITCHER? First off, no offense, he's not tall enough to be an SEC baseball pitcher that would get a full ride, especially to one of the top-tier baseball programs in the country. Still, I continued listening, sipping my beer, now calculating his facts.

"So then while I was in Clemson I ended up getting drafted into the Minor Leagues for the—"

From here he said some ridiculous team name and I laughed and reminisced with him about how Minor League mascots are always the most ridiculous team names.

He paused for a bit laughing and taking a sip of his beer as if the story was over.

"Uh, wait—so what happened?"

"What do you mean?"

"You went to the minors. Then you worked at the GOP. Why didn't you keep playing?"

"Oh! I, uh, threw my arm out," he said, looking away.

"Oh, like had to get Tommy John surgery?"

"Yeah, yeah! Tommy John!" he said pointing to me as he sipped his beer.

Okay, *hold the fuck up.*

Did I just feed him that answer? And what about that Nantucket answer before, when he had the same reaction? Something was up. Yeah, I've had a few beers at this point, but there's way too many coincidences going on here. And cool things, quite frankly. First off, what's the likelihood this Barstool guy gets paired up with me, Court Does Sports? This guy has to be lying. But is he that dumb? I worked in sports. The information he is feeding me is all very easy to look up. SEC baseball? Easily can check. Breaking COVID Cam news on your Twitter? Easy to check. Portnoy texting you? Dream on.

Yep, this guy was lying. My new favorite response would officially be "cool."

I go to the bathroom to update Grant with all the new information. He texted back quickly.

"Yeah, no one is that impressive," he replied.

I came back out to our table and he said he was texting Portnoy and Kayce. *Cool.*

Then he got to talking about how he posted something pro Trump on Twitter, and how a family member and him got into a heated debate so he was checking in on that. *Cool.*

He ordered us another round, ordering a drink with Pink Whitney, a Barstool-endorsed pink lemonade vodka, in it.

"Yeah I'm supposed to order this whenever I can to promote the company, ya know?"

I tried not to roll my eyes. "Oh, that's—*cool*... You must like working at Barstool, then?"

"Yeah but it doesn't pay much. I'm only making $200K," he said looking immediately at me to see my reaction.

My honest reaction was I wanted to burst out laughing, but instead I took a sip of my drink and, to his likely dismay, had no reaction other than my very original new reply of...

"Oh, *cool.*"

No one makes $200K in the sports journalism industry unless you're freaking Michael Strahan or someone legit. Certainly not some no-namer at Barstool. This guy was running out of lines and lies to use and fast. Was he keeping track? Because I certainly was trying, but I was even losing count.

After settling our tab at Stats, he said we could walk to some more bars in Southie and he could show me around since it was really fun on football Sundays. Sure, Don was full of shit, but how could I say no to that? I'm Court Does Sports. And since I had moved here, Court hadn't done any sports.

So we walked to this bar called Playwright which was awesome and had outdoor seating. But there were no TVs outside.

"Uh, don't you want to sit inside?" I asked.

"No, why?"

"Well, the football games. I'm trying to watch them and don't you have to do a show on them later?"

"Oh, it'll be okay if we miss a little of them."

So we sat outside and ordered more drinks and he ordered another with Pink Whitney in it while I tried not to roll my eyes into my skull.

Eventually I convinced him we should move inside and we talked about all the bets and the odds of the games and who we thought would win. He gave me some total tool bag line about how sports betting was more of a sport for Barstool guys than actually rooting for their teams. This guy really was a poster child for a Barstool frat guy. Well, there was the one thing—I was going out in Boston finally and talking sports and getting free drinks. Was he a compulsive liar? Probably. But the booze was cold, the football was great and therefore the Sunday Funday-ing was good, my companion be damned. And really, was he so different from some of my guy friends from college? Also, there was still the faintest glimmer of hope that this guy wasn't actually lying about his connections to the sports world.

We quickly stopped in at another bar, The Broadway, and ordered some drinks to go courtesy of COVID rules. With drinks in tow, he walked me through the rest of Southie to show me some more bars, only to realize because of the no time limit at bars at this point of COVID, we probably weren't getting in anywhere. We decided to bop over to one last place, Union Oyster House, somewhere I actually knew from my previous trips to Boston.

We ordered some more food and drinks, and he told me about his three roommates he shared a small apartment in Southie with. When the bill came, he didn't flinch. Looked like this one was mine. Which is fine, since he had picked up the other ones, but I was laughing back on his comment about making $200K a year and splitting a small apartment with three guys. *Yeah, OK, buddy.*

We decided to hit the bar next door, the oldest bar in America, The Bell in Hand Tavern, for one last drink since it seemed to be poppin'. We ordered and now I was significantly toasty from all the mixed alcohol. I knew he was, too, since he was slurring a bit.

I hit the bathroom and noticed a text on my phone from him while I was waiting to go in.

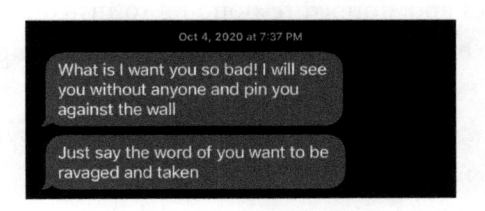

> Oct 4, 2020 at 7:37 PM
>
> What is I want you so bad! I will see you without anyone and pin you against the wall
>
> Just say the word of you want to be ravaged and taken

What the fuck. No dude, NOOO. At this point, I thought I had made our newfound friendship more of a "Hey, we're sports friends," or "Hey, we could be future coworkers maybe in sports," but apparently that vibe wasn't coming off clearly enough. Let's be frank here: He was decently attractive, but I was not into him like that. Like at all.

So I decided to pretend that his text didn't just happen and walked back to our table.

"Did you see my text?"

"Yeah." I said smirking, surprising myself that I was admitting to seeing it.

"So what do you think? Why didn't you respond?" he said smiling.

"No. Because... no, bro." I said laughing. "Absolutely not."

He actually laughed too and took the rejection pretty well.

"Ok, I get it. But hey I just dropped an Uber, let's go to your place to watch the last game since we're close to your house! And I know you gotta check on your dog. What's your address? Here just put it in actually since he's almost here."

I'm going to blame the booze and my desperation to actually have a friend to watch sports with on this one. He handed me his phone and I hesitantly, but unfortunately still did, typed in my address for our Uber to pick us up. *Cool, Courtney.*

We got to my place and for some reason my TV wouldn't turn on. Like at all. *What the actual fuck.*

Boone keeps bringing his tennis ball over to Don who keeps talking to me about God knows what now. I was laying on the couch, trying to get the TV on or trying to get the game on my phone at least but nothing was working. Finally, I just got on my phone and checked my fantasy scores and text messages and stopped responding to his conversation entirely. At this point, he had taken off my shoes and was rubbing my feet, which was as creepy as it sounds.

What the fuck, Courtney. Just tell him to leave. Why can't you just tell him to leave? You're not even watching the damn game.

But remember my optimistic plague and that stupid sliver of hope about him actually having sports world connections? I guess, deep down, I didn't want to offend him or something stupid. So my drunken plan to get him to leave? Have Boone do it for me.

I started giving Boone these crazy eye looks from him to Don, who was drunk and not paying attention and probably talking about Kayce or Twitter or the Chiefs game. Boone is super smart, like smarter than most people I know. And certainly smarter than this guy. I gave Boone the concerned look a couple more times back and forth from him to Don until Boone got the hint. His hair began to rise and he turned to Don and started growling at him.

"Woah, what's that about?" Don said, confused now, paying more attention to Boone.

"Looks like it's time to leave!" I said, probably too gleefully, finally having my excuse popping up from the couch.

"No, I think he just wants me to throw the ball?" he said, throwing the ball.

"No, it's late. It's probably time to go, I'm tired."

"Oh. Okay. I'll get an Uber."

When his Uber arrived, I gave him a peck goodbye and said I had a fun night. He said he did too and he'd let me know about what Kayce or Portnoy said. *Yeah, I won't be holding my breath on that one.*

I woke up the next morning with a nasty headache courtesy of the beers, Pink Whitney, mixed drinks, and I think Jameson sprinkled throughout our day. I decided to text him thanks for a fun day to follow up, but after I sent it all my memories began flooding back. So many ridiculous claims. Even beyond the whole Barstool bit. The dad and the black card. The vacation house. Breaking Cam Newton news. $200K a year. The GOP. SEC baseball. Minor Leagues. SO MANY CLAIMS.

I also remembered my friend Kassidy had a new subscription to this service they used for work to do background checks. I called her and told her everything, and said we got to look this guy up.

"I'm on it," Kassidy said.

I gave her what I had: phone number, Bumble info, and his Snapchat. As I gave her that information, I realized I already had caught a couple clues right there. His bumble account said he was from a city in South Carolina that was nowhere near Charleston.

Kassidy searched him with the phone number and BINGO. Not only did he have a criminal record, he had multiple! One for fraud, one that included the potential for abuse to an animal, and so many drunk in publics.

I flashbacked to him telling me one of his stories with Barstool was a video of him getting drunk and getting in a fight outside a bar and the video went viral. *Tool. Cool. Cool, tool.*

She then found his social media. Ah, the breaking of Cam Newton having COVID, you ask? He had shared on Facebook an article link from ESPN about Cam having COVID saying how much this would suck for the Patriots.

She then found his so-called Twitter battle with his family member, which apparently did happen, just on his private Facebook page.

At this point, I started freaking out. This guy was a pathological liar and now he knows where I live!

Kassidy kept digging and things went from being dark and scary to more just really freaking sad. She found the dad's Facebook profile and he posts like a fiend. Apparently he's unemployed, divorced, and eight months sober. Needless to say, his parents were definitely not getting wasted in Southie that weekend with him, picking up tabs with their black cards before looking at summer homes to buy in Nantucket.

Then Kassidy got a hold of photos of where he had supposedly grown up, and let's just say it wasn't Charleston or anything glamorous like the life he dreamed up to me.

But I still had lingering questions. Why Barstool? How did he know I would love sports and know Portnoy and Kayce? He didn't follow me on Instagram. How would he know that?

And then it hit me. He added me on Snapchat. @CourtDoesSports. I'm @CourtDoesSports on everything. It wouldn't be that hard to figure everything out.

Damn. So he literally looked me up the night before or morning prior and built his story and life catered to what I would like or be attracted to. Probably all to get laid, too. Sad. Really sad.

So I wasn't scared he knew where I lived anymore, just felt bad for the guy. He never texted me back, understandably so. How could he even have remembered all the lies he told?

The next weekend I was actually meeting some new potential friends after I finally sent a SOS text to my friend Melanie who had friends in Boston. She hooked us all up and I was going to brunch with this new group of girls. I showed up to my new friend Megan's house with a bottle of prosecco in hand and we all started getting to know each other. One of the other girls was telling us about two bad dates she went on when I jumped in.

"Oh let me tell you about the date I just went on! You know the show called Dirty John? I call him Dirty Don in honor of that."

I told them about all of our Southie day drinking escapades and all of his lies. They were in disbelief, but they were sure about one thing…

"I'm not surprised! That's Southie guys for ya!" one girl said.

"Yeah and they all look the same in their damn flannels," another chimed in.

"OMG, he was wearing a Patagonia vest and red flannel!" I said.

"Yep, typical! Watch out for the Southie guys."

NOTED.

4

Tyler

I woke up groggily in a dark room barely knowing where I was, then remembered the date.

What the fuck. Shit. Shit fuck. I slept here? What about fucking Boone! Jesus Christ. What time is it? I hate blackout curtains; they're so deceiving. At least I was alone. But then again, what did that say in itself? Never mind, I thought, shaking my head, shuffling around in the empty bed looking for my phone.

And I'm naked? Jesus Christ, Courtney! This is why taking tequila shots on the beach is not a great idea. Or maybe it's the best idea if you think about it? Ugh. But I really needed to blow off steam. I was very irritated at one of my professors, so when Tyler, one of my matches from Bumble, hit me up on that random Thursday I said fuck it.

Want to go to the beach? At night? Why not! What did I like to drink? I'll bring wine in a to-go cup, I said. He said he had Tito's and tequila too. But I was going to stick to wine because mixing with wine always equals blackout for me. Honestly, it's a known calculation for the body of Courtney at age twenty-eight: wine + any hard liquor = no memories. Like how sunny summer day + pale person = sunburn. So why do I think I'm more powerful than the sun aka the alcoholic elixir of mixing the two? Every. Damn. Time. When do people learn these things and grow up? I think I'm a late bloomer. Or maybe old dogs really don't learn new tricks. I don't know. But where is my phone? Where are my clothes? Where are my memories?

Ok, don't panic, Court. So what do I remember?

Well, obviously, Tyler picked me up. He got out of his car and opened the door for me, which was *so hot*. He was a really built, tall, broad-shouldered redhead with earrings. Earrings aren't really my thing, but totally not a deal breaker. He had a dope car by the way. Totally souped-up red Dodge Charger. As soon as I got in the car, I complimented it and he said thanks. Clearly, it was his baby.

We went through normal questions of what do you do, how's school, my teacher is a douche, etc., etc. He was a floor manager at the Encore casino, I was studying in grad school. We also joked about our first conversation a few weeks earlier via text, which was when I was waiting to get an Uber at the airport at midnight and they all kept cancelling on me. By the time I got one, my driver was driving the opposite direction of Boston and I joked with Tyler I was being kidnapped. So we shared locations for an hour so he knew I wouldn't get kidnapped.

About two minutes into the conversation he started coughing and making weird noises like he was choking.

"You got the 'Rona or something, bro?" I asked teasing, but actually kind of concerned. At this point, we are still in September 2020, so coronavirus madness had wound down and we still weren't at official mask mandates everywhere.

"No, uh, I have—(throat clear)—really bad allergies. Do you have a dog?"

Oh. My. God.

I remembered his profile said "no dogs" and I thought that just meant he didn't have dogs. *Shit.* This guy was so allergic to dogs that he literally was wheezing at Boone hair potentially on my clothing.

"Yes, I have a German Shepherd! Oh my God, I'm so sorry! I just bought this fur vest too, he hasn't even been near it! Are you going to be ok?"

Tyler insisted he would be fine and it would pass, hopefully. Glad we're off to such a great start. We haven't even gotten to the date and I've almost killed him.

As soon as we got to the beach aka his apartment overlooking the beach—(convenient huh?)—he said he just had to run in real quick to get a blanket and did I want to run up and take a shot with him? Now wine tipsy and feeling bad about his allergy, I way too quickly conceded.

"Sure!"

If my liver could shake it's head in disappointment at my idiocy, it did. I carried my Starbucks cup filled with wine and followed him into his apartment building.

His building smelled like cigarettes and was kind of sketchy honestly, but he was a big dude, so I felt happy to be with him at least. His place was small and still had Halloween decorations up and a gaming setup in the corner. I also spied a Millennium Falcon poster and a large fabric tarp with a mural of a shark on it.

"Yeah, I'm the guy who loves Halloween and keeps up decorations year-round..." he said hesitantly.

"Actually, I love Halloween. And is that the Millennium Falcon? I'm impressed. Also sharks are my favorite animal," I said pointing to the tarp over his bed. "I think we're going to get along just fine."

"Seriously?" he said, pulling up his shirt to reveal a shark tattoo with one hand while opening the freezer with the other, revealing bottles of Tito's and tequila. "Vodka or tequila?"

"Tequila, always. Vodka makes me crazy. Like I would probably make out with a wall kind of crazy."

"Hmm... You sure you don't want vodka then?" he said kidding.

"Yes!" I said laughing audibly. "Tequila, please!"

He poured my shot glass way too full but I took it like a champ. He grabbed a Yankees blanket and his mixed drink he made and I carried my wine cup as we headed to the sand. We were the only ones out, and it was a full moon. Plus, the weather seemed like just the right amount of crisp in the air. But once we plopped down on the sand it was actually kind of too chilly.

"Are you cold? Shit, I'm not wearing a jacket or I'd give it to you. I'll run and grab another blanket for you!"

"What! No. Are you sure? You don't have to!"

But he was already up and at it.

Well, that was sweet. I then realized no one knew I was on this last-minute date though, so I should text Kassidy at least. I told her and she texted me back quickly.

"Which one is this?"

I went to Bumble to take a screenshot, but he wasn't there anymore in my matches. *That's weird?* So I just screenshotted the tiny image I had dropped into his phone contact earlier when we first got each other's numbers. As I was sending that he showed up with the extra blanket and I started laughing thinking he saw my creepiness.

"Checking in with friends to make sure they know you're still alive?" he asked.

"Yes, actually! Sorry, she wanted to know who I'm on a date with so I only had this tiny screenshot from your contact from Bumble. I tried to find more to send her but you weren't there in the app? Isn't that weird? Then again, I don't know how to work these damn apps I swear."

"No, that's actually my fault..."

"How do you mean?" I said sipping my wine.

"Well, I actually unmatched you..."

I'm sorry—what?

"What! You unmatched me!"

"It wasn't like what you're thinking! Not because I was uninterested! Only because we talked for a little and then exchanged numbers and we stopped talking, so I just thought you were over it so I deleted you."

I started laughing, realizing now all our conversations had been on text after our initial conversation dropped off on the app.

"Wow! Okay, petty!"

He laughed.

"Well if I would've known I'm unmatched..." I said, teasing.

From there we snuggled on the beach and talked about all kinds of things: our families, friends, even exes. Eventually we headed back up to his place and decided to take more shots. Because, apparently, I have no self-control. He showed me his gaming setup because I asked, lights and all. I told him the guys from my office loved to game. I didn't mind watching sometimes, but I was not a gamer at all. Every time I tried to play *Call of Duty* I ended up with my gun facing the sky and running in circles. Not great.

But now here's where things get B L U R R Y. *How many shots did we take?*

Suddenly I'm jolted out of my thought process in bed due to a shirtless Tyler appearing in the doorway with a glass of water. *And damn!* His body is like *really sexy*. Well done, Court!

"Hey!" he said, smiling, setting down the water glass and climbing back into bed.

Play it cool, Court. But also, help me with my memories, my new acquaintance. Since you have clearly already seen me naked.

"So, I have a bit of a confession?" I said to his back now laying in front of me.

"Oh?" he said now rolling over to face me.

"I don't exactly remember the end of the night... Care to enlighten me?" I said with a big grin trying to play it cool.

"Ah, I see. We did take a lot of shots. What do you remember last?"

"Oh, let's not play that game!" I said like I was Alexis Rose from *Schitt's Creek*, smirking like an idiot. "Uhm, just start off from the beginning and I'll follow in with my memories."

He recapped all I knew and then things got wild. Like *WILD*.

"So after we took that round of shots you got up on my bar top in the kitchen—"

"Excuse me, what? I got on your bar..."

"Yeah and started stripping and tossing your clothes."

"Ok... Because that's normal," I said cringing and dying inside. *Tequila, you little bastard. That's usually Vodka's devil ass playing tricks like this on me.* It was times like these where it made sense why my friends from college always called me a NARP, as in "not a real person."

"So yeah, then you were naked dancing on the bar top and you pulled my head over and we started making out and then I went down on you on the countertop."

"You went down on me! And I don't even remember it? Damn."

"Yeah! And you liked it, too! Well, at least, it seemed like you did! You hopped off the countertop and then gave me a blow job, which was awesome."

"Nice. Cool. I mean, good..." *Jesus.*

"And then I said you looked so hot and wouldn't it be hot if I filmed it and you were totally into it and said yes. But my phone was dead so I used my iPod."

"I'm sorry, WHAT! There's a video of me giving you a blow job!"

"Yeah on my iPod! It's really short though I think. I couldn't keep it steady and barely filmed."

Lovely.

"Ok, well that needs to disappear like ASAP."

He laughed and said no problem he'd delete it.

"Then after that we came back in the room and had sex and then passed out."

"We had sex too? And I missed it! Damn it!"

"Yep," he said trying to stifle his grin, probably because I was making him feel guilty.

I was pretty pissed I had missed the wild night in my recollection, but honestly really grateful he was being so cool about it and decided maybe I wanted to remake those memories. Like seriously, this guy was a super nice dude. I liked him a lot for this. And he's hot. So like...

"Well, since I don't remember it the first time, I think you're going to have to jog my memory of how it went," I said and rolled over and pushed my butt into his groin, which led him to turn hard for me instantly.

Hey, if he was already adding to my body count, I might as well remember it.

"I think I can do that."

Since I was already naked—*psh*—getting straight to it wasn't exactly an obstacle. He pulled my hips back into him and fucked me from behind until he came onto my butt and my back. After he brought me a towel and dried me off, he disappeared into the other room and I realized I still had no clothes in this room. Only undies and a bra were on the floor.

"Uh, where's the rest of my clothes?" I said, emerging from the room naked.

"You stripped down in the kitchen but kind of threw them around." He pointed toward the kitchen area as he headed to the bathroom.

Unbelievable. Fucking cute, Courtney. My God.

"Oh, right!" I said with finger guns his way. *OMG, just stop.*

I saw my clothes, flung about as promised. I grabbed my shirt and put it on and then my fur vest only to realize it was wet. Bravely, I smelled the wetness—*liquor*. Apparently, Tyler said I had knocked over a shot on it during my countertop dance. *Great.* I put on the vest and decided to wear my soggy shame.

He had already said prior to sex he wouldn't mind giving me a ride and I was worried about Boone, but he was taking a while in the bathroom. I turned the corner to see him sitting on the toilet with his head in his hands.

"I'm not pooping I swear, I'm just dying."

"Oh, you're hungover too? That makes me feel a little better, honestly."

"Oh yeah, like dying. I took more shots than you did! I'm struggling. I honestly think I'm gonna puke. I'm so sorry," he said, motioning to close the door.

"Hey, don't mind me!" I said.

Bro, I stripped on your bar last night and made a sex tape with you on a 2000s iPod.

"No judgment here!" I beckoned on.

"Ok, I'll be back." He shut the door.

I went into the other room to let him do his thing peacefully. Well, as peacefully as yacking up vodka shots from the night before could be.

He emerged and apologized and I said I didn't hear anything. I asked if he wanted me to take an Uber? Would I mind since he was dying? No, not at all. The Uber ride went decently quick, but in a mask it was nauseating.

I got home and ran up to hug my poor Booney and immediately took him out. But he didn't seem too fazed. I turned off all the lights I left on for him, grabbed a White Claw to ease my headache, and went back to bed. A few hours later, I woke up to a text from Tyler that said he had a good time. Yay—same here, despite blacking out. We should do it again sometime? Totally. Next week work? Yeah, let's do it. He'll come over here.

The following week, Tyler showed up and said he had taken five Benadryl so he could meet Boone. *FIVE.* The poor guy. I would be sleeping like a baby if I took five Benadryl. He came in and met Boone and instantly started getting a scratchy throat despite the Benadryl. *Yeah, even if I did like this guy, there's no way this would work.* Whatever, we can just have fun, I guess.

He wanted to see around my place, so I gave him a little walk through and he tried to hide a smirk.

"Your place is so nice. I better not fuck this up."

I laughed and said thanks.

"Oh! While we're down in the kitchen I have to show you something!"

I pulled out my shark-shaped shot glasses and my wine glasses with sharks in them that make it look like the shark is swimming in blood when you're drinking red wine.

"See! I wasn't lying when I said they're my favorite! Them and alligators. Guess why?"

Only one person has ever guessed this right in my life, but we'll get to him later on. I think Tyler guessed that they were both predators or something.

"Nope, it's because they're the closest things we have to dinosaurs!

Well, besides birds and turtles. But they're not exactly dinosaur-like in terms of size and shock-and-awe factor."

"Well, should we give these shot glasses a go?"

"Oh God! Here we go again!" I rolled my eyes. "But sure, let's do one before dinner!" My liver likely scoffed at me.

"I'm going to do Jameson. And—actually, you're doing Jameson too because that's all I have!" I smiled, holding up the large green bottle. "Sorry, haven't gone to a liquor store lately and Jameson is really my go-to."

We did our first shots out of my shark shot glasses, and the shot glasses were clearly more for looks than actual function as a quarter of the shots slipped out the sides of the sharks' jaws and onto our faces. We both puffed cheeks, awkwardly swallowing the liquor, trying not to spit it out or laugh at how ridiculous we looked.

We decided to walk down the street from my brownstone to Legal Seafood for dinner. I asked if we could sit at a table facing the Alabama game and the Washington State game, preferably. Since no one was really there to watch football, they said they could switch on the WSU game next to the Alabama game, which was sweet.

"Oh, is there any game you want to see? The Bama game will probably be over soon," I asked Tyler.

He started laughing, but I didn't get the joke.

"Oh wait, I just realized you probably don't remember this conversation. I actually hate watching sports on TV. Totally not my thing," he said.

What. Oh God, honey no. This *absolutely would never work*. And I think my face said all of that.

He started laughing. "But if it was important to someone I was seeing, I'd be game to go to bars. I just probably wouldn't be paying attention."

I played it off but reminded him that I lived and breathed sports, and made a joke that it would probably never work with a wink. I ordered a glass of Cakebread chardonnay, because I was feeling boujee, apparently. Did I want a half bottle that would save me a few bucks? Sure, *wine not!* I, apparently, have short-term memory loss and forgot I just took a Jameson shot.

Surprisingly, Tyler didn't order a drink off the bat, so then I just looked like an alcoholic. *Greattttt.*

Thankfully, that didn't last long. Eventually he ordered a peach Bellini kind of drink that was custom made by the bartender for him. It was a total foo-foo pink drink, and there's something about big buff dudes drinking little pink drinks that makes me smile.

My dad is one of them. He always likes the strawberry, sugar-laden, rum-something drinks while I always order the "manly" drink that's usually dark and filled with bourbon or a smoky mezcal tequila. So, my Dad and my thing at bars would be when his drink comes out with a little umbrella or a pink flower garnish, I always take it off and plop it on mine to make my drink look more feminine and, in turn, his less so.

Somehow Tyler and I got into high school favorites as a topic. I told him I won Murphy's Law and they wrapped me in caution tape and caution cones and, ironically, my best guy friend won it along with me. Tyler said every year he won best laugh.

"When I was a kid I was watching *The Lion King* and the hyena scene came on and my grandma said 'See! That's what you sound like.' I was scarred after that," he said, starting to chuckle, sipping his tiny pink drink to mask his laughter.

I brought up our last date and how I can't believe the series of events. Oh, and that I hoped he deleted *that video.* I gave him an eyebrow raise. But he's a man and I know how these things work.

He smirked. "Ok, I haven't yet, but I will. I actually watched it the other day to see it and it was super blurry and not very long, but still it was super hot. I actually ended up jacking off to it," he said guiltily.

"Shut the fuck up," I blurted out, probably too loudly.

"Seriously!"

"Why didn't you text me and tell me! That's kind of hot."

He burst out laughing at this. "What! Uhm hey, we went on one date and I just whacked off to the blurry video on my 2004 iPod of you sucking my dick. Are you joking? You would've been like, *this guy's a fucking creep.*"

"Ok. Well, when you put it like that I guess you're right. But you do need to delete it!"

"Don't worry, I will. But it's not like I can exactly send it to anyone. I'm not joking when I say it's on like a 2000s iPod. I don't even know how to delete it. I'll have to Google it."

There's *no way* he's going to delete it. This video is going to resurface for sure one day. Hell, it'll probably make its debut once this gets read. I hope not. But I am curious to see it. Actually, maybe not. I start picturing myself in a liquor-covered fur vest—err, wait, no I was naked at that point I guess—giving a sloppy Gluck Gluck. Yeah, no—pass.

We get some octopus and split it and another appetizer, and by the time the bill comes out I reached for my purse. Tyler reached for his wallet and said don't worry I got this. I put my purse back down and I said thanks, but then he started doing the good old pants tap. You know, the pants tap, right? I've done it a thousand times courtesy of my ADD. It's the one where you know you forgot something and start tapping all your damn pockets. Yep. He forgot his wallet. He seemed embarrassed. No worries, I'll pick this one up. After all, I did order Cakebread wine, and a half bottle nonetheless, so I might as well.

We came back to my place and played with Boone before taking our party to the bedroom. We were making out and then I dropped down onto my mattress—still on the floor, by the way—my eyes level with his hardness through his jeans. I unbuckled his belt and pulled down his jeans and then his boxers to reveal something I wasn't expecting.

His penis was unlike any others I'd dealt with. Well, there was this one questionable time in Vegas, but I digress.

"Oh, wow."

I didn't just say that did I?

"What's up?" he asked.

"I didn't realize you were—uh—how do I say it? Like this?"

What the actual fuck, Courtney! Please shut up.

"What? Oh, uncircumcised?" he smiled. "You didn't remember I was?"

"Oh yeah, sorry I guess, I didn't! Why did you decide to have it like this?"

I did NOT just ask him WHY HE IS UNCIRCUMCISED. How many glasses of wine are in a half bottle? Oh wait—that first Jameson shot too, *duh*.

"Uh," he laughed a little. "Because I didn't want to be?"

"Oh, that's cool. Sorry! I've just never done this with one like this," I giggled.

Idiot.

"Well, technically you already have," he laughed.

HAH! He wasn't wrong. A week ago, I literally had this elephant trunk of a thing all up in my face and my mouth, filmed on a damn 2000s iPod and I didn't remember. *Tequila, man.*

I laughed and decided to start making out with him, and pushed him on the bed where he flipped me over to put himself into me. Honestly, he's so strong and his arms are so buff so whenever he flipped me around it was always such a turn on. Uncircumcised penis and all. We had a quick fuck sesh for about ten minutes, which led to fireworks for him and a happy camper out of me. Not because I came, but more so because I like seeing a job well done and a guy finishing.

Afterward we decided to watch a movie and I got dressed and put on my pink tie-dye sweatsuit and my *Frozen* Elsa socks and my pink glasses. *Like what?* Who did I think I was? Honestly, *who is Courtney Schellin*? What a question.

I asked if he liked horror movies and he said he did. *SCORE!* I never get to watch them as often now because I live alone in a big, old, historic brownstone that I just moved into and that seems like playing with fire. We watched some slasher, gory, terrible horror movie and I started falling asleep. I woke up on his shoulder and he said he probably should get going in a scratchy voice, his Benadryl likely wearing off. I kissed him goodbye and said we'd plan something soon.

We talked for a little after that. One day I texted him I was going to the casino but he said he wasn't working there anymore, but that he was thinking about me the other day and wanted to see me. I responded, but then let it fizzle out because, well, mainly I forgot to respond (typical), but also... no dogs and no sports? There's no way that could work for Court. I mean, *Court does sports*. And Court definitely loves *dogs*. No matter how much *Star Wars*, shark obsession, or Halloween and slasher films you throw into the mix, those two dislikes of his couldn't be remedied.

Still, Tyler is definitely in top dates since I've moved to Boston. Honestly, he probably is in the top two? And the only one I've gone on two dates with. But maybe that says something in itself about my reluctance to commit...

5

Anthony

So back to the dating apps in Boston we go. *Yay.*

I'd probably gone on about five dates at this point while being in Boston and it was mid-November. I came across this guy on Bumble who seemed like an honest-to-God teddy bear. Lives nearby, photo in a suit, photo at a wedding, photo being goofy drinking wine, photo weight lifting. The usual suspects were all in attendance.

But, like, he was a fucking huge teddy bear. Like a 6'8", 300-pound teddy bear. What can I say? I've always been a sucker for tall, big, ogre-like guys. They make me feel tiny and cute and they can pick you up. *So hot.*

So 6'8"? That's going to be a yes from me.

"It's a match!" came across the screen after swiping right.

I sent him a message and instantly got excited after hitting send. But then I immediately started looking through his profile photos and started getting too picky.

"Ugh! I hate these stupid apps!" I said, throwing my phone into my bed.

Regardless, we started talking and eventually exchanged numbers. But the more we talked the more I was like—err. Not because he was a bad guy, but because maybe I'm a shallow piece of shit apparently.

For example, he would text me about how much he enjoys the first snowfall and his words would be borderline poetic, and I'd be gritting my teeth reading them. *Like what a double standard, bitch! I'm a writer for God's sake.*

Or he'd tell me he was cooking, which I loved, but then when I would say what I liked to cook or confirm our upcoming plans he always responded with, "Awesome sauce." I decided to look past it. But when I called my sister Hailey and told her I was being a bitch about something stupid her reaction was less than helpful.

"Awesome sauce?" Hailey asked. "How old is he again?"

"Thirty-two."

"Oh—(long pause)—well it's probably nothing," she said, trying not to laugh.

But then when I FaceTimed my best friend Kassidy and told her, she wasn't about it either.

"Awesome sauce?" Kassidy asked. "He actually texts that to you."

"Stop. You know he does, I showed you the texts!"

"Right, right—(long pause)—well awesome sauce then," she said, raising her wine glass.

Fucking bitches. Damn it. I shouldn't have told them.

"Ok stop. He seems like a really great guy! And he said he's taking me to a 'classy restaurant' because I'm such a 'classy gal!'" I said with finger quotes, raising my eyebrows.

"Ooo, where? I'm looking up the menu now."

"It's called Tuscan Kitchen. Seems super swanky."

"Ok, pulling up menu now. Got it," she said, deep into her investigation on her computer. "Oh, I already know what he's going to order—tomahawk steak."

"What's that?"

"What! Courtney. You know what a tomahawk steak is. Dude, it's the one that is huge and comes with a bone in it and it takes up the whole table. I will bet money he orders this. Big guy, big steak."

He made us reservations at Tuscan Kitchen at 8:00 p.m. I curled my hair and did my makeup on point, wearing a sweater dress and boots. I was looking good. My Uber pulled up to the restaurant and I saw a large man waiting near the door. Like very tall. It had to be him. And he didn't have a mask on, which was also a plus in itself. I, unfortunately, did at first, because, Uber. I hopped out and ripped off my mask as soon as I could.

"Hi! You must be Anthony?"

"Hi! Yes, how are you? You look beautiful."

"Thank you!" I said, looking down smiling.

He opened the door for me and we went upstairs to the restaurant. It was swanky, indeed. We got seated, and a server came up swiftly asking for our drink orders. I deferred to Anthony, asking what he would be drinking—wine or cocktails? He said it was up to me, so I decided let's go with cocktails and start with martinis. I don't drink martinis often, but nice restaurants make damn good martinis. So I ordered a martini extra, extra dirty with bleu cheese stuffed olives and extra cold, as taught by my best friend Carly on how to order a martini that I actually liked. Anthony ordered the same. We had some small talk and I asked what he was going to order since I was intimidated by the price points next to the dishes on the menu.

"I don't know yet, actually. Oh wait—never mind. Yep, that's what I'm getting."

"What?"

"Tomahawk steak."

I tried not to laugh. Kassidy was right.

He ordered his tomahawk steak cooked rare. I decided to order a steak too, but a much smaller sibling in this scenario, the ribeye. Our waiter asked if we wanted another round of martinis, and since we were about halfway done, we said sure. *Coming right up.*

I thought we'd dive back into small talk, but Anthony hit me with the big dog questions.

"So what are you looking for in a partner?"

I was caught off guard and flustered. "Uhm, I don't know!"

"You don't know? Uh, I feel like that's something you should know..." he said.

"Well, *OK,* I do *know*. But it might sound stupid. The last guy I dated was great, but the biggest thing was that he wasn't the adult. Like, he wasn't the responsible one. I know that sounds stupid, but I need someone who is going to be the responsible, designated adult."

"No, I get that!" he smiled.

"What are you looking for in a partner?" I asked.

I'm not going to lie, I can't remember what he said. But it was super heartfelt and so well thought-out that it terrified me. That's probably why I don't remember it. His answer was so prepared and well-spoken and I started out with, "I don't know." Jesus. *Should I even be dating right now?* No wonder I need a designated adult.

Our waiter came back and asked if we'd like another round of martinis because the bar was closing.

WHAT?

We literally had full ones in front of us and I still had a sip of the first one. But Anthony looked at me and shrugged.

"Well if the bar is closing and this will be our last one for the night, I guess!"

So another round it was.

They brought out our food and Kassidy was right. His steak was *insane*. The giant bone hung off the plate by a foot. My steak came and was absolutely fantastic as well. It was dry aged and just so damn good. They had asked if we wanted sides with our steaks and I thought that meant regular sides on the plate, but they brought out full blown side dishes for us. This was so much food. And I suck at eating a lot. Like really suck.

Growing up, going to restaurants I would order something and my sister would strategically pass on ordering anything substantial, because she knew I'd never finish.

I started getting nervous about how much food was on the table. *Sip the martini.* Err—*don't sip the martini*, and *save space*. Too late for that.

I asked Anthony about weight lifting and how he got into it.

"Well, it's kind of embarrassing, but my ex broke up with me so it was kind of a revenge 'I'm going to get looking good' until it became a true passion of mine."

"Well, hey! Sometimes that's how it works!"

He told me more about lifting and his goal weight to reach this summer, and although I don't remember the number, I know it was enough that I stopped eating and set down my fork.

"Wait, that's got to be some kind of record? That's a ton of weight."

"Yeah, it's actually what the world's strongest man can squat right now."

"And that's *your* goal?"

"Yeah, but I'm not that close right now! I was much closer before quarantine."

Still, damn.

We talked about his passion for cooking and his family's meatball recipe, which sounded oh so delightful. He told me about going to school in New Hampshire and working at a bar and as a bouncer to pay for school. While doing that, he lived in a friend's walk-in closet and shared it with someone—err—*something*.

"A raccoon!" I nearly spit out my martini.

"Seriously! I started hearing things above the closet when I was sleeping, and one day I noticed this hole. This freaking guy jumped out the hole and attacked me, so I punched it."

"You punched a raccoon... That you happened to be sharing a living space with."

You can't make this shit up.

"Yeah. Well, he was there first, so we just ended up getting used to each other."

I shook my head. "Unreal."

Our server came up to interrupt again.

"Hi there, we'd like to give you this gift card to our restaurant to say we are sorry, because we are closing in ten minutes and we are going to need you to wrap up..."

Huh?

"...The governor issued a new curfew for the city because of COVID, so we are closing promptly at 9:30 p.m."

Ah, so now the rushed drinks made sense. Thanks, Gov. Thanks, COVID. But instead we said thank you to our server and we'd be on our way, but could we get to-go boxes? I know people say that's a no-no on dates, but I couldn't leave behind this beautiful steak. Anthony didn't need one because he took his steak down like a boss. We received the boxes quickly and our check which Anthony grabbed and swiftly denied my offer to split. I said thank you, even though I saw him look at the bill with wide eyes.

We were shuffled out by two servers and heard the door lock behind us. We both rolled our eyes and started laughing.

"People be acting all sorts of crazy! New curfews and everything," I said.

"Yeah it's super lame. Hey, want to walk down by the water since I just realized we can't get a drink anywhere now?"

"Yeah that sounds good."

It was chilly and breezy, but pretty out. Anthony walked with his arm at my back and I interlocked arms with him to beat the bite in the air. Eventually we decided to start heading back as it was pretty cold and I ordered an Uber.

While we were waiting he said he had a great time and we reminisced on some dates we had been on previously from apps. He said he went out with one girl who was beautiful, but she revealed she was an escort as her full-time job and he couldn't get on board with that.

"That would be tough."

"Yeah, I'm not going to date someone who is getting it from someone else. Or showing it to the world. Like someone with an Only Fans or something."

Uh oh. I paused. How had Court Does Sports not even come up yet on our date?

"Well..."

His face changed. "Oh, do you have an Only Fans?"

"Yes, but it's not what you think!" I said putting my hands up defensively. "Everyone thinks porn when they hear Only Fans, but mine is for sports talk shows I do. I mean most of the time, I'm in a swimsuit at my pool back home doing them, but yeah. I have a sports following online and a sports website with multiple female writers that I run and our slogan is 'The best in babes, booze, and ball games.'"

"That's totally different from what I was talking about! That actually sounds really cool."

Just then, my Uber pulled up.

"Oh, this is me!"

He said he had a fun time that night and wanted to do it again. I said definitely, we'd text and set something up. I gave him a good night peck and then got into my Uber.

I don't know if it was the martinis hitting all the sudden or something but now I was horny as fuck. Plus, my Uber driver was cute (was he though?) and his music was good (that it actually was). I asked what it was, and he said it was his own rap and it was on Spotify, so I downloaded some. Then he asked if I had Instagram and he followed me and I think I followed him back? I even briefly thought—he's kind of cute... what if I... *no stop.* Now I don't even remember his name! I bet I could figure it out though by looking at my playlist. All I remember is that he drove a BMW and he had shoulder-length dreads. Anyways, I got out of the car and went inside for my heathen brain to take a rest.

But it didn't. I went to change into pajamas, but got a glimpse of myself in my big, gold mirror in my Calvin Klein's and curled hair and thought—*hmmm.*

I pulled out my phone and started taking Snapchat videos of me rolling around in my sheets giggling and showing just enough, but never too much, because—why not?

Who to send to? My ex Tanner, who I still talked to, and these other two friends turned Snapchat flings I messed around with on the phone. Rob and Cole. Normally I'd get some decently quick responses, and I did from two of the three almost immediately. Tanner and Rob were typing...

My ex's response was something simple that must've bored me, but Rob's was heart eyes emojis and an actual photo snap back which looked like he was in the car. So I persisted with sending him slutty-not-slutty snaps since he was eager and available.

"Ugh, you're killing me right now. I'm in the car and you look damn good," he wrote.

I smiled and then must have passed out. I woke up in the morning with a nasty headache and a response back from my third sendee. I opened it and read it, which probably said something like "lemme see those titties" or something so typical of him. But after I opened it, I noticed on my snap icon I had a story up. *Huh? I didn't post a story. Wait...* I clicked it.

NO. *Nonononononono.*

There was the snap I had sent to Rob, Cole, and Tanner. The one of me rolling around in my sheets without a shirt on, but no actual nip slips.

Fuckfuckfuckfuckfuckfuck. I panicked, my brain not moving fast enough with the keys to get to the delete button. But right before I clicked delete, I stopped myself.

Wait, calm down for five seconds. See who the fuck watched this snap.

I swiped up to see, to my dismay, ninety-nine people had already watched my story of me rolling around in the sheets. *NINETY-NINE.* One away from fucking triple digits.

Lord, help me for I have sinned.

I swiped as swiftly through the list as I possibly could, noting anyone important. No mom, no sister, no guy cousins, thank GOD. People who did stand out: sister's best friend, two girl cousins, and Tanner and Rob.

What the fuck! I deleted it immediately and waited until my icon went back to my Bitmoji of me winking with a Green Bay Packers ball cap on. *Yikes.* I realized I did have one person other than my usual followers who responded to it—Kyle, a guy I had just met in Boston. Heart eyes. *Great.*

Now to address Rob and Tanner. I texted them. "Uhm, that video I sent you last night... It posted it to my fucking story! And you watched it there! Why didn't you tell me!"

Rob replied.

"Oh shit! My bad! I didn't even realize it was on your story. I probably just thought I was watching your snap."

Yeah, ok.

I sent Tanner the same message.

"Well I thought you were trying to promote your Only Fans or something."

"What! I don't post shit like that!"

"Oh well I didn't know that! You still haven't given me my free subscription! ;) "

I rolled my eyes. Just then a text popped in from Anthony. He had a wonderful time and wanted to go out again soon. I flopped back down on my bed.

What the fuck am I doing? I finally go on a date with a nice guy, and I come home and rather than dwell on that, I drunk snap all the fuck boys in my Snapchat list. *That's saying something.* I put off another dinner date with Anthony, but said I still wanted to go on one. I'd motivate myself to be a better person before then. A good person, even.

But then Anthony texted me every day. Sometimes twice a day. Sometimes without me responding to the other texts. Soon I agreed to a date, but had to cancel it. I couldn't do it. I wasn't into him and I couldn't force it. He was too nice of a guy and I was busy texting fuck boys. My priorities were clear that I wasn't into him and that wasn't fair to anyone. But even after my cancelling, he persisted. So I took drastic measures and said I wasn't fully over my ex.

A lie, *sort of,* yet again about Tanner. Sort of a lie because... was I over Tanner? Absolutely. But was I still sexting him any time I got horny? Absolutely. And for that matter, was I messaging multiple people when I got horny? Absolutely.

So, yes, I was over Tanner. But that didn't mean I couldn't stop sending my boobs out to my boy band trio. I mean, hell, I was borderline about to create a snap group for my Quarantine Horny-tine group, because really I was over all three of them, just bored. And what do you call *that*? How can you be *over* some people you were never technically *under*? Well, virtually I guess I was? Obviously Tanner was another story, but still. What even counts anymore?

I felt a little guilty about snapping them all, but only because I felt guilty about me being a hoe after going on a date with a seemingly good guy. I didn't feel guilty at all for my fuck boy trio. Poor Anthony was talking up a storm with me and persistent about likely only talking to me and I was wasting my time with a group of guys probably sending out dick pics in mass volumes to other girls too. Honestly, was I really much better than them?

Well, a couple months prior my friend's little sister told me she was doing the same thing during quarantine and would send her boobs out whenever she got bored, so I guess I didn't feel so bad.

Hey, if I'm going to hell, at least my friends will be there.

6

Keagan

"Wait, you don't know Keagan Rossi?" my friend Ali asked through her braces. "Uhm—he's like only the cutest guy at Niguel Hills Middle School. And public school guys are, just like, so much hotter."

Ali pulled up a Myspace profile on her family desktop and showed me the profile picture which was an iMac camera selfie of a tan boy with long, dark shaggy hair sweeping over his forehead.

"Totally cute," I assured her.

So when Ali and I were headed to our private Catholic high school and found out THE Keagan Rossi was going to the same high school, you can imagine our excitement. Heading into our first assembly we walked into the gym with hundreds of people and took a seat on the wooden bleachers only to have—guess who—sit right in front of us.

We started pinching each other's legs and holding back laughter, giving each other looks.

A totally hot, tan and buff senior grabbed the mic and started telling us about what a great class we had. And—oh yeah, we had one of the hottest, new surfer guys joining our class. Ali and I both looked back and forth to each other thinking—no way.

"Keagan Rossi! My baby bro! Come on up here! Show the girls that handsome mug!"

Ali and I couldn't contain our laughter at this point and burst into fits. Keagan immediately turned around and looked at us and scowled, probably because he had no idea who we were.

Keagan and I didn't exactly ever *talk* freshman year, but we did have a moment.

Cue my first real high school party. My new friend Laura was hosting a Halloween party, which included strobe lights, big speakers, and a bottle of alcohol she snuck from her parents' liquor cabinet. I was dancing at one point when, guess who, comes up behind me and starts dancing with me in the darkness. KEAGAN. And by dancing, I mean grinding. I played it cool, even though I was absolutely dying inside. I turned my face toward his thinking I might get my first make out, but right as he started leaning into my face someone turned on all the lights. Party was over. He walked off and we didn't speak. What would have been my first make out would have probably been his 1,000th, so probably for the best, really. He didn't need to experience my first, sloppy, figure-it-out kiss.

We crossed paths again when Ali and I decided to join surf team and headed into the first meeting. Again, we didn't talk; I just tried not to stare at him.

It wasn't until sophomore year summer we really started seeing each other often, as our friend groups collided and we all started going to the beach to surf. One day after surfing some waves, I decided to go for it with Keagan before heading back out.

"Wanna ride tandem?" I asked.

"Hell yeah," he smiled.

I hopped on the front of the board and tucked my legs under his arms, with his face essentially sitting in my ass. I didn't think anything of it and started paddling, but apparently this is the moment Keagan says he knew I was different than other girls.

"I'll never forget that. You got right on in front of me with your butt in my face and started paddling. I was like, in awe, and you turned around, looked at me and said, 'You good?'"

Well, too bad for Keagan. He had to go and screw things up.

Junior year started and we started talking more and more. One day he asked me to come over to hang. At his house. *Holy shit.* I told him I'd swing by after the gym. I remember I was wearing tight volleyball shorts and a big soccer tournament tee of my sister's and my bright pink Victoria's Secret zip-up hoodie. I pulled up to his house and added a swipe of mascara and saw my cheeks already blushing.

"Play it cool, Court. You're fine."

I walked up and knocked, and he let me in and said his parents weren't home and smiled. Oh, *great*. I certainly was not prepared for this kind of "hanging out." We walked into his living room where he said we could sit on the couch and I noticed *Blue Crush* was on.

"Oh my God! No way. This is like my favorite movie ever."

He sat next to me really close, touching, and I felt my cheeks starting to get hot again, so I avoided eye contact and looked at the TV, despite his gaze fully on my face and him not saying anything to my previous remark.

"So, uhm, yeah," I stuttered awkwardly, still not looking at him. "I watch it all the time. Kate Bosworth is like me. But I—"

He cut me off mid-sentence and leaned in and started kissing me. In other words, *shut the fuck up, Courtney.* We started making out, but that was all I was really into, and thankfully he didn't try for anything else. He probably could sense my virginity.

A few weeks later, there was a big Halloween party after the football game. I had finished playing beer pong when I realized I couldn't find one of my best friends, Harley. Then I realized I also couldn't find Keagan. I opened a bedroom door and found the two of them in there alone not doing anything, but it looked like they had just walked in together. I looked at both of them, didn't say anything, and walked back out. Keagan and I had literally just started talking so it wasn't like I could call him out, but Harley? Oh, she knew better. Driving home in the car Harley kept apologizing saying nothing happened and she was drunk, but all of our friends were silent. The next morning I accepted her apology and told her how much I liked him and she should've known and she said she was sorry and agreed.

After that, Keagan and I started hanging a lot. Surfing. Parties. The beach. I even asked him to Winter Formal. I wore a show-stopping dress. Long, yellow, and silk with a low back. Everyone said it looked just like the dress from *How to Lose a Guy in 10 Days* that Kate Hudson wore in her famous breakup scene with Ben. It was the first time I got to see Keagan somewhat flustered over me, which was nice for a change. Valentine's Day came around, and he planned on celebrating it with me. I decided I'd have a small party that night, regardless of whether he had plans with me or not, and he came over to my house and surprised me with a tub of my favorite cake batter ice cream and a case of beer, since my friends told him I was definitely not a flowers or stuffed animal kind of girl.

From that point on, I really started liking Keagan.

Spring break rolled around and my family headed to Mexico. As soon as we were back in the States, texts started rolling in from some of my best friends. They needed to talk to me—something was up. Harley was being shifty and they found out she was hooking up with Keagan while I was out of town. Some friend she was.

I called them both out in separate texts and Keagan immediately tried calling me, but I let it go straight to voicemail. He started blowing up my phone apologizing and saying it meant nothing and he was stupid. *Yeah, he was.* I thought maybe the texts from Harley would be the same but imagine my shock when her texts came in telling me she wasn't sorry and that maybe I wasn't giving Keagan what he wanted and that's why he started talking to her.

A knock on my virginity? Niceeeee, Harley. Nice.

I told her to enjoy her new man, and she could keep giving him whatever it was that he needed. Little did she realize, he was begging for my forgiveness, and he wouldn't get it.

Going back to school was *fun*. All my friends knew what happened and it didn't take long for everyone else to find out. Keagan tried talking to me multiple times which I responded to by either opening my locker toward his face to block it, flipping him off, or rolling my eyes. He didn't deserve to talk to me. As for Harley, I didn't have to do anything really, since everyone else did it for me. My friends had thoroughly spread the word of what happened, including how she reacted when I called her out, and let's just say she was not a crowd fave. The first day at the lunch tables no one would sit near her and she started crying. I remember someone nudging me to show me what was happening, and I remember shrugging back to them.

"Don't cheat with your best friend's guy."

For months, Keagan kept trying to talk to me every time we crossed paths in the halls since I deleted every text or call he sent. I remember one time I was just getting out of chemistry and it was near the end of the year. I had just gone surfing that morning with my sister's boyfriend before class and we cut it so close getting to school on time that I came with soaked hair and wore my wet swimsuit under my uniform. I probably still had sand in my hair and it was wavy by the afternoon. I was walking to my last class and saw Keagan across the courtyard. He saw me and instantly started waving. Rather than my usual eye-roll and head turn, I decided to fuck with him and started smiling and waving back. With this, a smile came over his face and he started to jog my way. As soon as he was decently close I switched my wave into a middle finger and smirked. He slowed his pace and I started laughing and walked past him.

Summer was coming and my sister was having a big graduation party. Keagan came up to me at my locker one day and asked if he could come. He said he figured we would see each other at my sister's boyfriend's graduation party too since they were best family friends and he wanted to come and congratulate Hailey. I scoffed, but decided I wouldn't be the one to hold him back and look petty.

"Sure, Keagan. If you want to go, come on over," I said, laughing and closing my locker, walking off. Why did he think being at my house would change anything?

He walked into the party like a lost puppy then lit up when we made eye contact.

"Hey Court! I—"

I smiled and put up a hand as if to say hello and continued walking past him. This left him slightly discouraged but he saw my sister's boyfriend and his friends and went up and cracked a drink with them.

Later I'd find out that sometime during the party my dad said "hi" to Keagan.

"You know, you've got a lot of balls to show up here after everything," my dad said to him, then walked away.

Keagan decided to leave shortly after. Maybe he had finally gotten the hint.

Summer breezed by and soon came senior year. I was living it up with the football guys and was now the team manager of the football team with my best friend Carly. We filmed practice every day and survived on sour gummy worms and Pick Up Stix in the filming tower, accompanied by whichever players were injured at the moment. There was no *one* boy at this time for me, and I was really just having fun. Homecoming came around and someone was talking about how one of our good friends, an offensive lineman, had never been to a dance yet. I was baffled. I considered myself the queen at matchmaking my friends and getting them invites to my dances, yet somehow had missed this. Usually the guys ask the girls to homecoming, but I said fuck it. I would ask him.

We were both die-hard football fans and I made a sign that said, "Can I Pittsburgh steal you for my homecoming date?" and the whole football team got in on it and I asked him after filming practice one day. It was awesome.

At this point, Keagan had spent the summer hanging out with the well-known party girl a grade below us and I'd see him walking over to her locker occasionally, likely still hanging or banging out with her. Only to see him go up and talk to another younger girl and see her blushing and batting her eyelashes. All this would do was make me laugh.

Second semester came around and after a crazy New Year's party I had finally lost my virginity. About time, really. It was almost starting to feel like a burden to me at that point and I was pretty dead set on wanting to lose it to someone who wasn't my boyfriend, because I saw how crazy all my friends got when they would do that. Texting, crying, screaming, phone calls. *Yikes. No, thanks.*

I was in yearbook class, which wasn't a surprise since it was my second year I'd made the team. What was surprising was Keagan walking into class. I had managed to avoid having a class with him the whole damn year and now I had yearbook and marine biology with him. Thankfully, in marine biology we walked in and chose assigned seats, and I was dating one of my best friends at the time so we sat next to each other in the front. That ended up being funny in itself because he tried breaking up with me via text message at lunch break, forgetting we had our last period sitting next to each other. He walked in with his head down and tried to turn away from me despite us sharing a wide science table.

I started dying laughing. "Did you forget you had last period with me before you decided to try and break up with me over a FUCKING TEXT!"

His best friend behind us started dying laughing. Typical, fucking boys.

Anyways, in yearbook we had semi-assigned seats, where you were just assigned to sit at certain tables. Even though we sat at art tables on bar stools, guess who was initially seated next to me? Keagan. And thus, there's only so much electricity that could be held off. We started talking again, mainly just in class but all those feelings started building up whether I wanted them to or not.

One day, Keagan asked if I was going to Zoe's party bus party. I was. Did we want to drive together? I mean, we did live like one neighborhood apart, so I guess we could do that. I told him I'd pick him up. The ride was normal even though I was feeling really nervous which annoyed me because I knew what it meant. We got on the bus together and almost as soon as the doors shut, we were all over each other. I was sitting straddled on top of him and we were making out, unaware and unfazed by anyone else on the bus.

Driving home from the party, Keagan immediately wanted to talk all things *us*.

"Ok, so what does this make us now? Are we dating? I just need to know. I don't want to screw things up."

"Woah, slow your roll, bro," I said.

"I mean, I don't care if we're exclusive. I want to be. I just want to do this right."

"Ok, well I'm not even sure how I feel about this yet, Keagan. So I need some time."

But I already knew what I wanted. It was him. It was always him. But fuck, I didn't trust him anymore. Did I?

But Keagan kept proving himself time and time again and whenever I walked into the room his eyes were on me. And he always had this stupid grin whenever he watched me talk. So I decided, let's do this. We started hanging out again and prom was around the corner. I found out one of his best friends wanted to ask me, which I thought was pretty funny. When I told Keagan about this, he did not think it was very funny and immediately tried to put an end to it but his buddy said, "Fine, we'll just see who she picks first." With this, Keagan came over.

"Courtney, I want you to be my girlfriend."

"Ugh, do we have to do this?"

"Yes, Courtney. Shawn is trying to ask you to prom. I want you and me to be known and official."

"So serious," I smirked.

"Courtney."

"Fine. I guess you can be my boyfriend."

Keagan came up with his plan to ask me to prom. He knew I loved scary movies mainly because I never got scared by them, so he decided to take on that challenge and "scare" me. He came to my house and asked my mom about his idea.

"Well, she loves scary movies, so I want to kidnap her in the middle of the night, put a pillowcase over her head so she doesn't know what's going on, and then drive her to that dirt lot in San Juan and lay her in a ditch and start throwing dirt on her and say 'I'll bury you alive unless you go to prom with me?' What do you think?" he said excited, nodding his head.

Needless to say, my mom was not pleased by the whole plan.

"I see what you're trying to do honey, and yes, she does love scary movies, but I am not going to allow you to bury my daughter alive. But you can kidnap her and take her somewhere fun she likes and ask her that way."

He agreed, still thrilled, and decided to take me to my favorite pancake place, Harbor House Diner, after my kidnapping and ask me to prom.

How did the kidnapping go? Well, let's just say I don't go down without a fight. Keagan recruited six of his friends from the football team to help and they came in the middle of the night with ski masks on. I woke up to someone putting a pillowcase over my head, which I immediately ripped off, and instinctively punched my assailant in the face. One of the other guys tried stepping in to pull me from bed, but I gave him a swift kick to the nuts. He crumbled on the ground. I was kicking and screaming and clearly, things weren't going as planned.

Pillowcase guy reapproached and I delivered a blow to their nose that we later discovered I broke. My sister who was having a "sleepover party" with me by staying in my bed that night, something we often did, was well aware of the plan but still looked horrified at me because of the fear in my eyes. I yelled at her to HELP ME but she yelled back to me things like "You're ok!" and "Do you have your phone?" which was so confusing to me. All the masked men had retreated at that point except for one of the guys who successfully managed to put me in a headlock from behind and was carrying me out in it. But I continued to punch him on the head. I tried flipping my legs up toward my head to try and use my cheer high kick to knock him out. The only thing he had on me was height because I couldn't reach the ground in the position he was carrying me in.

The only reason I stopped resisting was because my mom finally peeked her head out of her bedroom door. I started screaming at her to HELP ME and she said back, "Shh! You're going to wake your grandparents! And stop hitting him!"

I resisted my assault and admitted out loud whoever these "kidnappers" were must have been in the good graces of my mother, so that was enough for me. I was hauled out in my "headlock" position without my pillowcase on my face as a car full of eager and excited boys approached. Their faces turned to instant disappointment when they realized I could see their identities perfectly.

"Oh my God, dude! Where the fuck is the pillowcase! This is fucked! Now she knows! We can't even finish!"

"Oh, you're going to finish all right. Whatever you thought was so awesome and so great on how this was supposed to go down will be fucking finished all right. Because I will likely be scarred for the rest of my damn life being FUCKING KIDNAPPED FROM MY ROOM. SO YES, WE WILL FINISH."

The boys reluctantly agreed and made me wear a blindfold so at least I didn't know where we were going. We pulled up and as I was getting out of the car my new surroundings sounded loud and I thought we might be at a party. I instantly realized I was in pajamas and I wasn't wearing a bra.

"Are we at a party?" I asked.

"We're not telling you."

I became panicked and went off, "Someone needs to tell me if we're at a party or in public because I'm not wearing a bra!"

I heard the boys get flustered until Alex said, "Here, wear my sweatshirt." He handed it to me awkwardly.

"Thanks."

I was brought in somewhere hustling and bustling. I hear plates and cups clattering about before I'm seated in what feels like an old vinyl kind of puff chair. Like the kind you sit in at...

My blindfold is pulled off to reveal me sitting at Harbor House Diner, my favorite. With my go-to in front of me: chocolate chip banana pancakes, except this time they had "Prom?" written in whipped cream on top of the pancakes.

I smirked at Keagan. "You're stupid. But yes."

After prom, we were back on and better than we ever had been before. We were *that couple*. He'd grab me at the lockers to kiss me. Hold my hand in front of his friends, even though how many times had I insisted I hated PDA? Hot and heavy might as well have been an understatement.

We were having sex so much and with my ADD I kept missing my birth control and had to take Plan B right before our graduation ceremony.

Plus, I got my first yeast infection on top of that because we were fucking like bunnies all the time. I remember having to get the medicine for it and I had to shoot this lotion up into my vagina which was just so not cute when you're still trying to have rampant sex with your boyfriend. I wasn't supposed to finish the medication for another day, but I remember not wanting to wait that long. So instead of waiting like I was supposed to, I just shot the lotion up there the night of my friend's graduation party when I knew I'd be seeing Keagan and so be it. I remember wiping the majority of it out of me anyways at the party before Keagan and I snuck out to his car. Such horny teenagers. But the way I was starting to feel about Keagan was a feeling I had never had before with another boy and I knew it wasn't just because of the sex.

Later that week at another friend's graduation party, we snuck upstairs to have sex. Once up there, we collapsed on a bed and I rolled over and he was just looking at me with that grin again.

"So," I said, looking up at him with my chin resting on his chest.

"So," he kept smiling.

"I think I've decided on something."

"What's that?"

"Well, you know when you like someone a lot. Like a lot, a lot. Like really a lot. Like a ton."

He started smiling, seeing where this was heading. "Yes."

"But—like—when it's more than that."

"Yes," he said, now amused, propping himself up on an elbow.

Ugh, he's going to make me say it, isn't he?

"Well, I just wanted you to know that, I like you a lot, a lot. And you know how sometimes people use another word for it? Well, that."

"Hmm. I'm not following. What's the word?" he said, now smirking.

"Well—I—," I turned my face into the pillow trying to hide the fact I was having so many feelings and emotions.

This was me we were talking about. Courtney? In *love*? Was that even possible? For the first time ever, I guess it was. I turned back to face him.

"I love you, Keagan."

Before I had even finished his name, he responded back. "I love you too."

"Well, what the hell!"

He started laughing. "I've known I loved you for weeks now. I just wanted you to say it first," he said.

I threw my hands up theatrically and got up to go join the party again and he pulled me back down and kissed me. We started making out and taking off each other's clothes. Quickly, of course. After all, we were still high schoolers at a party. I guess technically this could be my first time I "made love" if you want to call it that. It certainly felt like that despite it being at our friend's house.

That summer, we were like magnets to each other. We may have been about to leave for different colleges across the country, but that didn't faze us. Every party we went to, we only had eyes for one another, and despite our past, we trusted each other with our whole hearts. Because Keagan looked like, well, Keagan, and had the track record of, well, himself, he still had the usual suspects approaching him at parties trying to get him to reminisce on long nights in jacuzzies and whatever else. I never minded it or paid attention to it, and would walk off to go play beer pong. He'd always come find me or I'd overhear him say to a girl, "See that beautiful blonde babe? That's my girl." And he'd walk over and pick me up or do something cute.

Sometimes Keagan would just show up to my house. One time I was mad at him for something silly and he came by the house and left a vase of hand cut roses, likely from his yard. There was a small Post-it Note reading "BELLA" with a heart (the nickname he called me because it meant beautiful in Italian). At this point, everyone joked Keagan and I spoke our own language, because I'd make funny faces at him and he'd make them back at me or start tickling me.

Our last trip of the summer, Keagan was going to come with me and my family on our houseboat to Lake Powell. We lived in swimsuits and drank beer every night and truly spent the time like it was our last weeks together forever. But this was when it started to hit that Keagan and I would soon be apart. Like thousands of miles away. One night Keagan and I got drunk on cheap sangria and slept on the roof of the houseboat, looking at the stars. I cried when we started to talk about college. There wasn't going to be anyone like him. I knew it in my bones.

The day Keagan had to leave, I did everything in my power to make sure I didn't cry. And as poetic as it could be, the skies opened up into the biggest monsoon we had ever seen on our two-hour boat drive to the marina.

Dating each other long distance didn't suck at first in terms of me meeting guys to invite us to their frat parties because my roommate started dating a guy off the bat so we had parties we could go to with him. Plus, I had a bunch of guy friends from high school that came to Southern Methodist University too and they all knew Keagan. And two seniors at SMU were good friends with Keagan's older brother, so when it came to going to fraternity formals, I wasn't left out.

The hardest part was not being able to see each other and touch each other. It killed us. And mind you, this was before FaceTime. We would set up Skype dates every week to catch up. I was swamped with school and now filming for the football team as the assistant video coordinator, all while trying to make friends and connections with sororities. I sucked at communicating and thankfully Keagan knew this. He'd even text me occasionally in all caps and say HELLO EARTH TO COURTNEY or leave me voicemails like "Hey, it's your boyfriend Keagan. Remember me? Anyways, it's been a week so just checking if you're still alive or if we're still dating. Love you."

Sometimes Keagan would just Skype me randomly if he knew I was on my laptop. Those were the best, but also the worst. I'll never forget the first time I cried on Skype with him. He said he missed me and started playing "Little Wing" by Jimi Hendrix and tears instantly began welling up. I missed him so much.

So when I had the option to come home for Thanksgiving and surprise Keagan at Chapman, I was damn well going to take it. Plus, it was Chapman's undie run, basically a school tradition where you run a one-mile section on campus in underwear. Aka, it would be an epic time to come visit him.

I got in touch with his roommate and we planned the entire surprise out.

When Keagan got out of his first class and opened the door to his dorm room, I was sitting right there on his bed.

"Hey Stranger!"

He instantly grabbed me off the bed and started hugging me and burying his face into my neck. He kissed me and started ripping off my clothes before I could even tell him the plan.

"What about your roommate, Keagan!" I laughed, trying to get a word in.

He yelled out to the hall, "Come back in twenty, bro!"

The undie run was a shit show, as expected, and I wasn't fully open to the idea of actually wearing underwear out, so I decided on blue volleyball shorts and a sports bra with a zip-up jacket. After the run, while we were walking back to his dorm, Keagan said he wanted to show me something. We snuck into the outdoor stadium, his mecca. He was one of the lacrosse stars on the team and I hadn't, and probably would never, get to see him play since all his games were in the middle of the semester. He looked proud showing it to me and I felt proud I got to call him mine, and ran up and jumped on him, wrapping my legs around him, kissing him.

"Wait..." he said, setting me down, pulling me up into the stands. "Let's have sex in the stadium."

Naturally, we got into one of the stadium seats and got right to it. At least now he could think of me in the stands when I couldn't be there, right?

That same weekend, Keagan and I were hooking up in his dorm bed, he asked me if I wanted to try anal. I had never done it, but he had. He said he would be gentle and I decided ok, we could give it a try. The minute he got close to trying to put it in the pain was so bad I donkey-kicked him off of me and into the wall like straight out of a *Charlie's Angels* movie. I immediately started apologizing, but he seemed more impressed than hurt and we both ended up laughing it off and deciding better not on that front.

Coming home for Christmas break just weeks later, Keagan insisted that he wanted to be the one to pick me up. I remember walking out of the airport with my friend Kiki who had gone to high school with me and now was at SMU with me, and Keagan was standing on the sidewalk waiting for me. He instantly ran up and picked me up and started kissing me, and I was instantly beet red. He loved embarrassing me with PDA. I said bye to Kiki, apologizing, but she just smiled and said, "I get it. Hi Keagan!"

Second semester I made it into the sorority I wanted, and from there it was date parties and formals galore. I was really missing Keagan and since I wasn't coming home for Easter, my mom bought a flight for him to come see me. Finally, he would be able to meet everyone and go out with us. And as expected, everyone loved him.

"Oh my God, do you guys think you'll get married?" Kiki asked us out one night.

"What? Oh my God. No," I responded, chugging the rest of my beer.

"Wait, why not?" Keagan asked.

I looked back and forth to them both. "You guys are stupid. We're eighteen and just started college. C'mon."

Later that night before we went to bed Keagan said he didn't like how I always said that as a response when people asked about marriage. I asked if he was serious and he played it off like he wasn't, but I started realizing maybe he was. And I mean, I loved Keagan, and sure, maybe I would marry him if we were still together, but that was like ten years away—wasn't it?

I finished out the school year partying hard with the Beta Beta Beta frat and my Kappa Kappa Gamma sorority, and I was loving life. As a sorority girl attending frat parties, I was also really getting the hang of flirting with guys without doing anything touchy. I had to imagine Keagan was probably doing the same. But it started to become apparent where our priorities were starting to go: College. Partying. And flirting. And being dumb. And being drunk. We wanted to have the "college experience" but couldn't stand the idea of not being with each other. Obviously, we were still in love, but maybe we needed some new rules of engagement going back to school for sophomore year. So, before going back we decided to have a sit-down on what we could and couldn't do going forward in an attempt to achieve more of a "college experience." Our rules would essentially be based on "Don't ask, don't tell" and "We're together when we're together, and we're not when we're not," but with more guidelines. Two we absolutely agreed on.

1. **Under no circumstances, no sex.**
2. **No bringing a guy/girl back to your actual bed, because that's where we visit each other and stay.**

"Ok, no head either?" I asked.

"Uhm..."

"Keagan!"

"Well, c'mon, Court! You're the one who wants to experience college and open us up to these rules."

"Ok, fine. Well that means guys can go down on me then, Keagan."

"Without having sex? Good luck with that."

I gasped and shoved him and we both started laughing. It did irritate me slightly since I knew he was right and it reminded me of that one time he told me guys didn't like going down on girls because it was "gross." *Like choking on a giant hard curling iron that guys pee out of was any better?* Still, it always stuck with me as a self-conscious thing hooking up with guys into adulthood.

"And no hooking up with anyone we know," he said. "I don't want to hear about it from someone because I'll fucking lose my shit."

"Ok, that's a good one."

3. **No hooking up with anyone we know.**

"Anything else?"

Nope. That was it. We had created our list of rules. There were other moments with asterisks and gray area like what did hooking up with someone we know mean? Could we make out with them? Could we go to a formal together? The line blurred there for me and I broke my first rule. I went to a formal with someone from high school and we made out. Thankfully, that was all we did. But still, it weighed on me that I had broken a rule.

When it came time for me to visit Keagan back at his college house and I jumped into his bed for the first time, I rolled over and looked at him and asked...

"So! How's it feel to have a girl in your bed again?"

His smile toward me immediately turned and he dropped his eyes to the floor. Instantly the bed I was sitting on felt wrong.

"Oh my God, Keagan. What the fuck! You broke a rule! And that rule! You brought a chick back here to your bed?"

"Oh, Courtney stop! Don't tell me you haven't broken a rule yet either."

"Well, I did but not really. Not a big one. I just made out with Gordo Paul."

"Are you kidding me! That'll be fun running into him," he said upset.

To distract us, I decided we should go out. But he wanted to stay in and just hang with me. I didn't want to though, not in that bed. We ended up going out and having a good time, but I couldn't shake the feeling.

I still loved Keagan. But fuck. Something had to change. Something had changed. A couple days went by, but the feeling just kept getting bigger and bigger. I finally knew what I had to do, but knew I didn't want to. I was still at home on break, so I texted him I was coming up to Chapman to talk. It felt like I didn't breathe the entire drive there. I didn't even listen to music, but I did have my best friend Briana come in the car with me because she knew I probably wouldn't be ok to drive afterward.

I knocked on the door and he opened. Without anything being said, we both instantly started crying. He pulled me into his arms and we stood there crying and hugging each other before I muttered out the words, "I just think it's time." We agreed it was mutual. We talked for about an hour and cried the entire time. But we promised we had to remain friends. We *had to*. And so we agreed we would.

Except here's the problem with that... I decided a week later I wanted to come up to Chapman undie run and could I stay with him? Totally, he said. Why did I think coming up to my ex's house to go out with friends in my underwear and get drunk would be a good idea? No feelings attached, right? *Right.*

Me and three of my girlfriends got to his house and this time we weren't messing around on the costumes. We were all in Christmas-themed, hardcore lingerie, since it was, after all, Christmas break and the undie run. We came in with a bottle of tequila and said hi to everyone. First and foremost, I went up to give Keagan a hug. Everything was fine with us, so the girls and I started scoping the room and saying hi to who we knew.

After some drinks, I went to the bathroom and overheard two girls talking in the hall.

"Oh, yeah she totally sucked Keagan's dick last month and he just stopped talking to her."

I instantly stopped in my tracks. Technically, that was fair game in our rules. And not like something I hadn't also done. But it still hurt to hear someone say it *out loud*. Like really hurt. *Shit.* Why did I think this was a good idea? I came out and told the girls it was time to take shots and we started taking them like it was our job. After profusely drinking, I saw a girl I despised who had always been trying to get with Keagan show up to the party.

"Are you kidding me... Look who's here," I said, nudging my friend.

"Kathy Pecky. I hate that girl."

"She's been trying to get with Keagan the entire time I've been with him. Not surprised at all that she's here. Let's go."

We decided to go to the next house party and then the undie run, but walking to the next house party, I was incredibly drunk and started bitching to my friends about Kathy being there.

"Ugh, I just hate Kathy! Of course she's here to hook up with Keagan as soon as he's available. How pathetic. She's just such a fucking cunt!" I slurred out, basically yelling to my three friends as we were walking on the sidewalk, I thought alone. I never used the c-word, so that was even more of an indicator at just how drunk I was.

Just then Kathy stormed past us, passing our group on the sidewalk in the street and then running to catch the group ahead of us.

"Shit," I said, suddenly feeling like a bitch.

I ran up after her to apologize and tell her I shouldn't have called her that. But as soon as I started to jog ahead after her, someone grabbed my arm. I turned to see it was Keagan.

"Let go of me, Keagan."

"Courtney. Don't do this."

"Let go of my arm," I started struggling to wriggle loose.

"No, I can't let y—"

Without thinking and clearly belligerent and irritated about being held back, I punched Keagan in the face. And much harder than I had expected, because as soon as I did it, I lost my balance and landed my tailbone directly to the curb.

The next morning I woke up in a room with one of his best friends beside me in the bed and was very confused. I couldn't remember what happened after tequila shots in the kitchen after hearing that girl talking about sucking Keagan's dick. And, damn, was my head spinning. I sat up to go to the bathroom and was instantly overcome with a wave of pain in my butt. It took my breath away, it was so bad.

"Fuck me. What the hell?"

I looked down at my attire to see I was in Keagan's Chapman soccer sweatshirt and his sweats. I got up and hobbled to the bathroom looking for my friends or anyone who could paint the picture for me of the night's activities. I went to go pee and had to hold myself up using the shower rail since I couldn't sit.

I found the girls, one on the couch snuggling with someone and the other on another guest bed. I told the girls I was hungover and we should get Harbor House, our fave diner down south. They were down. I asked them about the end of the night, but they kind of laughed and said it was a blur for them too. *Damn, no answers there.* I figured it couldn't be that bad if no one else remembered anything, so I just chalked it up to a crazy undie run night out. *But why did my butt hurt so much?*

I walked over to the next room to find Keagan in bed alone just waking up.

"Hey!"

He blinked at me.

"So we're all going to get Harbor House for breakfast since we're hungover. You should come too. And then maybe we can hang at my pool or go to the beach."

"Are you fucking kidding me Courtney?" he sneered.

Uh, oh. Things weren't ok.

"Sorry, I was just inviting you to brunch. If you're not hungry you don't have to come. I just thought it'd be fun."

"You have no idea what you did last night, do you?"

I stood in the doorway trying to decide what to say. I clearly did something to piss Keagan off and I felt bad. Why I thought this was my next thing to say, I don't know.

"I'm sorry. Did I hook up with one of your friends?"

"Pff! No! Jesus."

"Oh, sorry. Did I—"

"No, you punched me in the freaking face!"

"I did?"

"Yes!"

"Why'd I do that?"

"Does it matter?"

"Well sort o—"

"You were about to go fight Kathy Pecky so I tried to stop you and you punched me in the face."

All of the sudden all of the memories came flooding back and I remembered calling her a cunt and wanting to apologize. And blood pouring from Keagan's nose as soon as I hit it.

"Oh, yeah!" I said, overly enthusiastic about the revelation of the pain in my tailbone, glad it wasn't injured due to a sexual encounter. "That's why my butt hurts so bad. I fell on the curb. And for the record, I wasn't going to fight her, I was going to apologize. But I'm sorry."

"Sure you were."

"Ok, well I'm really, really sorry," I said grimacing.

He rolled his eyes and pulled his sheets up over his head.

"I'll buy you pancakes to make up for it? And I'll wash your clothes I'm borrowing and give them back to you when you come back down."

He pulled down the sheets again and just looked at me, mad, and I tried not to laugh.

"Ok, well… I can see that you're still tired… So I'll let you sleep. And just remember, I'm really sorry."

I started to see a smile crack over his face and he tried to hide it by smirking.

"And uhm, yeah. Thank you for letting us stay here. And we had a fun time! And if you want to go to the beach with us later then just text meeeee!" I said dragging out the "e" and shutting his door and waving.

I flagged the girls that we should leave, and I cracked open his door one more time. "But seriously, text me if you change your mind and you want to hang. And… we're good, right? Like, we're ok?"

"Ask me later," he said groggily rolling over into his pillow. I looked to make sure there wasn't blood on it from my Mike Tyson moment, and thank God there wasn't.

A month went by and Keagan and I were barely talking, but we were about to start running into each other again like always with our similar friend groups, so I decided to hit him up one night to hang out. This ended exactly the way you'd expect—hot and heavy, mind-blowing sex. And eventually joking around and messing with each other.

The truth is though, Keagan and I were never really just friends. I mean, sure, now running into each other we say hi and catch up, but more as exes and acquaintances. Even how we started out, if you think about it, there were always feelings attached. And even after our breakup there were feelings attached. Eventually they dwindled away, but I don't think we ever stopped caring for each other. Hell, I haven't talked to the kid in years and I'd say I still care about him as a person. He's a great guy.

And funny enough, he's now engaged to a girl we went to high school with that he always thought was hot.

The other day while driving in Boston, a total throwback song came on. "Ultimate" from the movie *Freaky Friday*. I was singing along and thought about the lyrics.

'Cause I been waiting all my life, for someone just like you!
'Cause you're it! You're the ultimate you!

I realized I was now screaming the lyrics. But who was I singing them about? For some reason, it made me think of Keagan. Which made me feel awkward because so much time had passed. Then I realized I wasn't singing it about him in a wanting *him* kind of way. It was different. Like a hopeful thing looking to the future. And I realized, that's what Keagan means to me now. Our love is the standard I'm aiming for. That first love kind of love. Not with *him,* but *that* kind of love.

They say your one true love should make it feel like it's the first time again. And, damn, I hope that's true for him and his fiancé and true for me. Because, as far as first loves go, we certainly changed the game.

7

Matt

"Are you dating anyone?" a family friend's dad asked me at a birthday party, officially moving our small talk into the good stuff.

"Yes, I'm still dating my boyfriend Matt. We're coming up on three years now!"

"Well that's great! Is he the one?"

I guess Matt was what anyone would consider my most serious boyfriend. We dated for three years, minus breaking up for a couple weeks somewhere in there. Does the length make it serious? How are these things justified? Also, why does *everyone* ask *this* question? *How the fuck should I know?*

"Hmm, I don't know!" I said fake smiling.

"Oh, if you don't know by now then he's not the one. You would know by now."

My heart sank to my butt and so did my stupid grin trying to appease this invasive conversation. Before I could respond, my dad popped up out of nowhere and jumped in.

"That's not true. I didn't know I wanted to marry Cathy until the day I bought the ring."

A well-established lie, that I am at least aware of, but this man dare not go against it as my parents' relationship is as strong as one can get. The family friend rolled his eyes and walked away. I turned to my dad to say thanks. He responded with a grin and a lift of his beer. Still, that question would linger with me. *Why didn't I know if Matt was the one?*

Our relationship had changed drastically over the course of three years, but there's something nostalgic about thinking about the first times. Like the first time Matt invited me up to Lake Tahoe with his family, I came a few days after him and drove up with one of his best friends. As soon as I got there he handed me a cracked Coors Light and introduced me to his parents and their friends who were visiting too. Matt said I was his girlfriend, and I took a big gulp of my beer when I saw the shocked smiles all come to their faces. Matt told me he hadn't dated anyone seriously since college and, as much as I detested "labels," I said why not before our trip to Tahoe. So I knew I'd endure those awkward questions from the moms.

Matt offered to help with my bags but really it was a ruse so we could go have sex. We popped into the smallest bathroom in the entire damn chalet and got to it. If there was one thing Matt and I were always good at with each other, it was sex.

The night was New Year's Eve, and we went out to the casinos. When the ball dropped, we kissed and he dipped me down theatrically. We decided to head home early because he couldn't keep his hands off me. After someone on the shuttle bus insisted I was Elle King and to sing "Ex's and Oh's" for the bus, we got off at his house and ran inside, where Matt threw me down onto a bunk bed. His parents had designated us and his friends to the bunk room, a room full of single bunk beds. But that clearly wasn't stopping us. Matt ripped off my jeans and immediately started burying his face between my legs. As soon as he got me off, I tried pulling him back up to meet my face, but he locked his arms around my legs and looked up and said he wasn't done. He said he was going to make me cum more times than anyone ever had before. He was successful. About five or six times successful.

The next morning we woke up and hit the mountain to go snowboarding. We had never rode together, so he was shocked when he realized I could keep up. At lunch, we hit the bar and ordered Bloody Marys and shots. I ordered them for us standing up at the bar while Matt sat on a bar stool, his knees on either side of me. We took our shots and just smiled at each other and then started laughing and looking away from each other. I looked into my Bloody Mary and used my straw to swirl it around, trying to avoid getting emotional.

"Just so you know, you could really crush me if you wanted to."

I looked up to see him looking directly at me. The sun was reflecting off one of his eyes revealing the green, blue, and yellow in them, similar to mine.

"You could crush me too, Court."

Even before Matt and I made things official, he always could make me laugh like no one else could. One of the first times we hung out after college, my friends were going down to the beach and asked if I could pick up Matt on the way? Sure. I put on music I thought was decent and he got in the car and I didn't even realize I was singing along to the music as we cruised the Pacific Coast Highway with the windows down into Laguna Beach.

At one point I could tell he was looking at me. He turned down the volume and kept staring at me, confused.

"Hey, I like that song!"

"Has anyone ever told you that you might be tone-deaf?"

I dropped my jaw and shoved his shoulder trying to hold back my laughter.

"Oh my God! Shut the fuck up! You're so mean!... But yes, they have."

He started laughing and I started singing again, more tone-deaf, and as loudly as I could.

Only a few weeks later, our friends would try and push Matt and I together to go on double dates and I insisted no. I told them they really needed to chill on the matchmaking. They tried everything though. Soon enough, Matt ended up texting me about a party at his buddy's. He got a bottle of wine and said we could go together.

We went to the party and at one point headed outside and started making out. I glimpsed a trampoline in my peripheral and insisted we get on it. We bounced around before collapsing onto it and I heard a big tear. The rip in the front of my jeans had gone from a knee hole to a rip up to my crotch and down past my knee. We both burst out laughing and proceeded to take off our clothes anyway.

Honestly, I have to say, hooking up on a trampoline is really fun.

Matt and I started hanging out as often as we could. But we both still lived at home. So I would leave my parents' house and say I was staying at a friend's when really I would head over to his parents' house where he would sneak me into the back pool house where his room was. The only problem was, he didn't have a bathroom in there. You'd have to enter the main house to use one. And I did not want to be caught by his parents. So every morning I'd book it early out of there and floor it to the beach parking lot where there was a public bathroom, barely making it, holding my crotch with all the little middle school surfers laughing at me.

Right around this time post-college, I decided I was going to move up to my grandparents' house in Walla Walla for a month or so to help out with some things up there and just get a change of scenery. Matt and I actually were starting to feel serious, despite not making things official, and he even told me he might actually miss me. But it was pretty good timing because he was going to Europe for three weeks. I told him to have fun, and even encouraged him to have butt sex with someone, since lately he had been trying to get me to do it. After giving it a try with Keagan, I told Matt the only person I'd do that with was my husband. He called me late and drunk after the first party they went to on the beach and said a girl wanted to hook up with him, but he said he didn't want to because he only wanted me.

We started FaceTiming every day. One night things even got sexy. I had never had FaceTime sex or anything like that, because as an aspiring journalist, that was one mistake I'd never make! No pictures or videos of anything. Ever. No exceptions. Not even at Mardi Gras in college. Well, except to that one bouncer that kicked me out and said he'd let me back in if I showed him a boob. Just one? Fine.

Needless to say, FaceTime sex was new to me. I pulled out a little vibrator I had and I only showed him my face and my cleavage as I came. No nipples or anything. Some habits are hard to crack. Still, I guess that was good enough, because he came too. Later I asked him if he had ever done that with someone and he said he'd rather not answer. *Greattt.*

I got back home and so did Matt, and he said he wanted to take me golfing at his club. He said hole 12 was going to be my favorite. We got there and midway through the hole he pulled off to a random house and opened the gate to their backyard.

"What are you doing!" I whisper-yelled to him.

He opened their outside fridge and grabbed a few beers out.

"Matt!"

He waved me from the cart and pointed to the sign on the fridge.

"Take what you need, leave a few bucks or whatever."

I laughed. He was right. This was definitely my favorite hole. We finished the round and walked up to the clubhouse deck overlooking the course.

"So... I think you should be my girlfriend."

My face dropped. Not because I didn't necessarily want it, but because the last real boyfriend I had was Keagan. And everyone after the fact was just not him.

"What?" I asked.

"Geez! Try not to look so excited!"

"I'm sorry. It's just—is that necessary? I feel like it's just a label really?"

He leaned on the railing smiling at me. "I don't know. We've been hanging out for a while now and I know I like you. And I think you like me."

"Ok."

"Ok? So you're my girlfriend?"

"And you're my boyfriend." I smirked. He leaned in and kissed me.

From there, things took a life of their own. We hung out incessantly except when I was off on trips with family or friends. And every time we hung out, we almost immediately were ripping each other's clothes off.

One day Matt and I were driving up to Tahoe talking all things sex, and I told him I wanted to know it all. I had just finished giving him road head on our lengthy eight-hour drive and decided I wanted to get into it. He said he didn't feel like it was a good idea but he told me anyway. He said he didn't know how many girls the exact count was, but somewhere around seventy-five probably because he knew he was way behind his best friend who was easily over one-hundred and probably up into the 120s by now.

"Damn! Ok—be honest—who was best sex ever?"

"You."

"Aww. Best butt?"

"You."

"Best boobs?"

"This girl from college. Damn, they were huge and real. So nice."

I turned and looked at him.

"What! You said be honest! No, no, no. I'm done now."

"Ok, do you want to hear mine now?"

"Absolutely not."

I don't know why I'm fascinated by hearing my boyfriends' past sex stories but I just am. And why not get it out of them in an eight-hour car ride where they have nowhere to go. I turned up "Closer" by the Chainsmokers and joked, asking if he had hooked up with this chick too. After all, it was about someone who went to school in Boulder (close to his alma mater, Utah) and who drove a Rover, like he did.

Despite being candid about former hook ups, what's funny is that it took a couple months into our relationship for me to bring up to Matt that we had hooked up before in high school, well made out, on a party bus going to a concert. Best part? There was a photo. I finally found the photo and, let me tell you, it was pure gold.

Matt has a faux hawk, is in a black V-neck and jeans, and I am straddling him on the party bus with one leg out revealing my boot with a broken-off heel. And I am sticking my tongue out holding a "rock on" symbol on one hand and my other hand is reaching into a potato chip bag. Honestly, not much has changed.

I showed him the photo while we sat at his parents' table attempting to play chess. He started dying laughing.

"That photo is ridiculous. But I totally remember this night. I just didn't put two and two together that you were the friend from another school!"

Matt was really good at chess and I was just starting. But after he beat me probably three times in a row within a matter of minutes, in our next game when I actually started to see a path for myself to win, I kept my mouth shut. Finally, I had him in check. But I didn't want to tell him because he'd move it, so I didn't. I bit my lip hoping he wouldn't notice and he moved a pawn, missing the realization. I immediately pushed my piece and knocked over his queen.

"Ah-hah! Checkmate!" I said, standing, holding up my arms.

"What! You never said check!"

"But I won!"

"That's not how it works!"

"I won!" I ran around the house, twirling and laughing as he chased me.

To say Matt and I were competitive was an understatement. Combined, we played nearly every single sport growing up. Even on the mountain, we were both looking at each other with racing eyes, despite Matt being a hell of a better snowboarder and skier than me. Matt had grown up hunting and fishing, and now even spearfished and lobster dove. Which made me want to do all of the above even more. Anything he could do, I wanted to do better, or just do, really.

Things were building in our relationship and Matt invited me to a wedding with him in Tennessee. He was a groomsman and his college buddy happened to be someone I went to high school with and knew well. I said hell yeah.

We'd fly into Knoxville and meet up with the group at a lake house we were staying at, and let me tell you, I was in heaven. It was a big cabin with a deck overlooking the water and cicadas humming all around us.

That night we played beer pong and all jumped into the lake for a night swim in the dark abyss. Later, the guys all started talking about how they might have a friend who could hook it up for us to go on the football field of the University of Tennessee tomorrow.

"Are you serious? Peyton Manning's mecca? That would be so sick," I chimed in.

Matt seemed a little sheepish that I was so into it because none of the other girls would be going. Thankfully, all the guys knew me growing up, so they knew I was gung ho sports everything and that I worked for ESPN. Of course, I could come.

I put on my "My daddy taught me about Jesus and pass interference" tee shirt proudly and was ready to go. We rode down the river and arrived to the stadium by boat, pulling up to one of the many docks out behind the stadium. I was seriously in awe and on cloud nine. At that point, I didn't even care if we got into the stadium, but we did. We walked out onto the field, and despite it being College Football Saturday, we were the only ones in there since the Volunteers were away. Someone pulled out a football and immediately the guys started tossing it around and running some plays and routes. I decided I wanted to run a drill against Matt, because, *me*.

"Fine. Prepare to get owned," Matt raised his eyebrows at me.

We lined up and took off with the cue of his friend. I immediately stiff-armed Matt off and jumped to try and get free to catch the pass, but he blocked it. Still, I had run a route on the grass of the University of Tennessee. *Hell-freakin-yeah.*

After that trip, Matt posted a photo of us on his Instagram from the wedding, which was a huge deal. He didn't have a single photo of a girl on his feed, and I felt proud that he wanted people to know about me finally. Even his family took notice.

Apparently my dad, my cousin, Matt, and his dad all wanted to go golfing together. On the first hole, Matt's dad decided to jump straight to it, I guess.

"You know the answer is yes, Jay."

My dad just looked at him confused.

"About Courtney! Absolutely yes. We couldn't be more excited to make her part of the family whenever Matt's ready. She's great."

My cousin called me after their round to tell me this and I was turning beet red just thinking about how palpable the embarrassment must've been for my dad and Matt.

"He said what!"

"Yeah! He was just joking around, but I actually think he was serious. Matt was dying. He was trying desperately to get his dad to stop talking."

"Jesus."

I wasn't ready to walk down the aisle with the kid, but I definitely was falling for him. Matt could make anyone laugh at any time, especially me and it was a trait I loved. But I didn't want to tell him yet because I felt like it was too soon. It had only been a few months. But then again, wasn't it like that with Keagan too?

We went to Tahoe for my birthday weekend and while dancing at the Cabo Wabo bar in the casinos with some booze confidence, I finally decided I wanted to tell him. A song came on that we were all jumping up and down to and Matt was shaking his head around being his typical self.

"Matt!" I yelled.

He stopped his head banging. "What!"

"I wanna tell you something!"

"Ok!"

"I love you!"

He smiled big. "I love you too!" We laughed and tried to kiss each other despite the jumping.

Naturally, Matt and I started going on more trips together. So when he got the invite from my parents to come to Palm Springs with us and golf with the dads, I wasn't surprised. The following day the girls would join up and while shopping in the pro shop at PGA West I saw a shirt I liked and realized it was the same as Matt's.

My mom said I should put it on so we matched and I nearly spit on her, I laughed out so quickly. "Matt would die. But I'll do it."

Surprisingly, he didn't die. He actually thought it was kind of fun and even took a picture with me on Hole 18. That day was fun because Matt bet me one-hundred bucks on the floating green hole I couldn't get on the green and guess who did and guess who didn't? There's a video of me dancing and swinging my club around and then storming over to Matt yelling you owe me one-hundred bucks.

We got back to the hotel and decided to take a "nap" but as soon as we shut the door we started going at it with each other and snuck into the shower. Matt pulled me back into the bedroom and went down on me shoving a pillow up to my face so he knew I would be quiet. We were never lacking in the sex department, let me tell you. Rain or shine, below freezing or over 120 degrees, happy or raging at each other, the sex was always going to happen.

The first time he came to Catalina with my family was off-the-charts fun. We swam and floated and drank all day on the boat with the family, went out to Luau Larry's at night, and emerged the next day bright and early, probably still drunk, in our large, obnoxious straw hats to go fishing. Matt helped me with all my lines and the fishes I hooked. The last day when we went back to the bedroom by ourselves we had, in my opinion, the best sex. There was just something about how passionate it was even leading up to it, and having sex in a quaint, old little hotel without air conditioning and the window open.

It's funny how quickly the fun things change, though. Or how memories like to play tricks on us.

* * *

While writing this book, I was actually doing some spring cleaning and came across a bag with a bunch of small pieces of paper in it. My sister was helping me clean.

"What's that?" she asked.

"I don't know," I said, confused holding it up and pouring some out.

"Go mini golfing. Ride bikes to the beach. Go indoor rock climbing. Go surfing." the slips of paper said in my handwriting.

Ah, yes. The random pieces of paper discovered in the old bag were from when I tried to get Matt to do a fun date idea with me when things weren't so good. The only rule was we had to say yes, I said to him while he picked out about six having an excuse for each one. He didn't say yes to any of them, so I gave up on it and we didn't do anything that day and I didn't bring them out again. I looked at the pieces of paper and set them on my desk and pulled out my phone.

I opened my phone to look at my Instagram, and then scrolled through some memories. I smiled at a video of us at the shooting range where Matt was popping his shotgun shells back at me making funny faces. It made me smile until I remembered, in actuality, I had been wiping away tears on that drive to the shooting range because Matt had insisted he was sick of me forcing him to go out on these elaborate dates.

I scrolled to another photo at the Beachcomber when Matt and I had gone down to get drinks on a gloomy Sunday. I had posted it later as a man crush Monday with the honey emoji and a bear emoji, but didn't tag him. Still, within twenty minutes of posting it, he called me and told me to take it down. Why would I post that photo of him? I told him it was cute. He said he looked huge. He didn't. Still, I took it down.

Everything seemed so happy and great in the photos, but it was all fake. Well, maybe not all fake, but there were certainly shades of gray in these memories. Once we were there maybe we were happy. Or maybe the upper of a margarita helped in one case and the upper of adrenaline helped in the other case. But it felt fake to me now.

I closed my phone and threw the pieces into the trash with the other spring cleaning items.

* * *

Don't get me wrong, Matt and I had some great memories and times together. And the beginning was so fun and full of love. But even then there were inklings of insecurities or things that would become problematic. All of those things would start to show their ugly face after our one-year anniversary.

We didn't want to do any old mushy-gushy normal couple thing to celebrate so we were going to go paintballing since I had never been. We drove down to Camp Pendleton in December and I wore my oversized camo jacket I had bought for fifteen dollars at a random Walmart in Alabama in college. I figured it'd give me a little cushion if I got hit.

We played our first round and as soon as the horn went off, Matt booked it in the opposite direction as me. *Typical, but I'd hold my own.* I was surprised how well I crushed it. I ended up staying in pretty long, even past Matt, but ended up getting unloaded on while running to the next station as our course got smaller. I threw my hands in the air as surrender, meaning you were hit and you were out. It hurt, but not as bad as I thought it would.

The next course, Matt and I split up again and I found a solid spot squished between a window and a door of a little shanty house where I was just picking people off left and right. I was hunkered down enough it was nearly impossible to hit me too. Until someone hit me with a dead perfect shot right to my goggles. It didn't hurt, but damn it scared me! I wiped the yellow paint from my goggles and raised my hand, seeing a person across the yard do a fist pump.

The next course was bigger and when the horn went off we took off running yet again, but as soon as I tucked behind an old burned-up car. I turned around to see Matt on the ground behind something with his hand already in the air. How could he already be out? We hadn't even shot yet. Something was wrong. I instantly shot my hand up and ran his way. Naturally, little shits still came at me. I ran to where he was and ducked below his cover.

"What's wrong?"

"My leg. My leg."

He pointed to his knee and there was a small cut in his jean with blood on the edges. But not a lot of blood. So that was good. A marshal came over to see what was up, but he was just a kid.

"What happened?"

"I slid to hide and didn't see this under the dirt."

He pointed to a piece of rusted, flat edged rebar barely sticking from under the dirt. *Great.* He might as well have baseball slid over a rusted old knife.

"Uh, can you walk off the course at least?"

I had Matt put his arm around me and we hobbled out of the makeshift warzone. Because Matt was a big dude, the guy didn't really know how to handle the situation. I tried peeking through the hole in his jeans but couldn't see anything. And I really didn't see my hunting, fishing, surfing, and literally all sports-playing boyfriend to be the kind to freak out over a scratch. Eventually I looked at Matt and told him these guys weren't going to be able to help. We needed to get to the car. Could he walk? I'd help him. So he got up and we made way to the car. Once there, I said I needed to see the wound.

"Take off your pants."

"I can't."

"I'll help you."

"I can't," he raised an eyebrow at me.

"What?"

"I'm not wearing underwear."

I started laughing. "Of course you're not! Of all the days. Well, it isn't anything I haven't seen. Take 'em off."

Once I pulled his pant leg past his knee, I knew just how much shit we were actually in. There was a two-inch gash about half an inch deep directly into his knee and his skin was gaping open revealing something shiny and silvery white. Matt looked at it and I saw him start to go pale. I immediately used my hand to block him from seeing it.

"Don't look at it. Look at me. I'm going to go see if they have a first aid kit. Then I am going to patch this up and I am driving you to the hospital. Ok?"

"I don't need to go to the hospital," he said in the most unconvincing voice ever.

"Matt, we're going to the hospital."

I helped him put his pants back on and went to get a first aid kit. Which again, was a feat in itself. No wonder they had us sign waivers in case we might drop dead on the course. Once I got the supplies, I realized Matt wasn't at the car and found Mr. Macho in the paintball practice zone shooting off a few more rounds.

"Matt? What the?"

"I had rounds left," he said, limping back with me to the car.

We got to the hospital and I told the nurse our situation despite the ER being packed. I told her my boyfriend was in a lot of pain. She said she couldn't give him anything yet. I had to come up again and ask her and she looked at me and smiled.

"What's his pain tolerance?"

"High."

"Is it though? Men can be babies. Especially when they're sick."

This made me laugh. "I promise his is high."

"Alright, fine." She went back and got him some painkillers while we waited.

I will say, those words will resonate with me forever after the months that would follow. Recovery took months for Matt. He had torn his ACL and was stitched up by the hospital, but eventually an infection broke out in his knee, and it wasn't properly healing because there were debris left over. They had to re-open the wound and then he had to sleep with a suction-like machine that would slowly but surely close the wound.

I tried to be there for him most nights, but he would end up screaming about the pain or complaining he needed water or that he needed something, I don't know, all the damn time. I might sound like an asshole saying this, but oh my God, I was about to lose my shit. I could never be a nurse. Major respect for nurses, man.

Finally, one night he woke up yelling again and I got up to do whatever he needed me to do, but he kept yelling obnoxiously loud at me until his mom came in the room to help out. I couldn't do this shit. I needed a break. The nurse's words came back to me. *Men can be babies. Especially when they're sick.*

The worst part of the injury was the change in his personality. He wasn't the big jokester like he always was and he seemed so irritable. Plus he started putting on weight, something I didn't care about for him, but something he was always so self-conscious of. He started taking it out on me even asking about the things I would eat in front of him. Did I need that glass of wine? Did I know how many calories and sugars were in it? He even started asking about my weight. But I knew it was because he was upset about his own weight and couldn't work out, so I tried not to take it personally. But I did start the 21 Day Fix diet and Whole 30 and any other diets I could try after he made a comment that we were going to be the "fat couple."

For Christmas, I had already put a big plan in motion for his gift. It was going to be epic and, hopefully, cheer him up. Months earlier, I had already sent a jersey and Sharpie to Lambeau Field addressed to Green Bay Packers offensive tackle David Bakhtiari with the return postage already included. I told him my boyfriend really didn't have a favorite NFL team and I wanted to convert him to a cheesehead since my family were die-hard Packers fans. Like the boss he is, Bakhtiari not only mailed it back signed, he even wrote a note on it to Matt about the Packers. Matt was amazed by the gift.

Despite the fun gift, it couldn't hide the fact things were heading in the wrong direction for Matt and me. Even after the injury when Matt was on the up and up, he did not want to do anything. We'd stay in all the time. We'd order food. He'd play video games. I'd work on my laptop. We'd watch a movie. We weren't even really seeing any of our friends anymore. The only time we'd go out was to our parents' houses. And even then, Matt refused to take any photos. I started figuring out it was about the weight gain. But partially he would do it to himself since he would try going all day without eating and then eat a double-double from In-N-Out down the street. Since I have never been able to finish a meal since I was like twelve, when I didn't finish he would eat my leftovers. I tried to tell him I would want my leftovers to try and help put off those calories, but he'd always laugh and say yeah right and start eating my food.

Beyond this, my family and I are the type who are always on the go. Always traveling. And no matter how many events and trips I invited Matt to come on, he didn't want to. I had my cousin's wedding coming up, in which I was a bridesmaid, and he didn't even want to come support me for that. Even writing this now, I'm still confused as to why didn't it end here? Why did we stay together for so many more months? And I realize it now.

Right before the wedding, tragedy struck my family, and my cousin

Mark who had been like a big brother to me growing up committed suicide. And Matt was there for me. He was my rock and helped me through it. Beyond that, I ended up getting Boone—my German shepherd, and my forever love. Matt and I stuck together through the shit times and then through the fun happy puppy times, and I guess that was distraction enough, until it wasn't. Things were going back down a dark path, but I never thought they'd take the turn they actually did.

My whole life I've always been the competitive type and the literal spitting image of Hayden Panettiere from *Remember the Titans*. I remember arguing football plays in sixth grade with the boys in my class and getting heated in arguments and winning them only to have the boys' comebacks be, "Whatever! You don't even play football."

I knew from then on I wanted to be a sports reporter. And for someone who spent most of their career in a male-dominated industry, full of condescending, misogynistic commentary detailing things like what you were wearing or what you wanted to be, you had to have some tough skin to hang with the boys—contrary to popular belief. If you didn't, you wouldn't survive. Simple as that. Be confident or get out. Thank God, confidence and sheer volume of voice has never been an issue with me.

That said, you would think a girl like me would be the literal last person susceptible to a verbally abusive relationship that turned to a physically abusive relationship. *How could someone so strong-willed allow that to happen?*

Every time our friends would talk in college about ever being in an abusive relationship we would always say, "Oh my God, never. The minute he even tries to lay a hand on me, I'm out!" or "Oh, if he said that to me or ever grabbed me, I'd call the police—or worse, my dad!"

I remember my mom even saying to my sister and me back in high school, "Girls—if you ever are in a situation where a boy or your boyfriend puts you in an uncomfortable position or he hits you or grabs you wrong or does anything wrong, you will immediately come to me and tell me. And we will deal with it. You will absolutely not tell your father. Because if you do, you will now be responsible for your father going to prison for the rest of his life, because he will probably kill them."

We would always look back and forth to each other and smirk at her seemingly ridiculous antics, knowing that wouldn't happen to us.

Once when we saw some news story come across the TV about a woman being attacked and forced into a car, I said I would kick a guy's ass and throw myself around vigorously before ever getting into a car with someone, ignorantly not knowing the situation. And my dad responded, keeping his eyes on the TV, "Obviously, I hope my daughter would never be in a situation like this. But I will say, if an attacker ever chose to kidnap Courtney out of anyone, I would pity the attacker."

He's not wrong. As per the Keagan chapter, I think that's apparent.

So this strong ass chick, who all her life would never allow something like this to happen… did. Just goes to show you, victims of abusive relationships aren't always the stereotypical victims you see on TV. *God, I hate that fucking word. Victim.* Truthfully, I didn't even feel like I was a "victim" of abuse. I'm no victim. I'm strong. He was just a fucking asshole who should have never laid hands on me.

The first time it happened, I like to think it went unnoticed. We were in San Diego at a ridiculously nice boutique hotel for his cousin's small wedding overlooking the ocean. I don't even remember what we were arguing about, but I was voicing my opinion about whatever it was (clearly, I do this a lot) as we were walking to our hotel room. As we entered the hotel room and the door shut behind us, he made it clear just how unhappy he was with my rebuttals. He launched himself at me onto the hotel bed putting his hands around my throat holding me down on the bed's brown patterned coverlet.

"SHUT UP! SERIOUSLY, SHUT THE FUCK UP. STOP FUCKING TALKING," he yelled with his eyes bulging and his hands snug around my throat.

He had this feverish look in his eyes. I didn't say anything while he yelled because, frankly, I was just in shock. Finally, his hands loosened around my throat but his body was still pressed over the top of me.

"Get your fucking hands off of me right now," I said defiantly, not blinking.

As soon as he unhinged his grip and stood up and flattened his now-wrinkled button-down shirt, I sat up in disbelief and redness rose to my face in anger. His face seemed to be in disbelief and maybe even embarrassment. But he didn't apologize or say anything. He continued fixing his shirt and headed toward the bathroom.

"If you ever touch me again like that I will fucking leave you in a second and everyone will know the type of person you really are," I said in a low tone looking directly at him with my eyes hooded by my eyebrows.

He was nervously smiling knowing he had done something wrong, but never willing to admit it. (Coming from the guy who has never apologized in his life and prides himself on it, seriously, why didn't I notice that as a red flag off the bat?) He didn't apologize. Instead, he said he had to go meet up with his cousins and check in and he'd be back shortly to get ready.

Alone in the room to think about what just happened, I decided not to. Instead I texted his sister who I knew would be attending the wedding as well and his mom to see what their plans were and where they were, to try and pretend what just happened didn't actually happen. Sometimes it's just easier that way.

As the ceremony approached, we got ready together, I drank wine and listened to music and he did his own thing. We walked to the bus to take us to the wedding and I remember at one point him trying to guide me with his hand on my waist, and I shrugged away from him. I couldn't get over my feelings regarding what had happened earlier. At one point, Matt's mom took a group photo of all of her kids and us, the respective girlfriends and boyfriends, and I remember saying "Cute!" looking at the photo. Really, I felt disgusted looking at the seemingly gentle gap between me and her son raging in the photo as what it truly was—a million miles.

I figured at the ceremony Matt would try to make up for it, maybe. I got up to dance and his mom got up too, and we were having a good time until the music got slow. Matt's sister, Chelsea, and her boyfriend, Jim, headed out to the floor. I waved to Matt to come dance with me so I wasn't a third wheel. He shook his head no.

"Seriously, come out here!" I yelled to him and tried waving him over.

"Nah, I don't do that."

I let my hand fall to my side, disappointed.

"Matt! Get up and dance with her!" his mom said to him from the table next to us.

"No."

"Psh! You know what Matt, you don't deserve her. She deserves someone better than you."

He responded by chugging the rest of his drink.

I was shocked she had even said that but, damn, was I doing a little victory dance in my head when she did. Once the reception ended we headed to post-ceremony cocktails at the little bar inside the hotel. We pulled up extra seats to a small high top table where his uncle was seated, a man I have actually known since I was in kindergarten. He had plenty to drink and was slightly slurring his words with a scotch in hand, but he was always jolly in spirit with a smirk of a smile just peeking out, showing his edge of tipsiness.

Two of the other cousins got up and it ended up being uncle Scott, me, and Matt alone at the table. They have a close relationship and the alcohol-infused night led me to start a bold conversation.

"Scott, I have a question for you."

"Sure, shoot honey!"

"Do you think it is ever ok for a man to hit a woman or lay hands on her?"

He immediately shot a sobering look at me and then a look at Matt. Matt glanced at me with a look of, *be very careful here.*

Scott immediately said while Matt was shooting this look to me, "Absolutely not. It's never ok under any circumstances."

I was surprised when Matt fired back almost immediately without pause and a sort of indignation. "Yeah, but what if she *deserved it?*"

***

The second time was the worst, in my opinion.

We had been fighting a lot lately. I was on a traveling bender, per usual. I had gone to Stagecoach Country Music Festival, the Hamptons, Washington, the Bahamas, Dallas, Louisiana, and more before he started to express he was irritated with all my travel. He said he felt like he didn't even have a girlfriend, despite my attempts to invite him. He had actually gone on two trips in there—one to Catalina with my family which we had a ball on, and even to Washington (finally meeting my mom's side of the family), but that trip was less than stellar since I basically had to force him to come. It wasn't until my dad made a side comment to Matt about missing the wedding and a few trips he was invited on that he actually bucked up and booked his plane ticket. Still, with no distractions and no separation now, there was no denying things were shit between us.

The last two weeks of seeing each other had ended with me crying and him yelling at me every night. To "make up" for this, I thought it would be fun if we went on a date night and got dressed up, just us two. (HAH—in hindsight, this disgusts me. Let's dress up this relationship and make it look presentable. Sick.) He agreed and said we would go to a nicer spot in Costa Mesa, Santa Monica Seafood.

I even curled my hair and wore my waist trainer with a regular black U-neck tank top, skinny American Eagle jeans, and black leather heeled boots with gold buckles so I'd look skinny and sexy. My mom said I looked cute before I left our house to head over to Matt's. Driving up the toll road, I was singing along to Katy Perry throwbacks and '90s girl power throwbacks, feeling hot and happy, and a little nervous.

I pulled up and parked with a sense of butterflies coming to me. The last few months we had really just been in sweats hanging out watching TV, so I was excited I was finally looking hot for my man. I found myself daydreaming about him grabbing me by the waist and pulling me in, saying I looked hot and kissing me before we went on our date. As this thought lingered I walked up the stairs of his house. When I got to the top of the stairs, I got a glimpse of him on the couch in a navy blue, ratty old sweatshirt with a stain on it and gray oversized sweatpants on. He had his hood on and looked like he hadn't showered. He shot his eyes in my direction when I appeared at the top of the stairs.

"Uh, what are you wearing?"

"Jeans, a tank top, and boots?" I said feeling defensive looking down at my options and instantly realizing my daydream would be just that.

He didn't respond.

"Are you going to change? Isn't our reservation soon?" I asked.

"No, I'm wearing this. Why are you wearing that? Why are you dressed like that?" he said, showing a visible face of his disgust like a two-year-old might to vegetables.

"I thought we decided to dress up for our date night!" I exasperatedly said, smiling through the pain even though deep down I just wanted to stab myself for being so stupid. I disallowed the tears to form in my eyes as I curled my toes deep into my boots to cause pain elsewhere and bit my lip when he wasn't looking. *Focus the pain somewhere else.*

"Alright, let's just go," he said, getting up and sliding on his old Vans with the heels pressed down and grabbing his keys.

After the week we'd had, I decided to not say anything in the car and hoped it would get better. We got to the restaurant without talking and he got out and shut the door immediately behind him, making swift strides to the restaurant. I barely got my door open before he locked it and the alarm would have sounded.

I hadn't worn heels in a while, let alone with a waist-trainer underneath my black tank top, so I was not as steady as I would've liked on my feet getting out of the car. I was kind of hoping I'd be walking side-by-side with him so I could lean on him if need be, but I noticed the restaurant door closing behind him. My knuckles started to ache, something that happens when I get overwhelmed with emotion. I felt tears wanting to come, but I would never let them.

I'm fine. And I look good. He's in the wrong. I look beautiful.

My fake smile turned to an instant frown, the one that happens when you know you're going to cry and that everything you're telling yourself is just a coping mechanism. Tears welled in my eyes. I felt stupid for thinking I looked pretty and for thinking that he would say so or acknowledge it. We had been together for years and I know damn well he's never called me beautiful. The tears welled bigger. I stopped in the parking lot to compose myself from my inner thoughts.

"Fuck that. I look good. Even if he hasn't noticed it." I said out loud to myself before walking in.

I walked in with my newly plastered joker smile and looked and smiled at the waiter who politely smiled back. I looked around for Matt and saw the back of his telltale sweatshirt seated outside at a table for four with two other familiar faces sitting at the table—his sister Chelsea and her boyfriend Jim. On our date night. I allowed my sadness to turn to blood-boiling anger, but I attempted to keep my face from showing it as Chelsea waved with a genuine smile to me as I approached the table.

"Yay, you're here!" she said as I looked at her and Jim's attire in sweats as well.

"Yep, I'm here!" I said trying not to sound sharp and dagger-like, but unsuccessfully. *Of course I'm fucking here.*

"Oh my God, wait! You look so hot! Why didn't we dress up? Wait—why do I feel like we're crashing a date night all the sudden," Chelsea said.

I sat down adjusting myself and smiled and just took a drink of my already arrived water glass. Matt didn't look up from the menu.

"Wow! I feel bad! We had no idea," Chelsea said awkwardly.

As genuine as Chelsea is, I couldn't let her feel guilty no matter how angry and sad I was. "No, no! I'm glad you're here," I said, reaching across the table grabbing her hand.

The waiter came by and I asked for a glass of chardonnay. *But really, just bring me the bottle at this point.* I didn't look at Matt the entire dinner. Maybe once, and it hurt too much. All I remember was Chelsea, a self-proclaimed healer and feeler of all things aura and whatever else, saying, "Wow the energy between you two is electric tonight! Like so many negative ions I can feel it all through me. Like I feel like you might even shock each other. The negativity is definitely radiating off of you."

Well yeah, Chelsea. Fuck.

I ordered my third glass of chardonnay and got my first eye-to-eye look from Matt as he judged me. When the glass came I gave him an unbothered glance, swallowing down a solid chug. He was drinking too, and I immediately knew, this was not going to be even close to the night I'd envisioned. We paid the bills and Matt got up immediately leaving me at the table. Jim followed Matt quickly to ease the situation with some golf or hunting talk while Chelsea and I took our time despite my annoyance in Matt leaving me behind, as always. Chelsea walked me out with her usual warmness about her, and we said our goodbyes. *I really do love her.* I waved goodbye to her and Jim, who was running up to catch up with her at their parked car on the other side of the parking lot. *As if Matt would ever do that for me.*

I turned my attention to the Chevy Tahoe already started and Matt waiting in the driver seat for me impatiently. I hoisted myself up, courtesy of the waist trainer, but once I was situated I instantly gave him a glare.

"What?" he said, irritated.

"I asked you for one thing. I needed a good night from you. I needed to have some alone time with you and some time for us to be intimate and just be with each other. And you blatantly disregarded that and blindsided me by inviting people. Inviting your sister and Jim!" A familiar feeling of salt lingered in my eyes and I tried to keep it at bay, but I knew it was fast approaching. "Tonight was important to me, Matt. And it obviously wasn't for you."

"Seriously? Well, I didn't think you'd show up looking like a hooker! Like what are you wearing? Jesus Christ. Let's just go home and go to bed," he said with a huff, looking away from me disgusted.

My lip started to quiver, but I wanted to be stronger. I turned to the window so he wouldn't see, not that he was actually even looking at me. *So much for looking beautiful.* The first tear fell. I wiped it quickly away.

"I told you I wanted one night together. I told you how important it was to me. You said you understood and agreed and I walk in to Chelsea and Jim sitting there?" my voice cracked.

"So what? I can't invite my family to dinner now?" he responded as if it was instinctual and he could never be wrong.

"Don't flip this on me. I needed this night for us. So badly," my voice sharpened to a point as a choke began to come. I turned back to the window to avoid showing my tears, but it was too late. The first one let loose and they began forming smooth streams down my hot cheeks.

"And then you start ordering wine like a fiend. You're embarrassing. And now you're just drunk trying to start a fight," Matt said.

Maybe he was right about having too much wine, but everything else that happened felt so unfair. I decided to stand my ground and explain why it was so wrong. He knew that night was important. And he should've told me he invited his sister and her boyfriend so I didn't have such high hopes. I felt like a loser. Like Drew Barrymore in the movie *Never Been Kissed* when she's so excited to go to prom with Billy. *He made me feel like that.* I laid everything out while attempting to hold back the rivers spewing from my eyes and hoping he would understand and give me a response of "I didn't realize" or even "Ok." Because everyone knows, even his family members, Matt doesn't apologize. So expecting an "I'm sorry" was even a pipe dream for me. I wouldn't let the possibility enter my thoughts after my earlier daydreams turned out to be just fantasies.

By the time I finished my well-thought-out rant, even saying it calmly without crying and choking, we had already arrived home and were sitting in his car. I had noticed he was texting while I was divulging my feelings to him, but despite the disrespect, I decided to keep going and finish what I had to say because it was important and needed to be heard. When I finished, he didn't say anything and was still looking at his phone. I waited a few seconds, and then longer.

"Did you hear what I was saying? I just need you to understand." I asked.

"Oh what?" he responded, looking up cavalierly. "I missed it, I wasn't listening," he said, turning off the ignition and opening the door and slamming it behind him, leaving me alone in the car. I sat in disbelief, sadness, betrayal, and *fucking stupidity*. The lights in the car eventually faded off.

What a loser you are. You're with someone who doesn't even care about you.

My mind started to spiral. I started to get vertigo and my knuckles panged. I kept blinking to stop tears from coming, looking up, but instead they just fell off my fake lashes sporadically wherever they could land as I leaned over my legs so they wouldn't stream down my face. They splatted to the plastic floorboards of the Tahoe's front seat floor mat. I couldn't stay in there, though. Too pathetic. Plus, this is his car.

I went inside the front door, surprised it wasn't already locked. I walked in the entryway and sat inside on the stairs that lead up to the living room. Thankfully it was a narrow three-story townhome, so the stairs seemed like a somewhat safe space for me to cry away from his roommates and, especially, away from him. *I should leave, but I can't drive. Plus my parents know I'm staying here.*

I sat and cried for a while. But the alcohol caught up to me. And the cries turned to heaves. And I was louder than I had hoped to be. And Matt was always the hero in everyone's eyes. I'd be lying if I said I didn't want Matt to come down. I wanted him to come down. *Apologize.* Say I looked pretty. Say he was sorry. Hold me. But there's me with my pipe dreams again. This thought made me sink my head into my hands and let out another whimper.

God, I'm pathetic.

Suddenly I heard a low voice behind me saying "Hey Court, are you ok? I wanted to check in on you? Is everything ok with you and Matt? Nothing happened to you, right? I just want to make sure you're ok."

Utterly embarrassed, I turned around, swiftly wiping the tears from my reddened face and eyes to see Chase, his roommate and house owner, with genuine concern on his face and that same smile and look of pity I had received from Matt's uncle Scott months before.

"I'm sorry, Chase. Yes, everything is fine. I'm ok, thank you. I'm sorry," I responded only to see seconds later a "concerned" Matt behind him.

"Hey Court, everything ok?" he said from up the stairs. "Sorry about this, man! Court, c'mon! Let's go up now." He said tapping his roommate on the shoulder with a reassuring glance telling him to buzz off. But he lingered a bit, which I appreciated.

"I don't want to yet. Just give me a sec."

"Come on up and we can talk in my room. You're ruining everyone's night," he said jokingly and embarrassed, looking at Chase.

I looked up to see Chase looking at Matt in rejection of the comment, shaking his head but not saying anything. I reluctantly lifted myself off the steps and went upstairs. Only to get into the bedroom to be berated by words about what an embarrassment I was and a bad person.

So, in my memory I always thought the second time things got physical was that night just because of how brutal he was verbally and how badly I was hurt emotionally that night, but really, that was just our first real breakup. We decided Matt said things to me that couldn't be taken back. Did he mean them? He wasn't sure. He needed time to think. A month went by and he decided he wanted to talk. He wanted to get back together. I had just lost my job courtesy of the "ESPN Apocalypse" as it was called. Over 500 employees were laid off, right before the holidays, nonetheless. On top of this, I had a lot of other things going on at this time. Needless to say, my vulnerable ass told Matt I would think about it. And then I made a decision that should've never been made.

We got back together and, almost immediately, fell back into our groove of unhappiness.

The night of the second time of physical abuse followed after whatever our night's escapade had been with friends. I remembered it had been a fun one, a happy one even. We came back and stumbled in together, hand-in-hand, to his bedroom on the third floor. When we got there, I was shocked to find he no longer had a bedroom door on the hinges.

"What happened here?" I asked.

He ignored me and laughed while taking off his pants and shirt and jumping into the bed. I joined in with the laughing, but more seriously asked "Wait no! Seriously, what happened to your door? You literally don't have a door!" I said, still smiling, but genuinely wanting to know.

He responded, "Nothing," smiling and rolling over in bed.

"Ugh, it's not exactly nothing," I said, now losing my smile.

No response.

"Seriously, what happened to your door, Matt?"

At this point he was ignoring me on purpose. Rolled over with a smirk on his face and attempting to be unresponsive.

"Matt, seriously!" I laughed.

No response.

I rolled over on top of his left shoulder, facing the wall, and pulled a piece of hair curling in front of his forehead slightly. "Hello?" I said in a funny voice, tilting my head. "What happened to your door! I don't want to sleep in here with you with your door wide open to your roommates!"

I looked out the doorway, the white door off its hinges and leaning against the wall, with a direct shot into his roommate's bedroom and Chase's bedroom just down the hall. Knowing Matt's sexual appetite, I wasn't exactly comfortable sleeping without a door.

"Matt, seriously." I said.

"Nothing. I don't know. Drop it," his tone had changed, darker and more hooded.

"Wait, what happened? You can tell me," I pleaded.

Now that he was somewhat awake and not drunkenly incoherent acknowledging me, I pulled the little piece of hair curling at his forehead again. And then again. It was wrong. And maybe I poked the bear and caused this, but he wasn't responding to me or listening to me and *why wouldn't he just answer?*

"Matt. Matt. Tell me what happened to the door. You can tell me. I won't care. I just need to know."

Clearly the alcohol was pulsing through my veins too, as I persisted on finding out the incident behind his door. Within an instant, he popped back to life after another hair tug and flipped me over on his bed to be on top of me with rage in his eyes. He grabbed my arm with one hand and used his other to jab me in the leg as he yelled.

"I DON'T KNOW WHAT HAPPENED TO THE FUCKING DOOR, COURTNEY! YOU FUCKING HEAR ME? I DON'T KNOW WHAT HAPPENED TO THE FUCKING DOOR! I DON'T KNOW. SO SHUT THE FUCK UP AND STOP ASKING ME!"

His grip tightened with every word he said and I could feel my pulse throbbing where his hands were. There's something about someone screaming in your face like this that instantly makes tears start to form. So here they were again. Those familiar, salty, stream-like fellows, tickling the back of my eyes, forcing their way into existence. I let them come as his hot, bitter breath flew into my face with every pointed *fuck*.

I responded back in what felt like the voice of a mouse. "Matt, you're hurting me. My arm."

He continued to yell he didn't care while keeping a firm grip on my arm.

I responded again smally and, to my utter dismay, with a serious crack of my voice. "Please Matt, you're going to leave bruises on my arm."

At this, he again declared he didn't care and moved on to his new exclamation of words and continued the grip on my arm. "You are so fucking stupid. Do you know that? You aresofuckingstup-," he continued his assault of words on me of what a pathetic excuse of life I was. And why would anyone want to be with the pathetic existence that was me. All while doing this he continually pounded his pointer finger into my bare thigh as he held me close to his face to yell at me with his other hand tightly grasped around my arm.

"Matt, you're hurting me," I squeaked out again, tears pouring from my eyes, hoping it would make a difference.

He released me violently and pushed me away and rolled over to fall asleep.

What just happened?

"Matt, these are going to leave bruises on me." I said to him while touching my arm and leg daintily in the sore areas that were just persecuted. "Why did you do that?"

"No they won't, you're fine," he said to the wall without rolling over.

I stared at the ceiling the entire night until the sun came up. Surprisingly, I didn't have to listen to Matt snoring the entire night, a sign that maybe he wasn't sleeping either. I felt the buzz of alcohol wear off and fade into a headache and dehydration from pouring every fluid out of my body through my eyes. I ignored the bruises and barely acknowledged them until the next day when we had to go to a Little League Baseball game for his co-worker's child. It was warm and I planned to wear a tank top, until I saw my arm.

"Yeah, you should probably wear a sweater or jacket over that," Matt said pointing to my arm.

"Yeah, well you did that, it's your fault," I responded pointedly, still grabbing a zip-up hoodie despite the heat.

Three days later was when it really hit me what had happened. I started my shower and, while waiting for the water to heat up, undressed in my bathroom. As soon as I was naked in front of the mirror, I saw it. There they were. Staring right at me in my bathroom mirror. The bruise on my upper thigh from where I had been continuously poked over and over particularly beckoned to me. It had now morphed in shade and color, and severely in size.

Rather than ignore it, I finally took the time to look at it. At all of them. I stared at the now black, grapefruit-sized bruise on my leg with interior edging of dark purple, spots of red and maroon, and hints of yellow at the exterior edges of the black abyss. I reluctantly, but curiously, turned my naked body in the mirror to reveal my arm and the back of it. Four distinct purple, gray finger marks. Like fingerprints even. I really didn't even think that was possible and thought that was only something they do with makeup in the movies. Why wouldn't it be just one big bruise? I touched them. They didn't hurt like the one on my leg did. The pain registered when these bruises were touched whereas I couldn't even run my fingers over the bruise on my leg. The more I stared at each impression on my body and traced my fingers along them, the more I felt absolutely disgusted. Not in him, but in myself. I instantly broke out into tears. *How had I not noticed it was this bad? How had I not noticed things were this bad?* But this time I made a decision for myself.

I am not a victim.

I won't let him have that.

I took out my phone and took photos of all the bruises on my arm. All four of the perfectly positioned finger marks on my arm. And then the hideous black hole of a bruise on the side of my upper thigh.

I texted my most-trusted friend Briana.

"Hey, I need to tell you something and I need to send you something that will be alarming, but it's fine. Just keep these if anything should ever happen."

I sent her all the photos, with tears still coming from my eyes and the shower still running in the background. It had probably been on for ten minutes at this point.

Briana started responding concerned texts, but first thing was first, I needed to call him.

"Hey babe! How's your morning?" he answered in his normal, upbeat way.

I answered back with tears and pants, hardly breathing. I told him I saw myself in the mirror for the first time with the bruises on me. How disgusting I felt. How I would never be this person. How *he did this*. Not me.

His voice choked up and started to crack back over the phone even though he was at work. He said he was so ashamed and was so sorry. *An apology.* He was disgusted. He couldn't believe it happened. He would never do it again.

"You're right. It won't ever happen again," I said defiantly, but sniffling. "I took photos of my bruises and sent them to Briana and told her what happened."

"YOU DID WHAT?" he said back in a fire, but still trying to keep his voice low since he was at work in his new office that was quite airy at the top floor of the financial building overlooking the ocean. There wasn't any sincerity or shame in his voice now, just concern for himself. "Court, why the hell would you do that?"

"Because Matt, I learned something when I looked in the mirror. I never thought I would be this girl. Hiding and covering up for my boyfriend. And then I realized, I'm not that girl. And I never will be. So I took these disgusting, embarrassing photos and sent them to Briana to show you, I will NEVER be that girl. I will never hide bruises. I will never hide what you've done ever again. And now she knows, too. And if you ever do it again, everyone will know."

Thankfully it was over the phone, and I didn't let my voice crack once despite tears consistently pouring down my face like an overflowing creek after a storm.

"OK," came over the other end of the phone. "It won't."

* * *

You know what's crazy? The inherent effect this had on me, yet I had no realization it did. I really thought I was fine and all hunky-dory after these things. I went through my iPhone photos to see where those bruise photos are and I have them favorited so they're easier to find. I don't know what that says about me needing to see them again.

I tried to get a better basis of how things got to where they did and how it led on after the fact. And shockingly, my pictures, or should I say lack thereof, proved to say it all considering I didn't take one single photo of myself for one month after the incident.

That said, Matt and I stayed together even after all this. We had a flight booked to go to our friend's wedding in Hawaii and I swear that was the only thing keeping us together at that point. Every time we hung out, I would leave in tears because of something he'd say to me. While all this was going on, Matt had me start looking at houses in Tahoe that I liked. He had enough money saved up and was thinking he wanted to move up there. When I had asked almost a year ago about us living together in Orange County he had laughed it off, but since we would be out in the middle of the woods, playing house, now apparently he was down.

We went to Tahoe again that winter, as usual. His mom and sister wanted to go down and get drinks at Edgewood Golf Club as a girls' outing, but what started out as fun turned into feeling more like an ambush by the firepits. They wanted to ask about Matt and if I thought he was depressed. *Maybe about his weight?* Or maybe *was I the reason he was depressed*? He was hardly going out and never wanted to do anything —what did *I think* was going on?

Duh. I would know. All he does is take it out on me. I lived it. But it's not my fault. *Is it?*

When Matt found out about the intervention, he freaked out. Like totally freaked out. And on me, of course. This was my fault apparently. Out of all things said, this might be the one thing I regretted telling him. Then again, maybe not, because if it wasn't for this tipping factor

I may have ended up playing house in the woods with him for the rest of my life.

"Depressed? I'm not fucking depressed. I'm not a fucking loser. And you guys were just talking behind my back? What'd you even say?" Matt fumed.

"I didn't know what to say, Matt. I said I didn't think you were depressed, but I knew your weight bugged you and you didn't like going out and doing things involving drinking or eating because it's more calories."

"What! That's not true! Why would you say that?"

"Not true? Ok, Matt. They were just asking because they care. I care. But we don't know what's going on. I just told them that."

He was so angry he grabbed my car keys and took my car down to the casinos that night and gambled the whole night. The next morning, he told me he lost thousands of dollars and it was my fault. He didn't know if he would ever get over the conversation that was had with his family.

The countdown to Hawaii began.

And it's no surprise, as soon as we got on our flight to Hawaii and all our friends on the flight started talking about golfing the next day, Matt said, no this is a boys' day, Court, even though we had already talked privately about how excited I was to golf.

"Wait, what? No. You said I could come golfing with you guys."

"Eh, no. Guys day. You can do something with the chicks."

"But I'm just as good of a golfer as everyone else. Why can't I go?"

The boys kept drinking their Jack and Cokes, and one of the guys even piped up and said he thought I should come. Why not?

Matt kept making jokes about it and said I couldn't until it finally got to me. I felt tears welling up. *Why did he get to decide what I could or couldn't do?* And why was he being such a dick about it in front of his friends? As soon as we got off the plane, I went to the bathroom and cried in a stall by myself only to hear a familiar voice and a knock.

"Hey Court, you ok? Sorry. Matt can be a real idiot sometimes. But I think he's sorry and just wants to have fun now since we're here! Yay! Hawaii!" Chelsea said through the stall door.

Great. Now I looked like that girl. I pulled it together and got rid of any evidence I was crying and put on my sunglasses. That would be the theme of the trip. *Mask it. Sweep it under the rug. Fake it 'til you make it.*

Sure, we had a good time. We both golfed with the group of guys and it was a lot of fun and not a big deal that I was the only girl, just like I knew it would be. We hung by the pool and drank with our friends, and went to all the pre-wedding cocktails and parties. Matt even took cute photos with me, which was a miracle in itself. One of which he dipped me down on the beach and I pretended to laugh. But no matter how cute the photos looked, it wasn't real. It was so fake it made my stomach hurt. I remember Matt even saying one of the photos was cute of us and I should post it, which was even more rare, but the thought of posting something so phony was sickening.

There was one thing Matt was right about—he said he was never going to get over that his mom and sister had consulted me about him being depressed. Our final conversation was a phone conversation and he brought it up again. It was just before Easter and I had family coming over and I told him it was important he make time to come say hi, but he said he didn't want to. Finally the conversation did what it always did, and Matt switched it onto me. I had just woken up and was lying in bed and switched my phone to speaker while I laid listening.

"Listen, I've been talking to my family, and they agree. You're just toxic. I'm not depressed or anything, you're just the problem. You're toxic for anyone to be around," he said.

He kept repeating the word *toxic* like he had nothing else he could think of to say. I grew furious with these comments, because I knew they weren't true. His mom was just texting me asking if I would be coming over for Easter and if I wanted to help her make the cherry pie.

I felt the ritual of liquid welling in my eyes and one broke free down my cheek. *How many mornings had started with tears because of his words? How many nights had ended with tears because of his words?* No more. I was fucking sick of crying. I finally interrupted his rant.

"Really, Matt? They think I'm so toxic? Well, if they think I'm so toxic, then I'm done. You think I'm so toxic? Let me make it easy for you. I'm done with you and I'm done with this. With us. We're done. Goodbye, Matt."

I hung up and slammed my phone into my comforter. As soon as I did, I broke out into heaves and put my face into my hands. All of the sudden, I was startled by mom pushing open my door. She must've been listening outside.

"Get up and get dressed. We're going for a walk. Oh, and you're never getting back together with him."

She told me I wasn't going to reach back out to him even if he texted me. I said he wouldn't and she rolled her eyes since she had seen this play out once before and, let's be real, mom was always right on these kinds of things. But this time, there would be no getting back together.

"If it's like this at three years, just imagine what six years looks like. Ten. Twenty."

This shook me to the core. She was right. And she didn't even know all the details of how bad things had gotten. He tried calling me multiple times that day which I rejected.

"You're just going to give up? Just like that. Just gonna dodge my calls and not even going to try? You're so typical. Call me back."

Yeah, actually. I was. I didn't call him back.

*　*　*

Until this year, I hadn't told anyone about the first choking incident because I didn't feel it was significant. The second incident, the bruising one—yeah, I had told a couple friends after the breakup. But the first one, I didn't even think of as abuse. When we grow up we learn about abuse as a man slapping you in the face or punching you or shoving you into a wall like in the movies. But what qualifies as abuse? If there's marks left over? If there aren't, does that count? It seems stupid, but when do you know if it counts? The choking incident lasted mere seconds and he didn't leave marks behind, so does that count? Apparently, it didn't register too harshly in my brain, because there weren't marks and I didn't want to overreact.

However, I guess some people do define abuse differently. After getting eye-bulge reactions from some of my friends upon telling the choking story, I realized maybe I'm just the one who didn't know the definition. To me, the choking didn't reflect nearly as bad as the second where bruises were left. *Evidence.*

"What? It's not as bad as the other story?" I'd say.

"...he had his hands *around your throat* and was *screaming in your face.*"

"Yeah, well he didn't leave any bruises behind or anything? It was just a quick reaction."

Ew. Bile lingers up in my throat reminiscing. I defended the act, him, because *he didn't leave bruises behind* and that must mean everything that happened was OK. Could be masked. Covered. Swept under the rug.

Who the fuck am I? Honestly, at this point, I still don't know, but I'll tell you one thing—I'm not a fucking victim. I know that may seem insensitive, but I can't let myself see myself as such. Not because of him.

That said, I think it's only fair to reveal even after Matt and I had been broken up for a few months, guess what I did? I asked to meet back up with him and talk about us. *Yep, I really did that.* I remember I started the conversation by bringing up a funny song that came on shuffle that he introduced me to. He laughed and I asked if we could talk.

He was busy. He was golfing. Couldn't I just call him? He was so busy. No. I was really hoping to talk in person. He said he didn't need to, but if I needed to that was fine. I could come over to his parents' house, where he was at for the weekend.

So, why did I need to talk to him? I felt like we made a mistake breaking up and we should get back together. I was heartbroken still and thought we needed to get back together. And I was so determined. As much as I hate revealing this part of the story, I think this is an important detail because so many girls go through this exact thing. Toxic relationships are real and common. And feeling like you need that person who was so wrong to you is disgusting, but also, so real. I felt disgusting and hated myself, but I still thought being together was better than apart.

I'll never forget how nervous I felt driving over there thinking we would either get back together or I'd be heartbroken all over again. To me, it was a fifty-fifty shot. So when I showed up and he barely got up to greet me in the house and looked like he had lost twenty pounds, I was even more nervous. I sat on the couch and tried to have small talk, but he basically said let's cut to the chase. So, I started to say my feelings and as soon as I said I thought we should get back together, he laughed under his breath and asked why? I tried to tell him I felt like we were so good together. Made each other laugh. Loved the same things. Loved each other's families. But it was no use. He was looking at his phone, his watch, around, anywhere but at me. Just like in the car that one night. I finally stopped talking and waited for his response, digging my nails into the underside of my hand so hard I'm surprised it didn't start bleeding. *Feel the pain elsewhere.*

"Court..." he looked at me like he was about to start laughing, like I was something to pity. "I'm sorry you feel this way. I really am. But the truth is, I'm better than I've ever been. I've lost weight, I'm feeling great and I just don't think it's a good idea. I don't feel the same way at all, really."

He finished with a smirk that I swear nearly broke out into a toothy grin that should be on a toothpaste advertisement. *He was better than he had ever been.* And he definitely had lost weight. He looked really good. I was devastated. By all of it. He didn't want me anymore. In fact, he was better off without me. I couldn't help it when my head hung down.

"Well, I don't think there's anything left to talk about then," I said, getting up to leave.

"Aww, you're going to be OK, Court. Right? You're going to be ok?" he said, making a theatrically sad face at me.

With this, all my sadness turned instantly to rage. I felt fury grow inside of me, but I was not going to let myself start crying in front of this smug asshole. *What was I thinking coming here?* How pathetic! I could feel his pity, his smile, his dragged-out "aww" burning into the back of my skull as I walked out. *So pathetic.* But I wasn't pathetic. I was just sad and heartbroken and had a lapse in judgement coming here. Not pathetic.

I finally turned around, not letting the tears that were already starting to sting my eyes show, to defiantly say some last words to remind him who the fuck I was.

"Oh, I'm going to be just fine, Matt. You can count on that. If there's one thing you can be sure of, it's that you don't have to worry about me being OK," I said, even starting to laugh a bit. I shut the large glass door behind me as he followed me up to it. I got in my car and didn't allow myself to start crying until I was out of his neighborhood. Then the tears came like waterfalls.

* * *

I ended up going to meet up with his sister Chelsea, who I had actually become close with, and her friend to go crystal hunting one day for their business, and for me it was just more for fun. Plus I could ask her about Matt just one more time.

"So I went and talked to Matt, actually."

"Yeah, I heard about that. But he really is doing so well, Courtney. He's really happy."

This hit like a dagger straight to the heart. Because it made me think for a brief second, *was I the problem?* Just like they insinuated all those months ago in the ambush at Edgewood. We continued hunting for crystals when the girls wanted to go one way, but I said one tent was calling to me and I wanted to hit it up. They came with, and Chelsea's friend Amy ended up finding a Jasper stone, her favorite, at the tent.

"We wouldn't have found it if you didn't lead us to the tent! You sensed it!" Chelsea said.

"I guess!" I laughed.

We walked to one more tent and while we were looking through bins I felt something that called for my attention to my right, and looked up immediately to see a woman next to me holding a crystal and flipping it over in her hand, smiling as she held the crystal. Chelsea watched this happen as her attention was diverted that way as well.

"Oh my God, Courtney," Chelsea said. "You're an empath."

"What?" I laughed.

"You felt that. You felt her feelings just like I did. Her energy. And with Amy! You brought her to that table."

"Uh..." I laughed uncomfortably, knowing this was so Chelsea.

"Maybe? What is it? An in-path? What does that even mean?" I continued laughing. I know Chelsea can get real witchy-woo sometimes, but I do believe in positive energy from crystals and just love the way they look, hence why I was here. So obviously, I'd hear her out.

"Empath. E-M-P-A-T-H," she laughed, then explained it to me.

At first, I just figured she was on her same shit, but when she explained what an empath was, everything made a whole lot of sense to me. Empaths feel deeper than other people. They take on everyone's emotions and burdens. Sometimes unwillingly. Was I the kind of person that random people would just spill their guts to? Could I always tell when people were lying? Did it break my heart when I could feel exactly how they were feeling despite what they told me? Did hanging with certain people who were unhappy or depressed drain the hell out of me?

God forbid we go into the amount of times random people at events, bars, the DMV, the gas station, you name it, came up to me to talk about their ex-wife, their kid with an addiction, or getting out of jail and starting brand new. They fucking flocked to me. But I was always ok with talking people through things. That's why my friends joked I was the therapist of the group. It may seem like very bland questions and maybe not something everyone would believe in but, damn, it opened new doors to me, and I honest to God think I needed to hear it exactly when I did. Because hearing his sister tell me he was doing "the best he ever had" cut deep. The hardest part was making myself believe I wasn't the reason why.

I'd feel sick reminiscing on bad memories, contorting them and twisting them to resonate with Matt's final words to me. Did I start our fights? Did I drink too much? Did I go out with friends too much? Did I push him to do things he didn't want to do? Did I travel and up-and-leave too often? Maybe I was the problem. Maybe I was *toxic*.

After embracing my empath traits, it helped me get more in tune with myself and realize something important. Those thoughts weren't true. Was I flawed? Sure. But was I toxic? No. Was I the problem? Maybe partially, but not entirely. And, ultimately, I was so much stronger and better than this. His mom was right the night of that wedding—I did deserve someone better. I didn't need Matt. One of the harder parts of the breakup, honestly, was breaking up with his family too. To this day, I love them.

My mom always says: "Forgive, but never forget." So that's what I've done. I've forgiven Matt. But I won't ever forget what he did. And I won't forget all the good times, either. I like to think maybe Matt won't ever do that to a girl again. Maybe he has grown as a person. Maybe I am naïve for trying to see the good in people, but I hope it's true. I think deep down Matt is a good person with a dark side that he should address, but I don't hate him.

And no matter how hard this chapter in my life was to write, ripping my heart out onto the pages and wiping the blood around just to shove it back in my chest, this is the truth. This is what happened. And sure, it's dark. But it's real. And shit like this happens every day. And it's important. If anything, I just hope that maybe someone else can read this chapter and relate to it and be strong enough to leave. Or strong enough to take the next step out of a toxic relationship. Or even recognize a toxic relationship. That was the hardest part for me. I didn't even realize I was in one until after the fact.

Now that years have passed since my relationship with Matt, and I was able to have a great relationship after, it made me realize some answers to some questions I had earlier. How could I let this happen? How could I let things get to the way they were? How could I not recognize it? Partially, this can be attributed to the fact I couldn't let go of our good memories and used them to attempt to overrun the bad ones. I convinced myself it wasn't as bad as it seemed. But how could I not realize it was bad?

I realized some past incidents and relationships in college could answer that question.

8

Bradley... and Josh

The yin and the yang of my college relationships. Which, funny enough, neither were actually ever full-blown relationships. Still, they would define me in more ways than one and answer a lot of questions about myself.

Let's start with Bradley. The Hyde to this Jekyll.

***

"Want to do something crazy?" I said, drunkenly giggling.

"What?" Bradley turned around smiling back at me.

"Let's have sex in the fountain."

He looked side-to-side, checking if anyone was around. It was probably 2:20 a.m. Campus was empty. He looked back at me.

"Let's do it!"

We both stepped in the cool water laughing and, looking around nervously, plopped down in the water. I sat on top of him and kissed him, holding the back of his head and his full head of hair. He flipped me over so I was in the water, and I gasped, laughing as he tried to work off his wet pants. I tried to get off my wet jean shorts. Let me tell you, wet Levi's cutoffs are not an easy thing to get off. I ended up having to stand again to work them off, and started laughing as soon as I was bare ass in my pink Victoria's Secret thong in the middle of campus.

Oh yeah, did I mention which fountain we're talking about? The fountain. Like *the fountain*. The iconic fountain in the middle of SMU's campus, right in front of Dallas Hall. The fountain where everyone takes goofy graduation photos. The fountain that everyone tries not to drunkenly stumble into on tailgate Saturdays on the Boulevard aka the greatest college football tailgating ever. Yep, *that* fountain.

He smiled, looking at me standing in my thong in front of Dallas Hall and pulled me back down into the water with him. He pulled out his dick from his boxers, already hard and ready to rock, which was honestly both surprising and impressive since the water was pretty chilly. He positioned himself on top of me and pulled my underwear to the side, and pushed himself into me. I gasped and immediately started laughing. His face went from pleasure-filled to a goofy laugh too.

"We're having sex in the SMU fountain."

"Hell yes we are," he said smiling, leaning in to kiss me, the water sloshing around us.

But just as soon as it started, it ended. We kept giggling the whole time making out, grinding against each other, but soon we started getting paranoid thinking we might get caught so we decided we'd better take this somewhere else. We pulled up our wet pants, pushed aside our soggy hair, and jogged away from the fountain like nothing had happened.

But that's just my favorite memory with Bradley. Realistically, things were a lot more fucked up.

* * *

I had never been "hit" or hurt in any way in college—physically. But there was Bradley.

And he sucked. We, as in my college roommates and I, literally referred to him as "he who should not be named" in my household in college. He was the king of red flags, and, apparently, I was the queen of ignoring them. But really, it didn't start out that way. He had to hook me somehow, right?

It all started sophomore year. I still had my boyfriend, Keagan, but we were doing that sort of open relationship thing to try and ease out of our breakup. I was allowed to go to formals with guys and "hook up," but I wasn't allowed to have sex. And especially no hook ups in my bed. I had just become good friends with the Beta Beta Beta fraternity, since all my best guy friends from home had rushed there. I would just walk over to the house during my class breaks and have a beer and play Mario Kart with the guys. I became best friends quickly with a couple new guys—Grant and Perry. Perry's roommate was Bradley, who I always thought was cute.

We started hanging out innocently, since I still had a boyfriend. One day, we were playing video games and Bradley stopped mid-game and looked at me, chugging the rest of his beer.

"Do you want to go somewhere with me? An adventure?"

"Sure!" I responded without even thinking, excitedly. I clearly hadn't taken my Adderall and was at the mercy of video games, beer, and spontaneity, even in my SMU cheer practice clothes.

He grabbed a jacket and I grabbed my hot pink backpack and we went out to his small sports car and drove to Guitar Center. At Guitar Center, he picked up various guitars and began to play some notes into a tune.

"I didn't know you played," I smiled.

"Sometimes," he smiled back, eventually showing me how to run my fingers on the chords in the shop. We didn't buy anything, just browsed, and he and the store employee bonded over guitar lingo I didn't understand.

We got back into his car to ride back to the frat house, and he reached for my hand and held it tight. He looked at me and smiled. I tried to hold the gaze and the moment, but sometimes I get awkward in these intimate situations. I started blushing and had to look out the window, but I didn't let go of his hand. It was the first moment I felt feelings for a boy that wasn't Keagan, the love of my life. And that was *scary*.

* * *

With Josh, things started out nearly identical to Bradley.

Mario Kart and beers in the frat house in between classes was basically a lifestyle. And since Keagan and I had established new rules, I was technically free to do some sexual things now. So when the first formal of the year themed Hunt or Be Hunted was coming up, I thought about asking Bradley, but decided it was dangerous territory since I knew I was starting to get feelings for him and was technically still with Keagan. I decided I would ask a friend that I always thought was cute and a total flirt: Josh.

We'd usually hang during the day though because, at night, that boy was usually occupied with other female guests. That kid got more ass than a toilet seat. But honestly, he never acted like it. Needless to say, I was intrigued, even if I couldn't have him in that way.

Naturally, for the formal I didn't want to do the same old camo-and-deer act that everyone else was doing. I liked to be different.

Clearly, this is coming from the girl who wore all black and cat ears to a toga party and when people asked me what the deal was I would proudly say with a wiggle of my makeshift tail, "I'm a sphinx, bitch. Pretty sure all you toga people worship me." It didn't actually make any sense, but with enough beer and vodka ice luges, no one really asked questions, they just laughed and wanted to play with my tail.

So for Hunt or Be Hunted, I wanted to think outside the box and I figured out exactly what I wanted us to be.

"So I figured out what we're going to be for Hunt or Be Hunted," I said.

"Hit me with it."

"I'm going to be a dead lifeguard and you're going to be a shark."

"I love it. But how the hell do I dress as a shark?"

"I don't know yet… Maybe we will make you a fin out of cardboard and attach it to you."

I cut one of my white tanks to create rips all through it and splattered

red paint across to act as blood. Then I pinned a printed piece of paper reading in bold red letters "LIFEGUARD." Then I cut out a triangle from a cardboard box, painting it blue to act as Josh's fin. I even tied blue ribbons through the sides so he could use them as straps. Naturally, I made the ribbons too small for Josh's buff shoulders to fit through, but hey, I tried.

As soon as Josh got to our house for the pregame we were hosting everyone was dressed in the usual camo, etc., except for my roommate who I had lent my gold digger costume to and she was wearing it with her boyfriend who dressed as an old man. She wasn't into being like everyone else that year too, so the self-proclaimed "Courtney's costume closet" was raided.

The shark and lifeguard combo was a hit. Josh was in a cuddly mood and kept putting his hand on my waist or coming up behind me and holding me. After more shots though this behavior always commenced with a theatrical bite to my arm or ear because he was "the shark" that had bitten me.

Our friend Trent, who was like a big brother to me, thought this was hilarious and joked he was a shark. He bit my arm so damn hard I punched him back.

"Ow, Trent!" I screamed laughing. "That actually freaking hurt! I'm for sure going to have a bruise!" I playfully punched him again in his army vest.

"I'm sorry I didn't mean to that hard," he said, spilling some drink from his red Solo Cup.

That upcoming weekend was parents' weekend, and my parents would land the next day. I slept over at the Beta Beta Beta house with Josh after the formal, and since I was still technically dating Keagan in our way, this was fair game, just no sex. And true to my word, we didn't have sex, just did other stuff. I woke up early and realized I needed to make moves home, and walked across campus in my lifeguard outfit. *Walk of shame at its finest.*

Friday we did all the parents' weekend festivities with our sorority, but Saturday would be tailgating on the Boulevard. It was no wonder no one ever made it to the games. Tents and stations were everywhere and pretty much every tent had a keg and some kind of smoker going. And often, someone passed out underneath a plastic table.

I told my parents about this elusive place of heaven we would be attending and they really didn't believe me until they were immersed in it. My dad still brags about SMU Boulevard tailgating to his friends. This first one around, my dad had trouble getting his beer refilled because of the swarm of kids flooding the front table needing refills, but in the future, Trent, a one of my Beta Beta Beta besties, would assign a pledge in charge of always bringing my dad a beer when he was out. *Classic frat move.*

Instead of waiting for the beers, I had figured out the life hack that underneath the tablecloth there was almost always a backup thirty rack in case the keg ran out. So I always popped under there, pulled it away where the guy running the table wouldn't notice, and pulled out as many beers as I could hold or shove in various nooks and crannies of whatever dress I was wearing. Always a dress, by the way. People do football games differently in the South.

After getting us plenty of beers, my mom asked me what the bruise on my arm was from. I said I dressed as a lifeguard and Josh as a shark and he bit me to be funny. My dad pretended he didn't hear that and I wished I hadn't said it because guess who walked up to us right then.

"Hey guys! You must be Courtney's parents. I'm Josh."

I choked on my beer and tried not to be awkward. "Yeah, this is Josh! He's a Beta Beta Beta with Trent and the guys. Josh and I went to a formal together a couple nights ago."

"Fun!" my mom said exuberantly, playfully smiling. I knew she was going to say it.

"So you're the one who bit Courtney's arm?" she asked with a wink.

I turned crimson.

"What?! No! That wasn't me. That was Trent!" Josh said, the color of his face now matching mine.

My mom took a sip of her beer and smirked.

I immediately remembered Josh was right, and I was drunkenly wrong in my memory for blaming him earlier when my mom asked about the bite mark.

"I swear it wasn't me, Mrs. Schellin," Josh said again, embarrassed.

"I'm only joking, honey," my mom said, teasing Josh, who broke into a relieved smile.

Bradley...

Soon enough the biggest formal of the year was looming ahead—Beta Beta Beta Black Gold. Even if you didn't like the Beta Beta Beta frat or hang with them, it was *the* formal to go to. Every girl wanted an invite. I didn't know if anyone was going to ask me, as we all thought about who might get asked and by whom since it was now the week of.

Perry texted me that he got a new Beta Beta Beta frat shirt for me and he was going to swing by and drop it off. He said to come out on my balcony so he could throw it up to me from the driveway. I obliged. I sat waiting on our big, leather couch on the second floor of our townhouse, the room attached to the balcony, while my roommate worked at the kitchen table. All of the sudden, I heard guitar acoustics coming over loudly in the driveway and drums. Like too loudly.

"What the fuck?" my roommate said from the kitchen table, looking at me.

"Dude, Perry said he was dropping off a shirt for me. I'm confused."

She got up and we peeked through the shutters. There Bradley was—out the sunroof of his new Jeep Cherokee playing the guitar, and Perry with a set of bongo drums. Yes, bongo drums. *What the fuck, indeed.* I opened the door to the balcony and watched his face light up as he saw me and then frantically waved to Perry to start the actual jig they had prepared.

He played an original song, asking me to come to Black Gold with him. Lyrics and original chords and all. I wish I remembered the lyrics.

I said yes. Quickly of course and from the balcony, because I was mortified. And people were starting to notice. Perry then threw me a shirt he actually had for me and they drove off.

* * *

The night was perfect to start.

I had specifically ordered a black dress that was backless, but still had something fun going on in the front to show off the girls. I would wear it with my black baby doll heels. I also packed my overnight bag and gave it to Bradley before so he could put it in our room at the W Hotel, where the formal was being held.

That night, he held me close when we were next to each other, but never questioned too hard when I wandered off with friends to the dance floor. I liked that. I liked to wander and be free, and I was glad he didn't care that I was like that. I began thinking we might be something just off these thoughts alone, and the way that he looked at me across the room when we both held eye contact with one another and pretended to be listening to the people talking to us.

When the dance floor began winding down, he came up to me to see if I was ready to go, and I was. We headed back to the hotel room, but just before we could go up his eyes lit up with that same mischievous look.

"Wait, we've got to do this." He took off running, pulling my hand to follow him.

"What do you mean?" I yelled, laughing as he pulled me close to what was the edge of an ice rink that happened to be inside the hotel. *Oh, he so would.*

He jumped up into the ice rink and ran around it a bit, sliding around like a goofball in his black shiny dress shoes and tux. I was in six-inch heels and there was no way I could, but I started slipping one heel off to get out there with him. But just as quickly as it began, it ended with a security guard from the other end running to stop him, slipping on the ice like a fool, too.

"Hey, stop! You're not allowed out here!"

Bradley faked him out and then hauled (well, as fast as he could haul on the slippery surface) to me, and we ran to the elevators giggling, my shoes in hand.

When we got up to the room we had a bottle of wine waiting for us, courtesy of the Fraternity, with the Beta Beta Beta emblem on the label, and Bradley offered me a glass. We started drinking it and then he started to kiss me, which I was happy to indulge in. Things escalated to us undressing each other. Me unbuttoning his shirt and him hiking up my dress, eventually my head moving elsewhere to please him. After a quick bit, he pulled me up and laid me on the bed and got between my legs, only for me to quickly remind him I don't do that because I was still in my functional, dysfunctional relationship so I couldn't have sex.

"I can't have sex, remember."

This infuriated him.

"Why can't we just have sex? Like why else would I bring you to this? I've done everything right haven't I? Don't you think I deserve this? What's wrong with you? I know you want to, too."

Deserve this? And just like that, the night was ruined. I was disgusted.

He continued to try to convince me to sleep with him to no avail. He looked like a complaining and crying toddler. I had never had to deal with something like this to this degree in my life and, honestly, was a little scared. But I decided the best way to handle the situation was to stand my ground and really make him feel ashamed. Because, after all, isn't that how he was making me feel for something as simple as to understand as a woman's choice—*my choice*. Finally, I interrupted his tantrum.

"OK, Bradley. You're so upset I won't have sex with you, and this is all you wanted. Fine, take me. You want to have sex with me, here I am! Just come on over and have sex with me if that's what you want so bad! Go right ahead. I'll just sit here while you get what you want," I said, flopping onto my back into the bed, lifting up my legs spread eagle.

He instantly turned away and realized he was being a real fucking dick.

"No, I won't. I wouldn't do that. I'm sorry."

With that, we didn't say much more. He apologized again and we finished off our glasses of wine. I brushed my teeth and hopped into bed, where he joined me and we gently cuddled. He reached and turned off the lights and we fell asleep, doing nothing more. I was upset about his outburst but the next morning he apologized and I said it was fine. But really, I started to realize, Keagan and I might need to have a talk soon. Because I was starting to feel like the lines were blurring on what even qualifies that you're still in a relationship if you're out getting naked with other people.

I went home for break and Keagan and I finally called it quits. Coming back to school, I finally could have sex if I wanted to. And honestly, I kind of did. The only question was, would it be Bradley or Josh? But I think deep down, I knew who I wanted it to be: Bradley.

In the first couple weeks back, we had our Big-Little night for our sorority. My friends and I ended up back at the Beta Beta Beta house to party with the guys and I was in a tiny red dress looking hot. I'd be lying if I said I wasn't trying to run into Bradley.

So when we caught eyes in the main hallway as he was saying bye to someone, it was kind of a no-brainer. He whisked me away, us making out and barely getting up the stairs to his room, let alone, up to his top bunk. Once there, things were exciting and rushed and happened quickly. We ripped off each other's clothes while making out and Bradley helped me into his top bunk in my bra and panties, which then quickly were pulled off once up top in the bed. He pushed himself into me and thrusted quickly and it didn't last very long. Even though things seemingly happened fast, like, much quicker than I was used to with Keagan, I felt ok. Like maybe a little too ok. Feelings were brewing already with Bradley which made me feel somewhat guilty, because maybe they already were while I was with Keagan.

Still, I ignored my guilt and snuggled deeper into the big spoon that was Bradley behind me. He kissed my cheek at this.

A few weeks later, I started noticing Bradley out with this one Kappa freshman a lot, and soon rumors were flowing that they were an item. In one class, I overheard he had even taken her on a date. Like a real dinner date. I tried not to be jealous or think into it, so when Josh (and, really, my best friend and frat bro Perry) invited me to Mardi Gras weekend to stay with the guys, I was very much game. Especially since I knew the room Josh had invited me to stay in was not only with all our best Beta Beta Beta friends, like eight of them, but also because it included Bradley. The more the merrier?

Josh...

Let me tell you, New Orleans's Bourbon Street was a sight for us college kids. The streets were filled to the brim with people and beads, and tits were all over the place.

We were chugging hurricanes at Pat O'Brien's when Josh and I decided it was getting late and we better head back to the room. I walked behind Josh holding his hand with my cross-body purse slung over my body, lying flat on my butt. But I kept feeling a tug at it. The first time I ignored it because we were packed like sardines walking down the sidewalk but the third tug I had had it.

"Hey what the hell are yo—" I turned around still holding Josh's hand only to see the mid-torso of a very large man towering over me. He met eyes with me once I tilted my head up to even see them. His face was expressionless. I looked down at my purse and saw that all three *decorative* zippers on the front of it were all undone. Thankfully, the actual purse was still closed. I didn't say anything though and Josh putting two and two together had me walk in front of him from now on, with his hands on my hips, right up against my back.

We got back to the room to six drunk frat guys, four passed out and two still awake, mumbling and bumbling around. One was Grant, who would become my best friend to this day. He was wasted and in a cuddly mood. He kept trying to hug me and let his hands go places they shouldn't, giggling, and I laughed and basically said, "Yeah, not gonna happen Grant." He laughed and smiled and blubbered around the room and then would come back for more hugs and tried to cuddle next to me and let his hands drift again, until I finally looked at Josh and laughed while motioning to this playful little leech hugging my side so he would do something about it since I didn't want to be mean.

"Stop being creepy, Grant," Josh said and playfully shoved him off me, and Grant fell off the overcrowded bed and flopped on the floor laughing.

"What! What! Me, creepy? No. I'm not creepy, right Court? Not me." And with his final words waiting for a response, he fell asleep right where he landed.

Josh and I snuggled and fell asleep on the bed, eventually having a drunken Grant arrive horizontal across the foot of our bed throughout the night.

Morning came and everyone was hungover and seeking sustenance. Everyone went off to their respective plans. I went to brunch with some of the guys and then we hit a bar for some drinks, but then decided we should power nap and recoup before the night's festivities.

We got back and since there were now only three guys in the room, two of them still asleep, rather than our usual seventeen, I decided now would be a good time for me to shower. I headed to the bathroom and told Josh I'm hopping in the shower with a wink, leaving the door unlocked.

While I'm showering, I heard the door open and close and I peeked out the textured shower glass door to see Josh going to brush his teeth or something.

"Hey," I said with a smirk opening the door a little more to reveal my naked body. "Wanna join me?"

He looked at me in the mirror and turned around to fully face me to get a better look.

"Hah—you have no idea how much I want to join you, Courtney," he said, biting his lip.

"So then do," I said playfully, washing my boobs and spinning in the water coming from the showerhead. "It'll be fun. And we can be quiet."

"I can't. I'm with Katie now. Officially. So I can't," he said, looking down at his feet but not turning away.

I didn't realize things with him and Katie had become more official and was honestly surprised he was locked down, but he really did like her from what I could tell.

"Fine, your loss," I said with a wink and a shut of the shower door.

"You should lock this so one of the drunk guys doesn't come in and take that offer though."

I laughed and reached through the shower door to lock the door behind him.

I swore I heard him laugh through the door.

Bradley...

I'll just say this. You know it's never a good thing when at a boat party you kiss a guy who you have been hooking up with all summer and he makes sure no one saw the kiss and then pulls you aside to say...

"Wait—so you want to come over tonight? And have some fun," he said playfully running his finger on my bikini.

"Uhm yeah," I said, smiling back.

"And you're fine with hooking up? And we can still be friends?"

"Well, duh..." I responded kind of confused.

"So no attachments or anything? And we don't have to date?" Bradley asked, smiling even bigger.

My heart sank. Now my drunken brain put two and two together and saw past his stupidly perfect smile to where he was going with this. All summer I had been hoping he might ask me on a date like he had with other girls before.

Still, maybe if we hooked up more and I was cool about it, he would finally ask me on one?

"Sure!" I said, drunkenly with a nod, then grabbing his beer and taking a sip of it, trying to be cool. *Way to have standards, Court.*

"Wow, this is awesome." He grazed my waist with his hand, close to my purple scrunch bikini bottoms. "You're so cool."

I probably should've known right there that I had a major red flag on my hands. But with summer in full swing, and us being some of the only people around for summer session, animal instincts will be animal instincts.

Bradley invited me over to his house to have a *Harry Potter* marathon on a random Thursday that summer. He and his roommate, Perry, pulled out full-blown Hogwarts robes and wands and we ordered pizza and drank beers, reciting our favorite lines. Halfway through the night, Bradley was getting tired and he came over to the couch I was sprawled out on. He picked me up and flipped me over his shoulder.

"We are going to bed!" he announced to Perry with a salute.

I giggled at the sack of potatoes he had made of me. I thought it was cute, even though he really didn't give me a choice in the matter. Still, it was nice to feel wanted.

I kept hooking up with Bradley, and even let myself indulge in some of the cute moments we'd have post hook up. Whether it was us rolling around in his bed the next morning and him brushing away my hair and staring into my eyes telling me the colors he saw. Or the time when he reached to grab my hand while we were driving and almost got so distracted he rear-ended the person in front of us. I'll never forget how red he got and he pretended to fix his hair or something to brush it off.

I tried not to get caught up in the moments, but I was still convinced he might ask me on a date and that there was something between us.

* * *

"Court, don't talk to Bradley anymore. Or get attached or anything," Grant, my new best friend and frat brother to Bradley, said while we walked to class.

"Why?"

"Well, there's this joke about him going around the house. And—well —ok, you know that night you guys hooked up here at the frat house?"

How could I forget?

Grant basically told me as nicely as possible about this "joke" and something about that night I hadn't put two and two together, probably because of the alcohol. The said "bunny" he was pushing out the door was the girl he had gone on a few dates with last year. And that she wasn't just partying in the house with the guys like we were. She was there with him. *Hanging out.*

"So basically Bradley fucked her, pushed her out the door when he saw me, and then fucked me right after she left."

I felt disgusted. And stupid.

"I'm sorry, Court. I didn't know how to tell you, but yeah, don't get feelings for him."

Worst part was Grant was just telling me all this now a YEAR LATER. My first time having sex in college, I was actually just some sloppy second to another girl for Bradley. And now part of some permanent Beta Beta Beta hook up joke about him. *Yuck.*

But rather than get mad, I decided to get even. I was no longer going to dwell on him. And as soon as the school year started, I was going to be single as fuck.

Josh...

The first formal of the year came around and I knew I was asking Josh since he was single. I was a Rho Gamma this dance so I couldn't wear any sorority symbols, but that didn't mean I didn't go all out for the glow theme. Needless to say, Josh didn't hold back either.

I remember one photo specifically. My mouth was open laughing and I had one leg lifted around Josh. I was in a white tutu, neon pink bra, neon orange shirt, a yellow backwards hat, and my legs and arms had green paint handprints all over, plus some handprints in some more scandalous places. Josh is facing the camera giving an "I'm guilty" type of grin, holding his hands up to the camera revealing they have green paint all over them.

Josh and I still hadn't had sex, and, honestly, I wasn't even sure we would hook up at this one. But he made it clear to me as soon as we walked down to the garage to get an Uber. Once in the garage, he pinned me up against a wall and started kissing me.

"Wow, I wasn't expecting this, Josh," I giggled.

"Sorry I just can't seem to keep my hands off you tonight," he joked, putting his hands where the prints were and kissing me again, letting his hands come under my tutu. Just then another wave of our friends opened the garage door to leave too.

"Busted!" Perry yelled out and we all started laughing and Josh and I blushed and started moving again to the cars but Josh didn't let me run away without grabbing my hand first.

And that night, things changed.

Hey Google, play "Sex on Fire" by Kings of Leon.

It was almost like Josh and I had broken our seal and we couldn't help hooking up with each other. Like full on crazy sex, finally. It was like all our tension from previous years finally erupted. But the best part was, we still felt like close friends like we were before.

I mean Josh and I had made out multiple times and I had slept over in his bed in the frat house the year before, but this was different because now I was actually single, he was single, and I could have sex.

Also, I can now say in hindsight, he did things no other guys usually do on the first time.

The first thing he did that was a rarity was he kept trying to go down on me the next morning. I hardly let anyone do this because I was embarrassed, nervous, and scared of a man's head being down *there* that wasn't my boyfriend. *Oh, to be young and dumb.* But he kept persisting, laughing and holding my hands away from me as I laughed and wiggled around, his green eyes looking back up at me from between my legs. Eventually I grabbed his hair and used it to pull his face up to meet mine. He was already hard, his cock pressing into my hip.

Round two it is.

Josh lived in an off-campus house next to Bradley's that I used to frequent, just not recently. As soon as Josh and I finished round two I snuck off to go to the bathroom realizing there was no door, just a short wall separating me sitting on the toilet from him. Well this might not be an issue to some people, but a girl who was pounding beer all night and who has a slight gluten allergy that she ignores, would likely have to toot in the morning. Sorry not sorry.

But seriously, how the hell am I supposed to pee without letting a little one slip out? What if it makes a noise? I ended up grabbing some toilet paper and with one hand and held it to my sphincter so if one came out it wouldn't make a sound. I was able to pee and let out a little air without any sound. *Success!* Little did I know, I would use this trick for the rest of my life whenever in such situations, and mainly in the rest of my post-fuck situations at Josh's house. Honestly, you're welcome to all the sorority sluts reading this who needed a remedy to this situation. But I digress.

I came out in one of Josh's T-shirts, more like a dress on me, and got dressed. He offered to drive me home, which was rarity number two. And then on the way to my house, he hit the healthy drive-thru spot that wasn't that cheap either. He bought my breakfast and dropped me at my place and kissed me goodbye. Hello rarities three and four. What a guy!

Now that Josh and I were having our fun, it was almost possible to not think of Bradley, even though we'd see each other every weekend at parties. Now I would be winking across the room at Josh. Josh and I weren't trying to keep it a secret, necessarily. But Josh also knew it was no secret that Bradley and I had past shit, and since it was basically his next door neighbor and homie, best to not shove it in his face.

Bradley...

Boulevard season was now in full swing, and, as the designated Boulevard pregame house, we were the epicenter for the pre-party. We liked it that way. We congregated there and then headed to the tailgate scene, and as soon as the game started, we often retreated back to the place of pregaming for some post-tailgate fun.

My roommate and I stumbled back into our house and entered into the same horde, but smaller, of people still partying. We joined in. Suddenly we noticed the balcony door was being knocked on and trying to be opened from the outside. *Like what?* Who was drunk enough to scale the side of our damn building and come through the balcony when the front door was still open? The door was finally pushed open and Bradley was standing there with a Chick-fil-A bag in hand. His button-down was severely wrinkled at this point and untucked and his dark brown hair was tousled. And I hate admitting he still looked hot.

He looked up at me and rolled his eyes. "Ugh, what is she doing here?"

I swiftly responded back with, "Excuse me? I FUCKING LIVE HERE, CLOWN!" which he then drunkenly looked around and rolled his eyes again without a response, casually sitting at our kitchen table, kicking off his shoes, like nothing was wrong. That's Bradley for you.

More people came in and out as we hosted the postgame party, but the same familiar face refused to leave. My roommates and I all kept looking at each other, hoping he would leave, until he finally plopped down on the couch next to me to talk to me.

"Courtney," he said, trying to brush the hair from my face. "I just need to talk to you. You know how much you mean to me. Fuck, why don't you ever see that. Let's just go up to your room and talk."

"No."

I knew I meant about as much to him as his Chick-fil-A trash sitting on the table still.

"Court, c'mon. Please just talk to me," he said, grazing my arm now.

"Bradley, stop. I can't. You need to leave."

"You don't mean that. Talk to me. It's me."

I didn't mean to or want to, but all of the sudden I broke into tears. It was the first and thankfully only time I had ever cried in front of him. He looked astonished at me and immediately lost his words since he had never seen me cry nor had anyone really in college. Unless I was drunkenly crying over falling asleep and missing our Jimmy John's order or not getting queso or something like that.

Instantly my sober roommate who was watching over us like a hawk from the barstools in the kitchen, jumped to her feet.

"That's it. Time's up. Get out!" she said, grabbing him by the arms, her little body showing no mercy lifting him off the couch.

Not that she needed it, but her boyfriend, who was a well-established UFC fighter despite his smaller size, was ready to take down this fool if necessary. But he truly was the epitome of *The Karate Kid* in the fact that he would only use his powers for good and if necessary.

Bradley, still in disbelief, got up from the couch, and was led—well—pushed down the stairs by my roommate, who eventually shoved him out the front door as I sunk my head into my hands. He didn't go easily once out there. He kept knocking. She came back to the door and he said he left his phone. She brought it to him. And then he knocked again, saying that he'd left his shoe.

"Go without it!" she beckoned, slamming the door in his face.

A couple weeks later, we were hosting the pre-Boulevard and post-Boulevard party again. This time it was the white out, which meant everyone was wearing white for the game. We all stumbled back into our place. Our crew was small, but great. My best guy friends Greg and Kirk, also Beta Beta Betas, came back to our place plus several of our girlfriends. Until *he* came.

To avoid him, since I could tell he was wasted, I tried to stay in the kitchen talking with everyone who had accumulated next to the vodka and tequila bottles. Still, he approached me.

"Let's go upstairs to talk."

"I don't want to," I said, not making eye contact with him.

"Just for a second, Court," he urged, or rather forced, helping me up the stairs to my bedroom by nudging and gently pushing me.

We got up there and he pushed the door open to my bedroom and jumped onto my bed.

"How come we never come here? I like your place. We should come here more."

"Because this is my space," I said, annoyed. "I don't bring guys here." *Especially not you*, I thought to myself. "I'm going downstairs."

"No, come here. Come to bed. I want you," he said, patting down my white comforter.

I belted out a laugh. "No, I'm going back downstairs."

"Courtney, come here."

"No," I turned around, rolling my eyes and heading out the door.

"Courtney, come get in bed right now or I'll throw you down and rape you in this bed," he said so seriously to my turned back.

My skin crawled as I turned around. *Did he just say what I fucking think he just said?* I turned around with my eyebrows raised so high, due to my utter horror and shock at his words. I knew he was a dick, but this was just *dark*.

"Woah, woah, I didn't mean that. I was, uh, joking," he apologized, flustered and looking fearful at how I might react next.

Joking? K. Enough said. I said nothing and instantly headed for the door with haste. I heard the bed rustle beneath him and slam up against the wall, a telltale sign someone had gotten up too quickly from it, and he was following after me.

"Court! I didn't mean that. That was a bad joke. You know I didn't mean that. It's just, you know what you do to me."

He reached for my arm which I attempted to pull away from, but instead he just pinned me to the wall by putting his arms on either side of me, trapping me from going downstairs just yet. It was the first time since the Black Gold formal the year before that I felt that fear. Thankfully, this time I wasn't necessarily alone, courtesy of the party downstairs.

While he kept me pinned to my wall, he said he was sorry and didn't mean it, and how come we hadn't been hanging out, and he hadn't seen me for a while, and again, how we should come here more often. He kept drunkenly going in circles, and before he could take any more of my time I blurted out, "Because I'm fucking Josh!"

He immediately stopped his rant, and left his mouth hanging open. His mouth started to move like he wanted to say words but nothing came out. Before I could wait and see what happened next, I ducked under his left arm and made a run for the stairs. I sprinted down the stairs as fast as I could in my cowboy boots and little white dress, and felt him swiftly following behind me. I brushed past some people into the kitchen, which was still full of people, thankfully, and found safety with my roommate by the vodka bottle and shot glasses in the kitchen and amongst my ever-protective best guy friends from high school, Greg and Kirk. Bradley followed me, jaw and fists clenched, shoulders tense and white knuckles bare. Greg saw he was distressed and tapped his shoulder.

"Hey man, you alrigh—"

Bradley turned immediately on instinct and punched Greg square in the face so hard that blood sprayed across the kitchen onto my white dress and Kirk's white button-down.

"What the fuck is wrong with you?" Greg yelled at him, holding his nose. When he dropped his hands, he revealed a disjointed nose pouring blood out of it.

In disbelief, Bradley came out of his fire-fueled trance and began apologizing.

"Oh my God. I'm so sorry, Greg. My dad is a plastic surgeon. He can fix this."

Greg's nose continued to stream blood no matter how many paper towels we shoved to his face. I death-stared Bradley telling him to leave. The rest of the group was obviously in agreeance. Eventually, he did and we decided Greg needed to be taken to the hospital.

So now you think Bradley and I would never happen again... Right? How could it? He's scum! Trash! But apparently I'm the trash collector.

Our second semester formal with Pi Phi came around and since I had kind of been bopping around just making out with a bunch of people, I decided to nail my date down as someone who was always the life of the party: Bradley. Josh was starting to date someone anyways so it felt like the right choice despite what had happened. I hadn't told anyone about the words he had said to me drunk at that Boulevard party, and just decided not to take them to heart. I mean, *he was just drunk. Whatever, right?*

Needless to say, all my girlfriends were pissed and all my Beta Beta Beta friends didn't really care, since at least they knew they'd get to party with us beforehand. I remember consciously not trying to take too many photos with him to look clingy or anything, but also wanting to get some with the Pro-Flash photo guy when we were there. Which meant copious amounts of alcohol.

The alcohol didn't even help my case really, because despite being dates, Bradley and I were hardly touching at all. And when we got to the after-party, aka a club to party at the rest of the night out, he ditched me. Eventually I found a crew of our other friends and no one said they saw him, so I just left and went home. I cried in my Uber home and acted like it was no big deal when he texted me the next day.

I realized after this, it was hard for things to be normal between Bradley and I. I couldn't stop thinking about the words he had said to me at that Boulevard party and it was messing with me.

Kirk and Greg noticed something was up between us because I wasn't hanging around anymore. And if I was, I left when Bradley got there.

"You guys are weird. We don't all hang anymore."

"No, we don't," I admitted.

I ended up confessing only to Kirk (because Greg could be seriously protective) at a Halloween party they were throwing, what had happened between Bradley and I and why things were weird ever since the Boulevard party. Kirk was furious. He wanted to fight him. Although the thought of Bradley getting punched for once was very satisfying, I couldn't let other people fight my battles. I said no.

"I don't care anymore. He's fucked up in more ways than one."

But after that, Kirk didn't want to hang out with Bradley for a while. Kirk ended up talking about it again with me in front of our friend Mickey when we were all drunk and he suddenly looked sobered. After hearing what Mickey had to say from other girls, let's just say it's my opinion it's not the first time Bradley's done this to other girls... maybe even followed through.

It made me sick to think about, but he was impossible to avoid since he was still best friends with the majority of my friends. And to make matters worse, he started dating a new girl, Adaline. An older girl from my hometown who actually tried to recruit me for her sorority, unsuccessfully. She was two years older than us, and, if I'm being honest, just a real bitch overall. I remember telling my sister and her friend about her and, apparently, my sister's friend had gone to high school with her and said she was as cold and snobby as it gets, and how she screwed over their friend group in the past, time and time again, when it came to guys or anything really.

One day at a party at Bradley's house, Adaline decided to try and have pleasantries with me. Once she mentioned she went to my rival high school (oh, the irony) I told her how my sister was good friends with someone she might know. She exclaimed how *OMGwearebestfriends,* etc. etc., despite me knowing the actual truth. I decided to play with fire.

"Oh my God, no way! Ok, let's call her! It'll be so fun!" I clicked away on my iPhone and handed her the phone already dialing. She immediately pressed hang up.

"Why'd you do that?" I asked innocently, knowing damn well what I was doing.

"Oh, well it's been a while, actually. I don't know if it'd make sense."

Caught in her own lie. Maybe her and Bradley are a better match than I thought.

When Bradley and Adaline broke up, I was hardly surprised. What I was surprised by was how I got dragged into it. Apparently, Bradley had dropped into a serious depression, and even Kirk, who was pissed at him, brought me into the situation to talk to him. We confronted him. He was upset that Adaline and him had broken up. And that she was the love of his life. And he couldn't live without her.

Great. Why the fuck am I here dealing with this?

We tried to console him but he was in a bad place. He was popping antidepressants like candy and they were doing nothing. But it was just further acknowledgement that I was nothing. And why did I care?

God, how pathetic. You wasted so many years of college on this clown and now he gets depressed over another girl after saying he'd rape you when he was drunk and, yet, you feel sorry for him.

I didn't feel sorry for him. I just didn't want him to do something stupid and kill himself. Not on my watch. After everything else he had taken, not that.

It was finally senior year, and our first formal was looming and it was hippie themed. I hadn't really been talking to anyone romantically, but I also didn't want to bring just a friend.

"I think I'm going to ask Bradley since he's single," I told my roommate in the kitchen, avoiding eye contact, knowing what response I would get.

"*Dear God*, please don't, Courtney," she said, waiting for me to make eye contact with her. I didn't.

"It's our last first one!" I pleaded.

"Exactly," she said, rolling her eyes, no longer looking at me.

"Ok, I'll think about it."

"Whatever. We both know you already made your mind up if you just said it out loud," she said, annoyed, turning back to her economics book.

I had, in fact, made my mind up, so I asked him. *Even after everything that had happened. Why did I still feel like there was something between us?*

As soon as he got to my place in our hippie attire I wanted to take photos. And he immediately rejected this idea.

"What? No. We don't need photos together," he said, trying to walk away in front of everyone in the kitchen.

I was defiant though.

"Shut up," I said, fake laughing. "We need some photos for the night!"

We took a couple and I remember thinking I looked cute and that I wanted to post them, but I could feel the cringe off him in the photos. Shoulders tense, fake smiles, even though the photos actually looked decent. I thought better of it, not posting them to my Instagram. Maybe to Facebook in a big album.

As soon as we got to the bar, he went off to say hi to friends. Which would've been fine, if I wasn't already self-consciously replaying the scene of taking pictures in my head. I thought about my roommate telling me not to bring him, and him not wanting to be seen with me in photos, and now him running off as soon as he got the chance. Tears started to come, but there was no way I'd cry in public over my feelings for him.

I needed to leave. Like now. After walking into the bar, I immediately turned straight around and beelined back for the door I came through. There were already masses of people, and I bumped into someone I knew.

"Courtney? Hey, how have you been? Are you—" They were smiling, but if I blinked or made eye contact, tears were going to fall. I continued to the door not saying anything.

I burst into tears as the fresh air hit me, and I got in the first available cab.

Way to go out with a bang for the last first formal, Court, I thought, crying in the cab. I went straight home and cried.

What a waste of a spray tan.

The next morning, I was opening a delivery box with my new iMac desktop computer, which my mom had gotten me for my final year of journalism classes and my new jobs, when Bradley walked up my stairs, unannounced. Shocking, I know.

"Oh God," I breathed, exasperated at the sight of him, turning my back to him. "What do you want?"

"I wanted to check on you. You just left last night. You know, uh, I was looking all around for you asking everyone where you were."

I continued unloading my box not looking at him.

"Courtney, are you listening to me? I was worried about you. I *care about you*."

I laughed in a full-blown, hysterical villain laugh.

Pretty sure people who care about someone don't tell them they'd rape them in their bed. Pretty sure people who care about someone don't fuck them after fucking another girl. Pretty sure people who care about someone don't ditch them. Pretty sure people who care about someone don't toy with them and use them as a sex joke to their fraternity. The list goes on.

"Shut the fuck up, Bradley," I said, not looking up from setting up my new computer.

Bradley walked around to be in front of me.

"I was! Where did you go? I missed you! I *wanted* you!" I finally looked up as he said this with his hands out being all fucking theatrical like he cared.

You wanted me? Well how about how long I've wanted you, Bradley? And how about how long you haven't cared? I've just been your toy. And I pretended I was ok with it, because that's what the cool girl does. And now I'm just a fucked-up, broken toy.

"I left. Ok. Are we done here?" I asked curtly, finishing propping up my new computer onto the table, then putting my hands on my hips inspecting my work.

"Do you want me to leave now?" he said slyly, his one eyebrow going up like this was a game, thinking his so-called speech about caring had done something. "Oh, nice computer. Is that for your sports broadcast stuff this year?"

I looked to the computer and back to him, knowing he was trying to distract me from his initial question and paused.

Do I want you to leave now? Looking at me with that damn look? No. Yes. Fuck. I don't even know what I want anymore. Is this toxic? I wouldn't know. Do I want you to sit here on my couch and talk with me about everything we like that's weird about us and pretend none of the bad things between us have happened? Yes. No. To somehow prove to me you care? No. Yes. But maybe too much has happened now. And I know everyone thinks I'm just a joke to you. Maybe that even includes you. Does it? I don't know. So, do I want you to leave now? Yeah. I do want you to leave.

"Yes," I said.

"Fine," he said, throwing his hands up, turning and leaving.

I couldn't decide if I was happy he left or not, but really I just wanted to finish the discussion with this. *Thanks for fucking me up, Bradley.*

* * *

It was officially one of the last months of my senior year. I think one of the best weekends of my life was one where we went out to middle-of-nowhere Texas to our friend's house on the Red River and stayed the weekend. If you've heard of the Red River rivalry then you get what I'm saying. We were on the border of Oklahoma and Texas, and when I say this place was in the boonies, I mean *the boonies.*

They had this big lake house that was probably half a mile from the blood-red river. The red water was flowing down in such a way that it looked barely swimmable; it was so thick and opaque. *Well, maybe with enough alcohol it's swimmable.*

There was even this little shack they called "The Bar" that was quite literally a little bar with bar stools and old metal beer signs on the walls. The place was in a shanty-like, tin roof, wooden setup, situated next to the river on huge stilts clearly in case of red river overflow.

Our crew consisted of all our best friends we had been recently hanging out with, basically the same group from Ultra, the rave we went to in Miami. We lived in swimsuits for the weekend and drank cheap beer, overpriced whiskey, and vodka all day the first day. I thought it was just the group that was here that was going to be coming down when all of the sudden there *he* was. Bradley walked up to the house, carrying a case of beer. As always, I was conflicted on my feelings when I saw him. I knew the natural feelings anyone would tell me to have would be "Ugh," but really, I was down a beer-and-whiskey hole, and ultimately, full of smiles when I saw him.

I was happy to see him, which I hated. He hugged me. I probably hung on a little too long. He allowed it. We flirted the rest of the night. I was in an XL frat tank that said BETA BETA BETA ISLAND on it, probably his, honestly. I had a backwards hat on and was sipping whiskey straight from the bottle, leaning on that little makeshift wooden balcony overlooking the river. The lights hummed above our heads. It wasn't as dark as you would think and certainly was a sticky summer night.

I don't remember the conversation next or if there even was one, but I remember leaning my chin on his chest and looking up at him with my drunk eyes and sly smile, with my arms hanging limply around him. We both smelled like booze, sweat, and mud, and I wanted him to kiss me. To want me. Just this once. He smiled, but looked up and pulled away.

"Let's do something fun," he said with those mischievous eyes, letting go of me and walking off, making me want to follow.

By the tone in his voice I knew "fun" didn't mean anything sexual, but rather, the type of PG fun on our first adventure to Guitar Center. He had brought his car down to the river and led a few of us back to it, where we all stuffed in. Apparently, he and some of the guys wanted to go off-roading in the very wide-open field between the house and the river. The girls, not knowing this plan, hopped in, only to be invited on Mr. Toad's Wild Ride.

We all got in, barely situated, and he gunned it toward the open grassland ahead. Screams and yells erupted from everyone in the car.

"What the fuck!"—"We're gonna die!"—"Oh my God!"—"Oh shit, dude!"

We raced and flew over ditches, and at one point launched off one so high I don't think our tires were on the ground. It was like in a *Dukes of Hazzard* episode. We all screamed and flew into each other and into the ceiling. I, along with the other girls, begged to be let out of the car. The guys obliged, laughing their heads off, fulfilled by their adrenaline rush. The ride was over.

* * *

For years after college, Bradley and I never really spoke. Except for this awkward follow and unfollow game on Instagram we would play. Besides, he was dating Adaline seriously. Whether they still are, I wouldn't know since we are currently not following each other.

But the last time I think we ever talked he texted me or DMed me one of my first big-time articles I had written for ESPN. He said he had read my article and didn't realize it was my writing until he got to the end of it and saw my name. I think I responded how crazy that was, and thanks for sharing. I think I even said I hoped he was doing well. And I definitely didn't keep rereading it when he told me he hoped I was doing well too.

Josh...

"Can I kiss you?" I asked.

I turned around to face Josh, still holding one of his hands, tequila lingering on my breath. Even after all these years after college and not having seen each other for most of them, Josh still gave me butterflies.

He smiled. "Of course you can kiss me," he said.

I leaned in and gave him a kiss on his lips but didn't want it to be a bigger deal than it was, so I avoided any tongue action.

"See you tomorrow, maybe," I said, releasing his hand and turning to head to my Uber.

"Oh, you're definitely coming. See you tomorrow."

I smiled again and winked and got into the back seat of my driver's small car.

Instantly, I was overcome with emotion and burst into tears.

What are you doing? It had been almost three years since college graduation, and Josh and I hadn't seen each other since. So when I saw he was in town for the weekend and Matt and I had just broken up, of course I thought it'd be fun to see him. But I had only been broken up with Matt for two weeks. And I had just kissed Josh. *Josh.*

Josh was only visiting for this one weekend, and I just happened to know he was here from his Instagram story, so I texted him. He immediately responded. What was I doing? And also, *how is it always Josh after the big ones? Even after Keagan, it was Josh. After Bradley, it was Josh. And after all this time, was it still Josh?*

The weekend came and went but we didn't talk for a couple more years.

Bradley...

Ironically, Josh wasn't the only one who would pop up in my life again in Newport Beach. Perry aka one of my best friends had gotten engaged and decided to have his bachelor party in Newport. When I found out, I decided I had to meet up with the crew out in Newport for one last hurrah. Seeing all the guys out in Newport was a blast, but I couldn't help noticing someone was missing, but I didn't ask about it. About *him.*

Once we left the bar, we headed back to the guy's place to play drinking games, when someone mentioned Bradley. Apparently he was there after all, he was just passed out in one of the rooms. Being near him felt weird and wrong in a way, but I was kind of curious about what he was doing or what he even looked like now. After all, it had been probably over five years since I had last seen him, since running into him at an alumni Boulevard. At the Boulevard it was nothing monumental—he was still with Adaline and our "hello's" and "how are you's" were brief and awkward. But now I wanted to see him, not with her.

But he never ended up coming out of the room and I didn't dare peek in to say hi.

* * *

I won't blame Bradley for the reasons as to why I didn't realize things were so bad with Matt, but I definitely think he is part of what groomed me into my mentality. Hearing words like rape, or pushing me to do things I didn't want to do, or just generally treating me like trash didn't seem significant enough as something to "report," but they definitely should have been "reported" or flagged to my own self.

What I mean is, these incidents changed me as a person whether I want to admit it or not. They were part of what allowed a domino effect to somewhat form in what I was "ok" with in relationships. I tout being a strong woman who could never allow any of these things to happen to me, but I think that's part of the problem. Being raised as a tough girl with a "rub some dirt in it" mentality, I was taught to be stronger, which generally means not showing emotions that could be misconstrued as weakness or sensitivity.

So the first time I was confronted with conflict in relationships or with boys my initial thought was, "I don't care" or "That doesn't hurt me." So a man pushing himself onto me despite me shoving and saying no, from high school times to college times, was always a "Oh please, I can handle this" and a "I'm not sensitive and *I can handle it*." So when it continued to reoccur it almost made me think "been there done that" when something like that would happen again, including with Bradley. Which is sad. Because it should never be overlooked and shoved under the rug. Because, eventually, a big pile is going to form under that rug of all the things being *handled*. And you end up in a relationship where you're allowing things to happen and not even realizing they are bad because you're building an unsteady foundation on top of all the debris.

Don't get me wrong, there is nothing wrong with being the tough girl and being raised that way, but I think there is something that needs to be said about being ok with not feeling ok. As women we're taught to hide these kinds of feelings for worry of being called weak or emotional or irrational, but recognizing something is wrong is a gut feeling. And if you've been wronged, offended, or hurt, there is power in recognizing that and admitting that instead of brushing it under the rug. Even if you can't admit it to anyone else at the time, admitting it to yourself is where basic change occurs in your brain, and all that debris is exposed from under the rug and you don't continue to build on top of it. And if you ask me, that's a hell of a start.

Josh...

"I still can't believe you told your parents that I bit you."

I'm sitting on my bed in Boston when the text pops in from Josh responding to my throwback shark and lifeguard photo I sent to him, and it makes me laugh. Especially since it's coming roughly seven years since the formal, and he's still hanging on to that one memory.

"And it wasn't even you! Hilarious."

Our conversation was sparked by me getting a Facebook memory about a different formal we went to, a glow dance, which led to more pictures down memory lane from Facebook albums, including the iconic photo of him pretending to bite my arm as a shark and me pretending to be dead.

I wonder if he remembers the little things like this that I do. I wonder if most of these guys remember the funny little details and moments I remember.

Certainly not Bradley. Right? But I think if anyone would, it would be Josh. He's just that kind of person. I literally don't think I have anything bad to say about the guy. He's still single and sometimes I think *what if*. I even texted one night while here in Boston after likely drinking one glass of wine too many and told him to come visit.

He laughed and said he would, even though I knew he wouldn't.

We would just have to be in the same place at the same time to meet up again, just like the time he was in Newport Beach two weeks after I had broken up with Matt. And honestly, that moment really helped me move on.

Coincidence? I think not. *Well played, God. Well played.*

9

Kenzo

You know how they say "The one that got away"? This was the dick that got away. Like, not because he was a dick, but like the actual penis that got away. It really was a specimen, let me tell you. But isn't there another saying that you don't marry the best sex guy?

"Yo, Kenzo and I decided we're gonna drive down to College Station to watch SMU play. Wanna come?" my best friend Grant texted me.

Kenzo was one of his good friends who was totally hot, and used to play for the football team with him. Hell yeah, I wanted to go. How could Court Does Sports pass up the opportunity to go to a football stadium I hadn't been to? Not to mention, Johnny Manziel aka college football quarterback phenom aka Johnny Freakin' Football would be playing our team. Would we be crushed? Surely. But I would get to feel the sway of Kyle Field as the students crossed arms over shoulders, and experience Texas A&M's Aggieland.

So—uh, *yeah*—I was in. Grant figured as much, and had already got our tickets.

The guys picked me up in the morning in Grant's Jeep. It was going to be a scorcher, so I opted for my cut-up SMU red tee shirt, now a strapless shirt with cutouts resembling a bandana, and jean shorts, a large belt buckle, and cowboy boots.

"Well hot damn, Courtney. That's a hell of an outfit," Kenzo said cocking down his sunglasses with his arm out the window of Grant's passenger seat.

"What! It's supposed to be hot."

"Mhmm," he said, raising his eyebrows.

I tried not to bite my lip as I watched him look me up and down under his sunglasses.

Kenzo and I had never hooked up and were just friends. But damn, I wouldn't mind if it happened. I hopped in and we were off. Halfway there we would have to stop and hit a gas station to fill up which was the perfect stop for us to grab more beer.

"I got the beer," I said, hopping out and slamming the door, heading into the gas station. We weren't close enough to A&M to be in a college environment, and, frankly, just the opposite. We were in Podunk, nowhere-ville Texas and apparently this gas station was the happening spot heading into College Station and my outfit was turning some heads. Next thing I knew, I started to hear whistles encircling me, and some guys walked past me and dramatically turned around, yelling, "Pony up, honey!" or "Go Stangs!" as they smiled and laughed, thinking they had great pick up lines. But I was in a great mood and yelled "Pony up!" back to them. Shortly after walking into the gas station, I had Kenzo up behind me.

"I said I'd get it?" I questioned.

"Yeah, well I wanted to come in with you and make sure you were fine since you were causing quite a fuss out there," he said, protectively.

I smiled back. "I don't know, seemed like they were all SMU fans to me," I said, pulling a case of beer out and handing it to him with a wink.

We pulled into College Station and the grass lots were already packed with cars parked every which way. The plan was, we were going to a tailgate tent and Kenzo's parents would meet us since they didn't live too far away. Like truffle pigs, Grant and I naturally found the first keg at the tailgate and then made some friends with girls Kenzo had known growing up. They were nice, but really Grant and I were more focused on slugging some beers before heading into the stadium. Game time was approaching so we decided to head that way. Grant and Kenzo worked on filling a water bottle with whiskey.

This was way more subtle than the time that Grant and I went to the Alabama-LSU game in Tuscaloosa and Grant just had me carry an entire handle of Fireball under my oversized camo hunting jacket.

Which, honestly, is a story worth telling so let me sidetrack for a second...

How Grant and I thought sneaking a handle in was ok, I will just go ahead and blame the fact that we started drinking at like 8:00 a.m. And how we got away with it, is just beyond me. Our friend Ashley decided to last-minute join in on Grant and my Roll Tide adventure where we would be staying at the Alabama Beta Beta Beta house. Our sleeping quarters were courtesy of Grant, the SMU Beta Beta Beta social chair, calling and asking them if they could spare a few rooms or couches. We went out all night and crashed on the couches with Grant passed out on the floor until I woke up to something unexpected.

Tap. Tap. Tap. I felt a finger poking my shoulder. I opened my eyes to see a frat boy sitting across from me with a large plastic cup in his hand. He smiled when I opened my eyes.

"What the fuck? Who are you? Can I help you?" I asked, wiping my eyes.

He said his name and that he lived here in the frat house.

"I need you to try this though. I think I just made the best drink on earth," he said, shoving his drink toward my face.

"What the fuck! No. I'm not trying that. What time even is it?"

"It's 8 a.m."

"What!"

"Never mind that, it's game day. And what! Seriously, you're not going to try? I need someone to know about this creation I've made though," he looked like a boy whose toy was taken from him as he took a sip of his beverage sadly. I realized this guy wasn't trying to be date rape-y, he was likely still drunk from the night before and just excited it was the biggest game day of the year.

I sat up and sighed and looked at his dark, ominous drink.

"Alright, what's in it?"

His eyes lit up and he held it out again. I took it from him. "The simplest thing! I literally just did Dr. Pepper and Jack Daniels Honey!" He smiled with his eyebrows raised awaiting my reaction as I took a small sip.

"Damn, you're not lying. That's really fucking good."

With this, he stood up and threw his hands in the air like he had transformed water into wine. "Right!"

I took another sip looking over to Ashley and Grant, both still passed out, and decided, fuck it. The day had officially started.

"You said you live here? Want to give me a tour of the house? We can share this elixir you made while we do so," I said, standing, and he held out a cocked arm for me to join him, which I laced my arm through. And now you know why we thought bringing a handle of Fireball into a game was kosher.

But back to Kenzo and Grant...

So Grant and Kenzo wanted me to sneak their dark whiskey-filled water bottle in since they probably wouldn't check me. I rolled my eyes, but it was hard to say no to Kenzo's grin. I jammed the bottle into the side of my boot.

We walked into the stadium and, let me tell you, Kyle Field is something to behold. Sure, it's pretty old, but seeing fans fill up high into those stands is something. And when they start to sway, they aren't kidding when they say the whole stadium starts to sway. Our seats were damn good, kudos to Grant or Kenzo. We were front row on the thirty-yard line. We shuffled into our seats and I was on the end of our group, seated next to this guy who was certainly a fan of my outfit. He made sure to say so and as soon as he did I saw Kenzo turn his head and give him a death glare.

Uh oh. I tried to keep the overly talkative and flirtatious man to my left at bay with one-word answers and no eye contact, but I also didn't want to be mean. I mean, we were sitting so close we were touching. It's not exactly like I could just pretend he didn't exist. But this didn't stop the guy from continuing to talk to me. Really, it was innocent—just asking me about the game and occasional compliments. But then when he complimented something about my outfit again, Kenzo (seemingly out of nowhere) stood up and turned to face the guy. He was heated.

"Hey buddy—you need to shut the fuck up and quit talking to her. You need to leave her alone and back the fuck off," Kenzo said, boiling.

The guy stood up.

"Woah, woah, woah. What the fuck you talking about? We're just talking and having a good time," the guy responded.

I remained seated in between them on the bleacher looking up at them back and forth, wishing this wasn't happening. The dude was an older guy, but not too short compared to Kenzo, who was clearly still in his prime, freshly off his college football days. I grabbed Kenzo's forearm.

"Kenzo, it's fine. I'm fine, really," I said.

"No you're not. I'm sick of him hitting on you and making you uncomfortable when we're here to watch a game."

He wasn't wrong, but he wasn't right. I didn't want to deal with this guy the whole game, but the game hadn't even started yet. Maybe when it started he would ease off.

All of the sudden, Kenzo's dad appeared behind Kenzo and said, "You need to back the fuck off buddy," but when he got up and appeared behind Kenzo it caused Kenzo to push into the guy and the guy pushed back and just before things got ugly—mainly, for that guy, because Kenzo would've wrecked him in a fight—security guards ran up.

"That's enough. One of you is out of here!" They couldn't decide to take Kenzo or the guy and the guy was yelling, pointing at Kenzo and then yelling to me desperately, "Tell them I did nothing wrong!"

But the security guard insisted someone was getting kicked out, and so I just looked down at my boots and shut up.

So the poor, overly flirtatious man was dragged out kicking and screaming and we were left to watch the Ponies get whacked by the Aggies. At least we had the water bottle to subdue the hurt. Plus, we scored a touchdown and got to watch Johnny Football, so really, how mad could we have been?

We sauntered out of the stadium and said our goodbyes to Kenzo's dad who left me with a comment about not letting these boys run the show and they were lucky to be hanging out with a girl as pretty as me in an outfit like that. If I was getting anything from this day it was that, apparently, this outfit was one for the books even if it was one-hundred degrees in Texas.

On our drive back, we blasted Eric Church and hung out the roof of the Jeep when we were on dirt backroads. Dust flew in from all directions, blowing my hair up into a mess of a tornado above my head. Kenzo occasionally reached back to put his hand on my leg, but then when I'd go to reciprocate with a touchy hand on his shoulder or his arm, he played hard to get. I even decided to flirt with Grant since I already knew Kenzo was the jealous type. It worked momentarily, but I think we all knew Grant and I were not actually flirting. So we continued to blast Church and hang out the windows, cracking more beers. We arrived back in Dallas late and the boys dropped me off.

"That was fun. Thanks for bringing me, boys! See you tomorrow? Ice House day drinking for Sunday Funday?" I said with a wink.

"You know it," Grant responded, and Kenzo just smiled.

Funny enough, initially, I didn't become close with Grant or Kenzo on the football field while I was working for the SMU football team as the assistant video coordinator, despite them both being on the team when I first got the job as a freshman.

I was as fresh as a freshman could be in the college experience department and it was opening weekend of SMU, my first weekend in college. I was at the hotel my parents were staying at in the bar area and my dad had the paper out and was asking my mom and I who are picks were, a tradition we've always done growing up.

My dad would put out the paper in the morning on the kitchen table with all the college football games that weekend, and everyone in our family would make their predictions for the games. My mom and I were looking at the paper together and debating the Boise State game.

"Well, it's at home and the other team's QB is new, so I'm going Boise State for sure. That blue field messes with players," I said.

"True. But they don't have the point spread. Plus the opponent's coach is tough," my mom said.

"That's true too. I'm still going Boise State though."

"Me too," my mom said, circling our pick with a pen.

"Excuse me—" a voice from the neighboring table rang in and we turned to face a middle-aged Native Hawaiian man. "Sorry, I don't mean to interrupt, but I was listening to your debate, and it sounds like you girls actually know what you're talking about. That's impressive!"

My mom and I looked at each other and laughed, because proving people wrong or surprising people with sports was kind of what we did best.

Cue my interview getting into SMU.

I was asked to bring in a photo that represented who I was and why I should be admitted to SMU as a good fit. I brought in a photo of me at seven years old at a birthday party with a large Burmese python going up my shirt and up the shirts of several other party goers.

"What's this?" the interviewer asked, holding my photo at arm's distance as if the python would break through the photo.

"That's me at a birthday party when I was around seven. The birthday theme was reptiles and they brought in a guy who had a giant python. He asked if anyone was brave enough and wanted the snake to go up their shirt. I immediately raised my hand as high as I possibly could with a smile on my face, only to look around and realize no one else's hands were up and, frankly, everyone looked horrified. The memory is still so vivid to me. The man asked if I was the only one. 'Just this *girl*?' he asked. As if instantly triggered by the word 'girl,' the birthday boy became enraged and ran up next to me defiantly and said he wasn't scared, and he'd do it. With that, the majority of boys insisted they weren't scared and they would do it, too. I chose this photo because this represents the personality I've had my whole life. I've never backed away from a challenge and I've never been afraid to stand out or be different. I know I'm going to be a sports reporter, despite it being a male-dominated industry, and going to SMU and their journalism department will bring me one step closer to that dream. Since I was a little girl my dad used to mute the TV when one of my favorites, Pam Oliver, would go on and he would say, 'Your turn. Interview me like I'm the coach. Thirty seconds. Go!' If my questions weren't good enough he'd respond, 'Fired. Try again.' I know what I want and I know who I am and that's what this photo represents to me," I finished, coming full circle.

The interviewer raised his eyebrows. "So you want to be a sports reporter? If you become a sports reporter, what's the goal?"

I corrected him, "*When* I become a sports reporter..."

Needless to say, when the man who asked about our football picks that opening weekend turned out to be the SMU football team's video coordinator, it felt like fate.

That next week, I wandered the stadium until I made it to the top floor of the suites and found the office of the Hawaiian man named Pac with a large editing bay set up.

"Hey, Pac right?"

"Hey! Yeah. Hey aren't you the girl from the hotel that picked Boise State? You were right! They upset!"

"Yeah, that's me! My mom told me you worked here and I wanted to come introduce myself. I'm in school to become a sports reporter and I'd love to get some experience by working for the football team. Are you looking to hire anyone?"

"Unfortunately we don't have any extra money to hire anyone on right now."

"Oh, I'd work for free."

"You'd work for free? Seriously?"

"Yeah. I just want to get some more experience."

"Well, alright. Sure then! I could use any help I can get. When can you start?"

"Whenever you need me."

"How about this week? You can film practice with me."

"I'll be there."

And with that, I essentially created the first assistant video coordinator position. As the assistant video coordinator I would film behind the offensive line to record players' movements and habits. So one day when I was filming, carrying my camera and tripod around with me to the sideline I heard someone yelling my mom's maiden name.

"Ashland! Ashland! Ashland!"

I finally turned around to see the defensive coordinator, Mike, looking directly at me while yelling the name. I hadn't met him yet, but I knew who he was, of course.

"Actually, it's Schellin, now. Ashland is my mom's maiden name," I said, as Mike approached me.

"Well, I'll be damned. I knew it. Who's your mom?" he asked, removing his sunglasses.

"Catherine Schellin—err—Ashland."

"Yep. You look just like her, you know that?"

I looked at him confused but responded. "That's what I'm told! Did you know my mom?"

"Your grandpa is Jerry?" he asked.

"Yes," I said, curiouser and curiouser.

"Hah! Yeah! I know your family. Your grandpa coached me in college for football in Walla Walla."

"No way!"

"Yeah, I used to date your mom's cousin Jodi, too," he said with a smile. "How is she?"

When people don't believe everything happens for a reason or fate, it makes me laugh. Think of this... In order for any of these things to happen, this series of events had to happen: 1. Pac had to overhear my mom and I talking. 2. I had to go up and essentially create my assistant video coordinator job. 3. I had to be filming practice on the field for coach Mike to recognize me.

Once I called and told the story to my family, it was a no-brainer when my grandparents decided to fly out for Parents' Weekend. Coach Mike and my grandpa, his mentor and coach, would get to reunite. And what a cool moment that was.

After the football game, Coach Mike swung by our hotel. They had lost the game, but he was in good spirits upon sight of my grandpa. After embracing, my grandpa's first words were classic.

"Hey, who's teaching those boys to tackle? Because I sure as hell didn't teach you that," he said with a nudge to his former pupil.

But at this point, you're probably wondering what the hell happened to Kenzo. Sorry, me and my ADD.

Earlier that same game day, we went into the game to watch, but it was bloody hot so we left at halftime to grab beers and margaritas by campus at Banditos then Barley House. We met up with Kenzo and Grant outside of Barley House and, walking in, my grandpa didn't see a step ahead of him and fell. Hard. My heart stopped but before I could even react, Grant and Kenzo were on both sides of him, pulling him right back on his feet before anyone could realize he had fallen.

"You alright, man?" Kenzo asked.

"Yes, thank you," my grandpa said thanking them, but they both just smiled and said, "Hey, no worries, no one even saw." It may seem trivial, because you would hope any rational man would act the same, but it meant a lot to me and I could tell it meant something to my family too. My mom walked over to me and whispered in my ear facing the bar where Grant, Kenzo, and Dad had congregated to get us more beers.

"Who is that guy? Grant's friend?"

"That's Kenzo," I said.

"He's cute."

"Trust me, I know."

* * *

Kenzo and I continued to hang out on and off whenever we were all together with Grant, but I never pursued him in that way because: 1. *Thanks for wasting my time, Bradley.* And 2. He was kind of always on and off with different girls. It was hard to keep up. Still, whenever we'd hang out we'd always flirt like it was our job.

The first time we all went to Top Golf together I decided not to mention I had played golf in high school and was MVP on the team.

"I've got a bet for us," I said, eyeing the course mischievously.

"Let's hear it." Kenzo said.

"If you can hit your ball closer than mine to the pin in that circle there, I'll buy us a round of shots."

He started laughing. "Uh, yeah, I'm in on that."

I continued. "But! If I hit it closer, then shots are on you."

"Done."

"Best of 3?" I asked.

"Sure."

I let them go first and they did decent, landing a couple in the outer circles of the target. I walked up to the platform and teed up my ball while they giggled about something. I grabbed Kenzo's 7 Iron and hit a perfect shot to the target, plopping it into the target's inner circle. Their laughter stopped as I turned around to face them.

"So, Fireball shots then, boys?" I said with a wink to Kenzo, walking over and pulling up a seat next to Grant and grabbing my Coors Light. "Thanks!"

Kenzo went to tell the waiter our new order.

"You guys fucked yet?" Grant asked, nonchalantly.

"Grant!"

"I'm just saying, Court! There's a lot there," he said, sipping his beer.

The school year came to a close and next thing we knew it was the middle of summer in Dallas, Texas. And in true Texas fashion, it was dripping hot. I was in summer school and working an internship at Dave Campbell's Texas Football magazine and life was pretty damn good. Not everyone stayed in Dallas for the summers, naturally, so I was at the mercy of hanging out with all my friends who were around.

Kenzo was around because he graduated the semester before and he was now living in a complex with an awesome pool. One day he invited me over to Sunday Funday with a group of people. Again it was Texas summer hot, so passing on a cool pool to jump into was not going to happen. When I got to the pool, there were some other girls I knew. We weren't best friends or anything, just more fun acquaintances. This became quite a crew for us that summer and we had a hell of a time. Kenzo was hooking up with Betty, the fun, pretty blonde with huge boobs, of course, and his friend was constantly flirting with me despite Kenzo doing that watching-over-me thing no matter who his hands were currently on.

He was a player. Bad news. But I already knew that, *right?*

Summer was coming to a close and Corey Smith was coming into town and we were going to get tickets and go to his concert at Billy Bob's, an iconic western bar in Fort Worth, but rather than designate a DD, we'd get a hotel.

Grant and Kenzo picked me up in the Jeep and we headed to the concert. I wore a white tank, an American flag bandana in my hair, cut-offs, and my cowboy boots. The concert was a hell of a time. I ran into a sorority sister and we chatted and took shots. I hopped on and off the dance floor, occasionally running into Grant or Kenzo sauntering around on the dance floor or buying drinks for some girls. I'd even been spun around by some lad on the dance floor myself.

But eventually I went back to the bar and was talking with my sorority sister again, when she asked if I was good with who I was going home with. *Sure! They were around here somewhere.* I went to the bathroom and wandered around looking for them, but I couldn't find anyone from our group. *Damn it.* I pulled out my phone to text them. I started typing the text only for the wheel of death to pop up. My phone was dead.

Fuck.

Then I realized the lights were on in the bar and, worse, they had been on for a while. How long was I in the damn bathroom for?

Fuck, fuck, fuck.

I ran outside to see if I could grab a cab. But where the fuck was

I going? The name of the damn hotel was in my iPhone notes. And to make matters worse, there were no cabs out front.

Fuckfuckfuckfuckfuck.

I needed a phone charger. I went to go back inside the bar only to realize the doors were now locked. They must have locked them right behind me leaving. *Oh fuck.* Why didn't Grant check on me? Fuck. This is not a good situation. I sat on the curb and started crying for a few minutes. *Where the fuck was anyone?* I was so fucked. I needed a plan and quick.

A large semitruck pulled over to the curb.

"Hey are you ok? Do you need help?" the driver asked.

I immediately wiped my eyes and got up and pretended I knew someone, anyone, because this was way too sketchy.

"No it's ok. I'm fine," I said, waving him off, avoiding eye contact.

"Are you sure? Do you need me to call someone at least?"

Wait... Yes. I needed him to call someone, for sure. What other option did I have?

"Yes, actually. That would be helpful," I said wiping my eyes again.

"Ok. Here's my phone." He handed me his phone down through the window.

But who was I going to call? I didn't have Grant or Kenzo's number memorized. I could call a few people, aka the only numbers I had memorized, but none could help me—my sister and my best friends from home didn't have Grant's number. Well, my roommate and college best friend did. I could call her.

I called her, but she didn't answer. I left a message. I was still fucked.

"Listen, I know you don't trust me, but I'm a good guy just trying to help. I have my own daughters so I get it. Do you need a ride somewhere?" he asked.

I looked around at the empty street and seriously hated the idea of getting into a truck driver's semi, but I really was pretty fucked over. So I decided to fill him in on the situation before committing. *I came with a group and we were visiting from Dallas, we were all staying in a hotel off the freeway about 20 minutes out. No, I didn't know the hotel name. And my phone was dead so I couldn't call them.* Unfortunately, his phone was an old flip phone so an iPhone charger was out of the question too.

"What's the hotel look like?" he asked.

I did my best to describe it and the big billboard next to it.

"You know, I actually know where that is if you're comfortable with me taking you."

"Ok."

I hopped in the truck and we headed to the highway. He talked about his daughters and how he would want someone to help if they were in my shoes and that he was unhappy my friends left me in that situation.

Yeah, me too. Mainly fucking mad at Grant. So much for being my best friend. I was going to kill him if I ever made it alive to the damn hotel. Sure enough, on the highway, the hotel was there sticking out like a sore thumb. Right where the truck driver said it would be.

"That's it!" I yelled. Never did I think I'd be so excited to see that sketchy hotel.

"Yep! That's the one I thought." He pulled off and into the hotel parking lot and I said I couldn't thank him enough.

"Here, take my number and let me know you're ok when your phone goes on," and he scribbled his number on a receipt.

"Thank you so much," I said, wiping my eyes free of all the tears from earlier.

I got to the room and banged on the door since those idiots hadn't even given me my own key. Maybe I was an idiot for not insisting on one. Then again, Grant was my buddy and supposed to stick with me. The door opened and Kenzo didn't even look to see if it was me, but maybe he looked through the gaping hole in our door where there was supposed to be a peephole. I was about to yell at him but instead watched him plop into a bed with two other girls sleeping in it. *Typical.* I made my way to the adjacent room's bed to berate Grant who was also in bed with multiple people.

"Oh hey, Grant! Remember me! Your best fucking friend who got left a Billy Bob's without a ride and a dead phone and was stranded!"

"Oh shit, Court," he said belligerently and still half asleep. "Sorry,

I thought you were already back here when Kenzo and I got back and when you weren't I tried calling you but your phone was dead."

"Ugh!" I plopped next to him on the bed that another one of our guy friends had come to crash in and got under the comforters and decided we'd take this conversation up in the morning. I was dead tired from all the damn adrenaline I had just endured.

"It's not fucking ok." I said rolling over, knowing this was in a major part, my own fault.

"Sorry Court, how'd you get home anyways?"

"A fucking semitruck driver!"

"Jesus."

The next morning I tried to stay mad at the boys, but really, I wasn't a child and it wasn't their fault. I just pretended to be mad crossing my arms and rolling my eyes at them. Kenzo tried not to laugh when I said I got driven home by a truck driver and I shoved his chest for laughing.

"You guys! This is serious! I could've been killed! Or raped! Or something horrible!"

"You're right, you're right. We're sorry," Kenzo said with a smirk and a look to Grant.

Ugh, that stupid smirk.

* * *

Alright—don't kill me for this one guys, but I don't actually remember perfectly the first night of how hooking up with Kenzo went down. Which is, like, *such* a missed opportunity because I've hyped you all up for it. But here's what I can tell you.

It happened during that same summer I was doing summer school sometime after that concert we all went to at the beginning.

It was a summer night and I came back to his place after a night out drinking. We went up to his room and instantly the electricity that had so long been there finally broke loose. He picked me up and flipped me onto the bed, and we started ripping each other's clothes off.

He pulled down his pants and revealed the hardest, biggest dick I'd ever seen. Like, *huge*. He pulled off my panties and started fingering me while kissing my neck.

"Do you have a condom?" I asked, which was ironic since when the fuck did I care about using a condom? I was probably just trying to seem responsible.

He said yes and pulled open his bedside table drawer and pulled out a box of Magnum condoms.

"Wow, you're so fucking tight. This is gonna be interesting."

Ugh, Magnum condoms? Hell yeah this was going to be interesting.

He kept fingering me until I was severely turned on and went to put his dick inside of me, but it wasn't fitting. So he spread my legs a little wider and used his hand to pull my vagina and my butt cheek further apart and eventually made his way in. I instantly lost my breath like I never had before. He let out a moan and started thrusting hard into me. I couldn't stop muttering "Oh my," throwing my own head back into the pillow as he continued thrusting, my chin reaching up further to the ceiling. He recognized my pleasure and spread me further with his free hand pulling my leg up onto his shoulder.

The sex was insane. And he was so sexy on top of me, his triceps flexed and his biceps so well-defined. And his jawline flexed with every thrust into me.

Fuck, he was hot. And this might be the best damn sex I've ever had.

Shit, *this was the best sex I had ever had* and he wasn't even playing with my clit, but damn. He told me he was going to cum and he moaned out, "Fuck, Courtney" as he clearly came, but continued thrusting into me. He collapsed next to me and we both sat heaving breaths for a little before we both started laughing out loud.

"That was awesome," Kenzo said.

"Uh, yeah. You could say that," I said, staring at the ceiling trying to hide my stupid grin. Kenzo rolled over and pulled me to him with his free arm like a Neanderthal man claiming his prize, but I was totally ok with it.

After that, every damn night of the week was Kenzo and Courtney time. Kenzo was working full-time and I was just working my summer internship a couple days a week since school was about to start. If I'd go out, he'd get me an Uber to his place when I was done. If I'd stay in, he'd get off of work and pick me up to go back to his place. Circumstances didn't really matter, just as long as we ended the night hooking up.

One night we came back to his place after we had been out at the bars, but he admitted his dad was visiting and staying with him, which meant his room was taken. So we got to it on the couch, but Kenzo was so big he always made me moan audibly when we'd have sex because I borderline couldn't handle him. But he never asked me to be quiet, because I could tell he loved seeing what he did to me. I tried so hard to be quiet this time, but instead my moans came out like whimpers. I tried biting his neck or his ear to keep from wanting to scream as he continued to thrust into me harder and harder.

"Oh fuck," I moaned, trying to grab a pillow off the big, brown couch to cover my face as Kenzo grunted on.

All the sudden a voice piped up from the other room.

"Seriously you guys! Go to fucking sleep! All you do is fuck! Isn't your dad right upstairs too? Jesus, man."

We both stopped dead in our tracks mid-fuck with Kenzo inside me and looked panicked, but we both knew it was his roommate Clark. I forgot poor Clark's door wasn't even a door really—it was a damn curtain. *Fuck*. Poor guy was listening to us fuck on the couch the whole damn time.

I tried not to laugh and Kenzo tried not to laugh too, but then he whisper-yelled back, "Shut up, Clark."

We finished up our shenanigans and I kept a pillow over my face.

A random Thursday, Kenzo got off work and wanted to hang out aka bang out again. I told him to pick me up. He needed more condoms so we went to the gas station and he went in and got a bottle of wine and a giant pack of condoms, which made me laugh since he held the brown bag up as he left the gas station like it was a prize. We headed back to his place and used two of the condoms that night and another one the following morning. That morning, once we finished, he rolled over and opened his phone to a text that looked like a small novel. It was from his ex, Sammi. I rolled over to lay on his chest.

"Damn, someone's in trouble," I said, eyeing the text.

"It's Sammi. She's fucking insane, dude. She wants to get back together, but she's honestly just so fucking nuts."

She basically stalked his ass and forced them to get back together because she knew they were supposed to get married or some crazy shit. As he continued telling me, he got up and pulled a Coors Light out of his mini fridge and cracked it open. I raised an eyebrow at him.

"C'mon! It's Friday!" he said, disappearing into the bathroom to get ready for work.

He re-emerged, getting dressed and polishing off the silver bullet, then brushing his teeth and fixing the collar of his shirt in his mirror.

I rolled over in his bed, watching him adjust his collar and sleeves. "Damn, you do look good in dress clothes."

He laughed. "Thanks. I'll see you later," he said with a wink and shut his room door behind him.

This was probably a week before school was about to start, so everyone was trickling back to campus. Thursday night everyone was going to Rio, a total underground club with bottle service. I went with my roommate and our girlfriends, dressed to the nine in bandage dresses and fake eyelashes. We hung out at one of our friend's tables as the music bumped, but then worked our way down to the basement. Kenzo was there and looking fine in his button down. As soon as he saw me, he took a sip of his drink and walked over. He whispered in my ear how great I looked and how he loved this dress, giving me a little wink and sliding his hand on my waist and slipping it just a little too low. He saw a buddy and went over to say hi soon after. I preoccupied myself with some new friends and a few guys who were giving looks that night. You know, the "I'm trying to get laid" kind of looks. I started flirting with one guy who had secretly had a crush on me for a while, because I knew exactly whose territorial eye it would be catching. Finally, after staring across the bar and chugging his drink, Kenzo came up and basically made the conversation awkward so the guy would end up leaving.

"Uhm, what are you doing?" I asked.

"Nothing," he said with a smile.

Kenzo walked off as soon as the potential candidate had retreated. I rolled my eyes. But I wasn't the only one noticing how good Kenzo looked. People had started getting back into town for school and the bar was popping with plenty of familiar faces. Including one in particular: his ex, Sammi. She was talking up a storm with him at the bar and he was just kind of smiling and looking around, but would catch eye contact with me occasionally. *Not this shit again.*

I looked at my phone at the time and it was just past 1:00 a.m. I grabbed my vodka cranberry off the bar, chugged it, and headed Kenzo's way. I walked with purpose and sass, fueled likely by one too many vodka crans.

"I'm leaving," I said, not giving him eye contact, scanning the room.

"Ok," he replied, sipping his drink with a smirk, avoiding eye contact as well.

I let my eyes find his.

"Kenzo, I'm leaving and it can be with you, or otherwise, I'll find someone else who wants to take me home," I said then scanning the room to a couple of the earlier potential candidates, ending my scan with a raised eyebrow his way.

He held my eye contact and started clenching his jaw. He grabbed his drink off the bar and tossed it back, then grabbed my hand without saying anything. Sort of rushed, he interlaced his fingers in mine and pulled me along toward the door and leaned down to my ear to answer my last remark before we left.

"It's going to be me."

As his words came out, I smirked to myself as the last image I had leaving the club was of his ex watching us leave the bar together.

In the cab home we were surprisingly not all over each other. We were just sitting next to each other as he held my hand. We walked into his place composed like this until we got upstairs to his room and I said I had to use the bathroom. I totally forgot I was wearing Spanx and needed to take them off before he realized. My neon yellow Tori Burch purse was literally the size of a cell phone, so that was out for a hiding place. But what about his drawers in the bathroom? They were also tiny and one was fake, so that was out, too.

But the bath mat. *Yes, the bath mat.* I could lay it on the ground underneath it and get it in the morning. *Yep,* that was the plan. I slipped them off and laid them under the mat. I finished my routine with a dab of toothpaste from his drawer into my mouth and headed into his room.

We started making out and naturally his hands started going up my dress and playing with me over my underwear getting me warmed up and prepped for him. He started to spread me out and pulled out his hard cock, but I stopped him just before and asked about a condom. I knew he would have one since we had just bought a gigantic box of them and had only used three.

He opened the drawer and pulled out the box and flipped it revealing it was empty.

"Damn, I'm out," he said.

Wait...

I sat there confused and looked at him until he realized he had fucked up.

"How could you be out? We bought those on Tuesday and it's Thursday night. We only used two or three and it's a six pack..." I asked.

He looked away guiltily. "Wait, I think I know where I have some."

"Kenzo, why is the box of condoms empty already? Hmm?"

"I can ask Clark if he has one."

"Oh my God! You're such a whore, Kenzo!"

"Lemme go ask Clark!"

"Don't bother," I said, getting up.

"I'll be right back. Don't leave!" he said, vanishing out of the room.

I pulled my dress back down and grabbed my phone and ordered an Uber.

"See! I told you I'd find one!" he said, holding up the condom.

"Too late. Just ordered an Uber."

"Wait, don't go."

"Ok—fine. Answer this: Why don't you have any condoms left,

Kenzo? When we bought a mega pack two days ago. Hmm?" I said, picking up the empty box from the bed.

"Court..."

"Kenzo..."

I tried saying his name without a smile peeking out and looked at my phone. I pretended to be mad even though I knew I couldn't actually be mad. It wasn't like we were dating. But I knew who the girl was. It was his ex. I saw the way she watched us leave together and I knew she was texting him. He caught wind of me pretending to be mad and instantly got up and flipped me back down on the bed which naturally led me to burst into giggles.

"You don't want to leave. I know it," he said smiling.

"No, I do," I said laughing now, knowing I was caught.

My phone started ringing on the dresser. "That's my Uber, I gotta go." I gave him a wink and got up to get it off the dresser but he jumped up and beat me to it, answering my phone.

"No, she actually doesn't need an Uber anymore."

I sat on the end of the bed and crossed my legs and folded my arms, rolling my eyes at him.

"Yes, I'm sure. Yep, I'll cover the charge. Thanks."

He hung up and looked over at me.

"You're the worst."

He giddily sat back down on the bed next to me and started kissing my neck.

"I shouldn't hook up with you. I'm not going to."

"Oh, yeah?"

"Yeah."

He laid me back down on the bed and pushed up my dress and started kissing my inner thigh.

Who was I kidding? Yep. I was most certainly going to hook up with him. He went down on me, flicking his tongue on my clit and thrusting his fingers into me before pulling his hard dick out and ripping open the condom.

"Clark probably hates us." I laughed. He pushed himself into me and made me audibly moan out just like he always did. And just like that the conversation was over.

After this, Kenzo and I never hooked up again, but damn there were plenty of times we wanted to. The only problem was, he got back together with—who else—Sammi. After he said all that shit about her being nuts, he must've not-so-secretly loved nuts. We went to New Orleans that year together and even when he was a drunken fool stumbling back to the hotel with me and the elevator doors closed we just stood there in so much sexual tension, mainly because Greg was with us too, but he was still with Sammi.

Kenzo and I stayed in touch and talked on and off for years. Him telling me I should move back to Texas when he was single and me texting him every weekend I was going back to Dallas when I was single. Grant even invited me to go on a trip to Florida with him and the boys while I was dating my boyfriend Tanner (who I'll get to later), but when he told me Kenzo was coming too, I had to decline the trip. Everyone knew single Kenzo and me together was bad news bears. Even though I wasn't a cheater, it was playing with fire. Even Grant said so.

From then on, every time Kenzo was single it was a running joke between Grant and me. But I have to say, the man was hardly ever single. He bounced from cute girlfriend to cute girlfriend like it was his job.

"Guess who's single again?" Grant would ask.

The answers would vary on whether I was single or not single.

"Oh, God. Guess who's not? Please tell me he's not in town when I'm there."

Or...

"Oh damn. Maybe I should hit him up again."

Even then Grant would warn, "Hey Kenzo is going to be in town."

"Yeah, but he has a girlfriend."

"Well yeah, but it's Kenzo..." Grant would say, starting to laugh.

After college, Kenzo bounced around to a couple different cities and so did I, but we always stayed in touch as friends. When the Packers went to play the Falcons in the NFL Playoffs, I knew he was living in Atlanta, so I hit him up and told him we were coming. My mom and I ended up meeting him for drinks, catching up. I hit him up when I was applying to grad schools and told him I was applying to the University of Texas. He said I should move to Houston.

"What's in Houston?" I texted back.

"Uh, me—obviously."

"Oh, that's all?" I teased.

I wasn't positive if he had a girlfriend at this point of us texting, but really even if he did it was just playful banter. He even Snapchatted me recently, saying he was coming to Boston for a trip, and I told him I had an extra Red Sox ticket if he was down. I knew he was dating a new cute blondie and I even told him I could try and get her a ticket too if she was in town.

Grant said Kenzo and his new girl are totally into each other and she's probably the one. Honestly, I hope she is. But if not, let's just say if he texted me out of the blue and asked why I hadn't moved to Texas yet, I would crack a smile.

10

Alex

It was Labor Day and my first weekend in Boston by myself. So what's a girl to do? I opened Bumble and started swiping with one hand and sipping white wine on ice with the other. A dangerous combo.

"Huh—this guy is kind of cute? What do you think?" I held my phone out to Boone, situated on the other side of the couch, who looked at me with the tilt of his head.

"I mean, why not, right?" I swiped right to reveal we had matched.

I used to have my go-to pussycat line as you're all aware now, but I decided now that I'm twenty-eight maybe I'm more mature? I should probably retire that line and be more grown up. Rather than keep swiping and put off sending an opening line only to realize days later the match was expired, I decided to send something now. I swiped through his photos again: dancing/wedding photos, one playing basketball, professional headshot, and one in front of an Equinox gym where he looked ridiculously tall. I took another gulp of my wine and typed.

"I feel like you're a really good dancer."

I pressed send. Then naturally, I did my ADD thing and typed again to finish my thought.

"Idk where this epiphany comes from but I hope it's true."

Throw in some emojis. I added some emojis and pressed send again.

I nodded my head in approval looking to Boone for reassurance, but he's back to sleeping.

Naturally, I neglected the app for a few days while getting caught up in work and school, which I learned quickly, I would never take more than the designated course load again on top of work and trying to have a social life and keeping a dog alive and myself healthy.

I opened the app to see I had two messages from my new match Alex. One from three days ago, and another from one day ago.

"I think of myself as the white Chris Brown, so ya. Think you can keep up?"

(Two days later.)

"Shit I thought that line was money."

I slapped my hand to my forehead and quickly responded in rapid fire.

"UHM OMG IT WAS MONEY!"

"SOOOO FIRE"

"but yeah, I can keep up (smirk emoji)"

He responded.

"Hahaha ok I'll start practicing head spinning now. Let's meet up for a drink and find out. Do you live in Southie?"

Our messaging continued on the app for a month longer, horrendously too long, I know, but I was drowning in work and only checking the app every few days. Finally, Alex made a revolutionary suggestion.

"What's your phone number? I want to be added to the list of guys in your texts."

Cute. I sent my number over and a text came in.

"Hey it's Alex not to be confused with Steve or Josh from Bumble."

Cute! Ok, ok, ok, Alex.

We finally come up with a day that works for us and decide on Saturday somewhere outside since it's going to be nice out.

"Let's go to Six West in Southie. It's a roof deck & I need a tan," he texted.

It really was hot out that day which I was totally at odds on how to dress for, especially for an afternoon date. I decided on a plain black tank dress with a flannel tied around my waist and converse. *Baseball cap? Nah, try and dress it up a bit, Court.* I ordered an Uber and an incoming call was ringing in from my Grandma aka G-MA.

"Wassup, G!" I said.

I filled her in that I was going on a date. *Who was this new guy?* Some tall guy. *Where were we going?* A rooftop bar since it was nice out. *Was he a nice man?* Who knows. *How were my studies?* Great. And you and Grandpa? *Good—bored.* Cool. I'll call you this week with updates, I love you. *Love you, too.*

I got off the phone right as we were pulling up and my Uber driver told me he talked to his grandma every week when he got his hair cut which happened to be today.

"Weekly haircut?" I asked.

"Ah, yeah. Gotta be staying fresh. You have a good day now!"

"Thanks, you too! Is this it?" I asked looking up at a high rise building.

"Yeah, it's a rooftop deck at the top. Just go in and tell them you're going to Six West."

I thought about our brief exchange: *A man who talks to his grandma regularly, hell yeah. Weekly haircuts though? I barely remembered to brush my hair weekly. City boys are certainly something.*

I headed up the elevator and emerged into a packed bar, socially distanced with clear plexiglass. Which, *thank God*, because weren't we trying to soak up some rays? I walked in and tried to find a single at a table, finally spying one in the corner with sunglasses on.

"Hi Alex? I'm Courtney!" I said.

He stood up and I had to go on my tippy toes to hug him. He was every bit of 6'4", as he mentioned on his dating profile, a rarity in itself. At 5'5", I don't necessarily need a giant, but I'm always a sucker for one.

We sat down and got to talking and the conversation flowed easily. He ordered an IPA and I ordered a jalapeno-something margarita on the menu. My drink came in a tiny glass with two gigantic Scotch-style ice cubes in it. More like three sips of tequila for eighteen bucks.

He told me about how he had a corporate job but decided to become a personal trainer instead, something he was more passionate about. That career path worked well for him, as he had a background as a basketball player and had previously been a trainer for some players on the Boston Celtics. I think he said he was a rehabilitation trainer, maybe? I'm not sure. But he ultimately returned to his financial roots and started day trading. *Ah, back to the finance boys we go.*

"That's risky," I said, pulling my near-empty glass to my face, waiting for the last licks of tequila to reach my tongue.

"Yeah, but I like it. And everyone warned me it's not a good idea, but here I am two years later and on the up and up."

"Hey! That's awesome. My ex was in finance and always wanted to day trade, but it's freaking hard! So that's awesome you've got a knack for it."

"What do you do?"

I laughed.

Like choosing an alcohol and sticking to it, this question always took similar twists and turns, even though it's an age-old question that will always be asked on dates. Because, *what do I do?* Everything, honestly. Sports. Social Media. Website Development. Graphic Design. Marketing. Writer. Blogger. Videographer. Photographer. Entertainment. The list goes on. But this guy changed careers a couple times, too. Maybe he'll understand a fellow juggler.

"Well, social media and website development for local businesses back home pays the bills, but I've always been a sports writer and blogger. I used to work at ESPN and kind of built up my social media after that and now I do a lot of blogs and video podcasts online."

"That's awesome! You laughed, so I thought you were going to say you were an escort or like had an Only Fans or something. Which, no hate, I dated a girl who did that a bit ago and she made a killing doing it and wasn't even really doing much."

Here we go again!

"Hah—yeah. Actually, I do have an Only Fans, but it's not like *that.*

It's where I post my full-length sports hot take videos. And like, some sports-themed swimsuit kind of shoots."

I stared at my empty drink as I waited for judgment.

"That's sick. Yeah, I'm totally into entrepreneur-brained people, so that's awesome you knew how to capitalize on that."

Ok, Alex. Liking you more and more, my friend.

We decided to walk and wander around until we found the next bar to go to. There was an outdoor patio nearby so we stopped in. The Fox and the Knife. We were seated and given a menu and I didn't recognize anything on the menu. Alex looked confused too.

"Yo, I don't know what any of this is," he said, holding up the menu.

I started laughing. "Yeah, me either, let's ask her."

Our waiter told us they were all liquor-type drinks. Did we want to try? Sure. She brought out some samples and they were pretty good, but totally not what we were looking for. We thanked her and ordered Stella's, the only thing we recognized on the menu. I got up to go to the bathroom and realized the hallway leading to the bathroom was labeled Platform 9 ¾.

What? We were we at a Harry Potter bar and I didn't even know it! I'm a huge Potterhead, for the record. A house-sorted and tested Gryffindor, to be exact.

I came out to exclaim the news to him. He didn't watch Harry Potter though. *Fine, no worries, that's an easy fix, right? Sure. That can be changed.*

After Fox and Knife, we decided to head back to my place in Charlestown to have a beer. We got there and he met Boone and I showed him around and he said he really liked my place. He wandered over to my oddities shelf, which always gets people raising their eyebrows at me. It used to be a lot of crystals, but now it's grown to incorporate other specimens and taxidermy, including a puffer fish, antlers, a wet specimen octopus in a globe, a diaphanized pink seahorse wet specimen, a fossilized Mosasaur jaw bone and teeth, an alligator head, a mounted butterfly collection, and countless crystals and other fossils. Plus there's tons of antiques like an old lantern, my great uncle's old typewriter, a Webster's original dictionary from the '40s and plenty of other fun stuff. Those are just the highlights of my collection for now though. My oddity wish list in my iPhone notes is forever growing.

"Yeah, I'm a little odd," I said, finally.

"You're a witch, aren't you?" he asked.

I burst out laughing. "No. But I do have a classmate that said we have one at Emerson and she was worried she got on her bad side and was going to be hexed or something. I found out she's in one of my classes."

I went on to tell him about the supposed witch in my class and about another girl from class who was a ghost hunter for years. While I'm telling him, my Google Home was still playing my "Mellow" Spotify playlist I put on for Boone before I leave the house. A good song came on, Alabama Shakes or Lumineers I believe, and he looked surprised I knew it.

"Do you want to dance?" he asked.

"In my living room?" I scoffed.

He raised his eyebrows, throwing out a hand theatrically. *This guy has seen too many movies.* But I'd be a total liar if I said I wasn't secretly swooning.

"How could I say no?" I joked, enduring his theatrics by reaching my arm out and dramatically tipping my hand to meet his.

He pulled me in close and we began to dance. Soon he lifted me off the ground and pulled me against him to bring me to eye level. My feet dangled above his, barely touching the tops.

Okkk.

He stared into my eyes and tilted his head sideways and kissed me, slowly releasing his grip, lowering me back down to the ground. Suddenly, I felt so short.

"I gotta say, when you first walked into our date I was like, oh wow," he said.

"What does that mean?"

"I mean, I thought you were pretty in your photos, but then you showed up and I was like 'oh shit, she's like really pretty.'"

"Oh my God, stop. You aren't too shabby yourself," I responded, getting on my tippy toes to give him another peck.

"Alright, let's try something fun," he said, now positioning me across the room. "Ok, you're going to run to me and I'm going to lift you in the air."

Normally, I'd have some interior thoughts here, but at this point, I had no filter and was letting them fly right at him.

"Excuse me, what? Like *Dirty Dancing*? You can't lift me. Trust me."

"Watch me," he said.

"I'm heavier than you think."

"I just lifted you now."

"That was different."

"Alright, ready," he said, planting his feet.

"No."

He unplanted his feet and started rushing to me instead.

"No, no no!" I repeated, holding out my hands, backing up and laughing. "You won't be able to."

He raised an eyebrow at me. I smirked.

"Ok, fine! Fuck! Tell me what to do," I said.

"That's the spirit!"

He wanted me to run to him and he was going to lift me and hold me in the air like I was some damn ballerina or eighty-five-pound figure skater, which I most certainly AM NOT. Also, many of you may be thinking this scene sounds familiar if you've seen the movie *Crazy, Stupid, Love* aka where Ryan Gosling does this exact same thing for his first date in a scene. Well, I had never seen that movie. Clearly, Alex had. But let me tell you, the first time I did see it I about spit out my drink laughing trying to explain to my sister someone had done this to me before. Anyways...

"Ok, go!" he yelled.

I ran up to him and he went to lift me only to get halfway to his face and have to bring me back down.

"See! This is a bad idea!" I said.

"No, I almost had it! One more time."

I obliged and went across the room. Sure, this would be the last time—successful or not. I trotted his way on call and bounced up into his hands, secured on my rib cage, and he lifted me up in the air and actually held it for a couple seconds. Until we both started laughing and he brought me down collapsing into him. We kissed again and he picked me up to be eye level with him, placing my feet on top of his. He walked me into my room like this, and we both flopped onto my mattress on the floor.

"Don't ask about the bed. It's a whole thing," I said.

"Hah—ok, I won't."

We started making out and rolling around taking off pieces of clothing. But not my panties. He started to reach a hand down there before I stopped him.

"Ugh, yeah, we can't do that—it's my time if you know what I mean."

"Oh, I see." His hand retreated back to safety and continued kissing me working his way on top of me, but I flipped him over to get on top of him and take charge. My turn to do the pleasing. I decided just because we couldn't have sex, courtesy of Mother Nature, didn't mean I couldn't give this guy a blow job. And besides, I liked giving blow jobs. There's something about being in control over a man and their desires and allowing them to cum that seems powerful.

Anyways, I got to work going up and down his shaft as he looked down at me, occasionally trying not to show his awe as I kept locking eyes with him. But soon after taking his balls into my mouth, I decided to take him deep into my throat. His body stiffened at this and he flipped me over and got on top.

"Are you sure you're on your period?"

"Yes," I said. smiling back up at him with hair in my face and my head buried between pillows.

"Damn," he rolled over.

"Better luck next time," I joked, maneuvering myself back on top to finish the job.

And after that it didn't take long. Some more bobbing and gagging and eventually a consistent locked lips on his cock and he couldn't take anymore.

"I'm gonna cum," he said. *Magic to my ears, you power thirsty, she-devil.*

I continued my lip lock and felt him cum inside my mouth, promptly swallowing what was exerted. Coming up for air after, with a swift flip of my hair and wipe of my hand to make sure there wasn't slobber on my face, I smiled while he looked astonished.

"Well, ok," he said.

I started laughing and shoved him back onto the bed messing around. We rolled around in the sheets a bit before we started talking about where I lived and where he lived. He lived in Dorchester, about twenty or so minutes away aka farther than the usual I would go out to. I'd only been when I went to my favorite Packers Bar there called The Banshee. He said he knew The Banshee but for soccer. I explained it's kind of a secret Pack bar because the entire upstairs attic-like area is decked out in green and gold.

"Well, I'm hungry now," he said.

"I'm not," I joked, raising my eyebrows, head still on a pillow. *Courtney, why do you have to be such a degenerate.* But he laughed.

"Are there any bars around here?" he asked.

"Yeah! Actually, there's this total townie bar down the street, Sullivan's, I'm trying to become a regular at! Let's go! It'll give me good brownie points!"

So we got dressed and headed arm-in-arm down to Sullivan's. We walked in and sure enough, the same white-haired man with dark eyebrows was behind the bar and told us to sit anywhere, no masks required. *Sweet.* We grabbed a menu and the only thing on it was a small pizza, ham and cheese sandwich, and a pretzel. I wasn't that hungry but Alex was. So he ordered a pizza. But they were out of pizza. How about a ham sandwich and a pretzel then? And some beers. The sandwich came out and Alex was thrilled about it, which I did not get.

"God, I love this place. This is like... a homemade sandwich. Like, you know he just was back there and whipped this together. That's my kind of sandwich," he said as he dove headfirst into the sandwich taking monster bites.

He looked ridiculously happy, sandwich in mouth, but it was cute.

"You could fit right in in Charlestown. Natural townie," I said, sipping my Guinness.

"Actually, this used to be my dad's stomping grounds about twenty to thirty years ago."

My eyes immediately widened.

"Wait, really? I'm so curious about that time period here in Charlestown. Because it's super safe and cute and all people popping bottles of champagne on the square Wednesday through Sunday nowadays, but apparently, it used to be all Irish Mafia bad in the '70s and '80s. Bank robberies. Big Italian and Irish Mafia beef."

"Yeah," he started bringing his voice down, signaling mine was likely too loud, like it always was. Dates telling me I was too loud was hardly new for me.

"He was basically part of that, I'm like as Irish as they come," he continued.

"Wait—so you're saying your dad was like C-town Irish Mafia?"

He shrugged guiltily, waiting for me to judge or flee.

"Is it bad that I think that's lowkey badass? Because it's like the movies. But like obviously not. So major Mafia? Like he's killed people..." I was thinking he would dismiss this thought and say I was getting theatrical, but he didn't.

"Well, I can't say for sure, but he definitely went to prison for dealing drugs when he was doing his time with that 'crew.' Heroin, I think. But yeah, gnarly stuff."

"That's insane!" I tried not to yell.

He took another bite of his sandwich and nodded his head. "Once he got out, he got his life straight, married my mom, etc. But the craziest part, to me, is that guy turns into the dad I know, who sends me pictures of his tomato plant and his flowers every week, so proud."

"Settled for the country life over the street life."

He showed me a photo of a little old man standing next to his tomato plant and then a close-up of the vegetables. Adorable. *Did this man really kill someone?* The world's a crazy place, man.

"That's actually adorable," I said, handing his phone back.

The bill came and he said he would take care of it and put out a twenty-dollar bill.

"Wait, random request, since you have cash—I need coins for laundry—can I Venmo you for the check if you get the rest of the bill in quarters?" I said guiltily, gritting my teeth into a smile.

"Sure! No worries!"

He picked up the tab and got the rest in quarters. What a guy. Even if his dad was a former heroin-dealing, Irish Mafia man. People change, right? And sons are not their fathers, certainly. We got back to my place and Alex decided it was late and he should probably be on his way. I said he could've got an Uber from Sullivan's and didn't have to walk me to my house.

"I wanted to," he said, kissing me. "Ok, so what's the rule then—I gotta wait five or six days or something until we go on a date?"

"Something like that." I said, shaking my head, looking up at him smiling.

"Cool. Well, my Uber should be here any second so I better go out there." He kissed me one more time.

Our 'had a good time' texts were the last messages from him until five days later.

"Has it been five-six days yet?"

"I believe it has," I replied.

We made plans on and off trying to coordinate schedules a few times. But also, in hindsight writing this, five or six days conveniently lined up with Mother Nature's timeline, didn't it? *God, I hate guys sometimes.* Anyways, one of our attempts to meet up again lined up and one time he even was down for me to come over right then.

"Unless you're free right now?" he texted.

"What for lunch?" I asked.

"Yeah, I'll cook. Bring Boon."

"Boone*, but good on you remembering his name. Let's do Sunday."

I'd like to think I wanted the date change because I knew he was using me as a lunchtime slam piece, but I also think that part of me just didn't feel like getting ready that quick and didn't read into it. *So, great, Courtney.*

He agreed to Sunday and it came around and I started getting ready early on because it was a big day regardless of him.

"Packers are on at 1:00 p.m. and the Masters are on. What's our plan Stan?" I know it seems weird the Masters Tournament was on during football season, but it was because of COVID delays.

He responded almost immediately. "Sorry gotta bail on today. I'm sorryyy."

Rats. Well, I guess I'm Packers-watching and Masters-watching on my own today. I didn't text him again after that, because I might as well follow my own rule: *If a guy wants to make it happen, he's going to make it happen.* So, to my surprise, when I sent a last-minute extra Red Sox ticket invite out to a group of people and included him, I realized we hadn't talked since November and it was now April. As soon as the text sent, I realized my mistake. I wished it never sent as I was driving through a rainstorm back to my place. Maybe the game would get canceled anyways.

A response came in quickly.

"Who is this?"

Fuck my life.

I responded and planned on never responding again. "LOL. Courtney Schellin. We went on a date a few months ago." Sent.

"I appreciate it but with this rain I'll have to pass."

Who is this? Oh I don't know, the girl who sucked your dick bro and you told me your dad was in the Irish Mafia and we shared a sandwich. Sick bro.

I shook my head disgusted while driving through the torrential rain. How fitting.

11

Kyle

"Ok, is it just me or is every guy out here hot?" I asked my new Boston girlfriends.

"Yes, but they're *Southie guys*. And we warned you about them. Plus, they all travel in packs of like six or seven."

We kept walking down Broadway Street to head to the next Southie bar on our Sunday Funday drinking escapades.

"I did notice that. Those guys at the last bar I had to get up and hit on them and give them our numbers! I feel like I'm back in California," I said.

"Yep, that's Southie guys for you."

"Whatever. I've never been afraid to put myself out there." Just as I'm saying this to our group of girls another group of guys passed by. The margarita tower aka giant, spouted vat we had just downed fueled my confidence and decided to speak for me.

"Hey, you're pretty cute!" I said, pointing to one with a wink as we passed by.

"Yeah, you're pretty cute, too," he said, turning around, getting a better look. Me and Jan, one of the girls, stopped to chat as the rest of the girls rolled their eyes and kept walking, laughing at our shenanigans.

"We're in the military," one blurted out.

Sweet opening line, bro.

"That's cool!" Jan said.

"We're heading to Stats though—here give me your number!" One extended his phone out to me and I typed it in.

"Bye!"

Jan and I jogged to catch up to the girls.

The next morning I was horrendously hungover, yet again. But that's what happens when you start with apple cider mimosas at the pregame, a pitcher of sangria at Monument, a margarita tower at Broadway, mix in some shots and beers at Playwright, and finish off with Loco's famous coconut margaritas for a solid eight hours of drinking. *Hasta luego, mi amiga.* Unfortunately, hangover or not, I had a hair appointment that following morning. So I made my way to South End, wearing sunglasses indoors, when a text popped up on my phone.

"Hey what's upp"

"Haha who's this," I responded.

"Kyle I got your number at the bar last night"

Kyle? Who the fuck is Kyle? I gave my number to that one guy at Playwright, I gave my number to the guy on the side of the road, and then I think there was that guy at Loco? I don't think the first guy even took my number down off the napkin, so I'm going to go fifty-fifty odds on side-of-the-road man and Loco guy. But he did say the bar... So Loco guy? Probably. I added his number into my phone as Kyle Loco Boston Guy.

I told him I was wildly hungover from our Sunday festivities and was at my hair appointment. He wanted a picture of my hair, likely to make sure his drunken stupor didn't lead him to give his number with beer goggles on. I sent him a picture of me smiling with my hair and he said "Gorgeous!" *Hmm, promising?*

I didn't respond, but the next night I had another text from him.

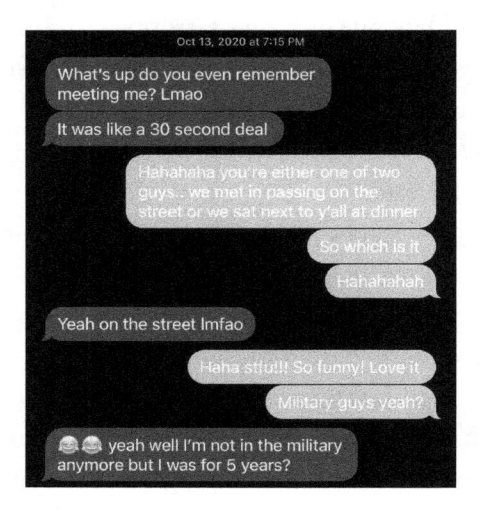

> **Oct 13, 2020 at 7:15 PM**
>
> What's up do you even remember meeting me? Lmao
>
> It was like a 30 second deal
>
> > Hahahaha you're either one of two guys.. we met in passing on the street or we sat next to y'all at dinner
> >
> > So which is it
> >
> > Hahahahah
>
> Yeah on the street lmfao
>
> > Haha stfu!!! So funny! Love it
> >
> > Military guys yeah?
>
> 😂😂 yeah well I'm not in the military anymore but I was for 5 years?

So, not the guy from Loco. Side of the road guy! Nice.

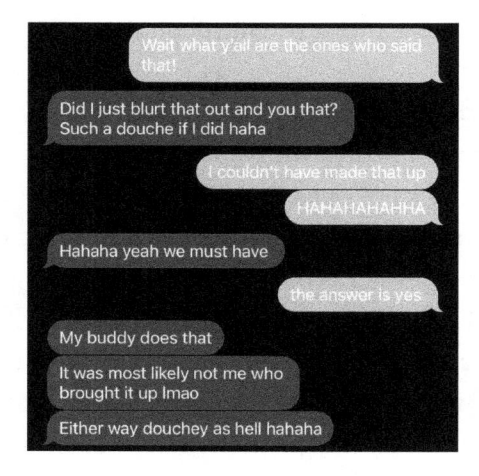

> > Wait what y'all are the ones who said that!
>
> Did I just blurt that out and you that? Such a douche if I did haha
>
> > I couldn't have made that up
> >
> > HAHAHAHAHHA
>
> Hahaha yeah we must have
>
> > the answer is yes
>
> My buddy does that
>
> It was most likely not me who brought it up lmao
>
> Either way douchey as hell hahaha

> Hahahah clearly we didn't mind
>
> The girls briefed me on southie guys being the douch Kong's of them all so maybe I was ready for it
>
> 😂
>
> I just moved here so I'm unfamiliar with all scenes lol

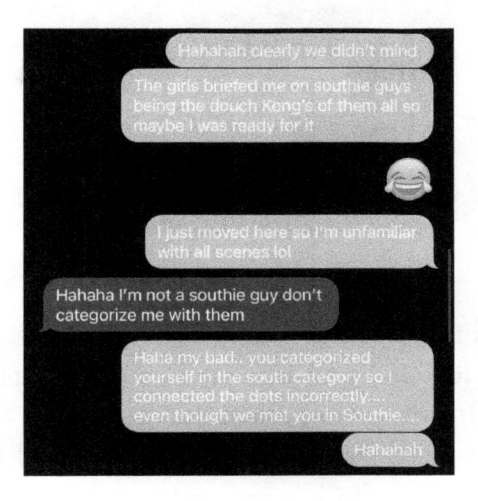

Hahaha I'm not a southie guy don't categorize me with them

> Haha my bad.. you categorized yourself in the south category so I connected the dots incorrectly.... even though we met you in Southie...
>
> Hahahah

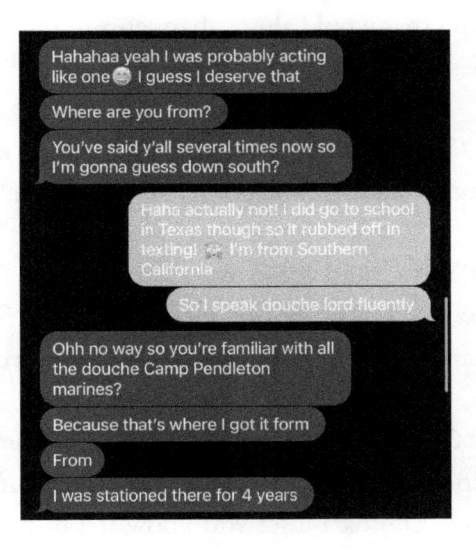

Hahahaa yeah I was probably acting like one 😅 I guess I deserve that

Where are you from?

You've said y'all several times now so I'm gonna guess down south?

> Haha actually not! I did go to school in Texas though so it rubbed off in texting! 😆 I'm from Southern California
>
> So I speak douche lord fluently

Ohh no way so you're familiar with all the douche Camp Pendleton marines?

Because that's where I got it form

From

I was stationed there for 4 years

[Text messages screenshot:]
Christ, here we go again
Haha but wait so you were there for four years like 6 years ago you said?
Oh wait no I read that wrong
When we're you in so cal?
No I was there from 2014-2019

This guy's actually pretty entertaining, but I really wish I remembered what he looked like. If I gave him my number though, he had to be decently cute, margarita tower be damned.

He eventually asked me on a date and we decided to go to a sushi place in the North End, which seems random because most people go to all the awesome Italian places in North End, but I heard it was good, so we decided why not? At this point I had already dealt with a slew of flaky fuck boys and dates that would almost happen and then didn't.

Some examples:

Douche #1: "Do you want to come over for wine night?" *Actually, I'm more comfortable meeting in public for the first time?* "Oh bummer..." (*Seriously?*)

Douche #2: "You should come over, I'm stuck on a zoom call." *Just call me when you're off and we can meet somewhere for drinks!* "Well technically only my face needs to be on the screen if you catch my drift..." (*SERIOUSLY?*)

Douche #3: "Can I take you out soon?" *Sure! What's your week look like?* "Oh I meant like now." *Uh, right now? I can't do right now but I could do dinner?* "Oh, ok I'll let you know if I'm busy or not later." (*HUH, SERIOUSLY?*)

Needless to say, I was equipped with men bailing or having unrealistic requests.

But Kyle hit me up as promised, despite having boxing and school to finish before dinner. I told him we could reschedule if it was too much, but no—he had it handled, he'd be there. *If a guy wants to make it happen, he's going to make it happen.* I Ubered to the sushi place and got us a table and he said he was parking.

I was getting nervous-excited when I realized I don't even remember what this guy looks like. *What if he walks in and I don't recognize him?* After all, it's beginning COVID times so he would have to walk in with a mask too, making my odds of distinguishing him that much harder. But he knows what I look like, this place is tiny, and my mask is off since I'm sitting. He'll know, so I'll know. *Right?*

Two guys walked in and I sat still so I didn't look like an idiot and, sure enough, they were just there for takeout. Finally a guy in a mask walked in, seemingly cute and a little shorter than expected, but came right up the table.

"Hey Courtney! Sorry I had to find parking," he said, taking off his mask, revealing a sweet face and a great smile. Not seemingly cute, he was *definitely* cute. *Damn, tipsy Courtney giving your number out—nice choice.* This has got to be the cutest guy I've gone on a date with in Boston!

We each ordered a beer and then looked at the roll menu. He admitted he was really only a California Roll kind of guy.

"Oh, we're going to change that. Trust me you're going to like these rolls if you're a sushi baby and don't like the 'scary' ones," I laughed.

I, on the other hand, liked it all. After a crunchy roll and some kind of shrimp tempura cream cheese rolls, I knew this guy would be happy.

While we waited for the food, he told me about his time in the military and the different countries he had traveled to. Now he's an electrician but also going back to school to get his degree. *Hard worker, clearly. Love that.*

He was hesitant when the food arrived, but said he wasn't a wuss and ended up loving all the sushi. *Knew it.* Before we could even order another round of beers, the place was closing, courtesy of the new curfew put in place for COVID. But this was kind of a pleasant surprise compared to my last few dates, which ended with excessive drinking. Memories would be fully intact for this one. Still, one more beer and some more time together would've been nice. I thanked Kyle for insisting to pay the bill, and he offered to drive me home. We just had to walk to his car parked a bit away. It was a chilly that night though, and Kyle was only in a tee shirt!

"Aren't you cold?"

"Yeah, but I'll be fine. I should've brought a coat," he laughed, shivering.

We finally got to the parking garage and he walked up to a big raised truck. *Swoon.*

"This is your truck? I love it."

"Thanks, sorry it's a little messy." It wasn't though.

He started his truck and the music came on loud, blasting some country music.

"Wait a minute—you drive a lifted truck and you listen to country music... Remind me why you're not actually a southern boy? You're not very Boston," I scoffed.

He laughed. "Yeah, I'm not. And I'd love to live in the South one day, all my family is up here though."

This guy might be a pretty damn good fit with me. And to think, I met him on the side of the road—not even from my dating apps. *Typical.*

We got to my house and as I pointed out the driveway to pull into, he pulled to a stop and said with a big grin, "So, did I do OK? Did I earn a goodnight kiss?"

This makes me burst out laughing, him sitting there, smiling, holding his steering wheel.

"In fact, you did." I said, smiling and leaning over the center counsel to give him a sweet kiss on the lips. I could feel him still smiling through my lips. "I'd invite you to come in for another beer since we only got to have one, but my place is a mess."

And it actually was. I somewhat purposefully left it messy so that I would not let this man over to my place, good date or not. I needed to reign it in and not be so trusting on these first dates since I really did just move here.

"Ah, that doesn't bug me."

"Trust me, not tonight." I said, trying to sound confident even though I really did want him to come in. "Next time."

We kissed one more time and I waved goodbye as his truck drove off, smiling to myself. As soon as I got inside and let Boone out, I told my dog all about my date night and how he even drove a truck! I decided to text Kyle thank you and that I had a good time and we texted on and off for the next few days.

I realized he had added me on Snapchat, God knows how long ago. I had been avoiding my Snapchat DMs considering only a few days earlier was the date with Anthony when I accidentally posted a video of me rolling around in the sheets to my damn story. Sure enough, one of the messages was from Kyle sending me the heart eyes emoji several times. *How embarrassing. Whatever, roll with it.*

The following weekend I went out with my friends Megan and Nisha to try a trendy Mexican spot in the city, Citrus & Salt. It was pretty cold out, so I wore my pink oversized sweater with a wide brim hat, and the girls were looking sexier than me; I would soon learn my lesson on overdressing because, one way or another, we'd always end up in Southie.

Citrus & Salt turned into dumplings and drinks in the South End, to beers at the hole-in-the-wall bar Anchovies, to liquor store Dr. McGillicuddy's nip shots taken on the side of the road, to an Uber to the staple sports bar in Southie, Stats. We walk into Stats and everyone was looking hot and ready to take on the Saturday night by the horns, except me. In hindsight, I probably looked fine, but I felt like I was sticking out like a sore thumb being so covered up.

The hostess brought us up to a table hidden away in a corner, which we hated because we usually liked to scope out the boy situation.

"I need to change," I said, sitting down and picking up a menu.

"I always tell you don't wear a sweater out, you'll regret it," Megan said, raising her eyebrows and grabbing a menu.

"I know. You're right."

Our waitress came over and got our drink order for a round of Bud Lights and I eyed her tight black tank top with the Stats logo on it before she smiled and walked away with our order. My smile turned into the Grinch's scheming grin.

"Oh, I'm going to change," I said, cheekily.

"Into what?"

"You'll see."

When she came back with our beers, I immediately jumped into my semi-prepared monologue.

"So I feel like I'm not looking hot enough to go out in Southie right now and I realized you look hot in that Stats tank. Do you sell those? And if so, can I buy one?"

The waitress just smiled and said reassuringly, "Sure! What size? I'll grab you one!"

I laughed and did a fist pump. The girls started dying laughing as she walked away.

She brought me back my T-shirt and I instantly started taking the sweater off and told the girls to block me as I changed.

"What! No! Just go to the bathroom and change, you weirdo!"

"Oh, yeah, I guess I could totally just do that." I shrugged and trotted off to the bathroom, slipping my arm back into its sleeve.

I returned to our table feeling like a new woman in my tight, black, somewhat see through, Stats tank. The girls did fake applause, commending my new outfit change.

Eventually a table opened up in the middle of all the fun on the bottom floor of Stats, so our waitress let us move there. Nisha was immediately hit on by a tall, dark and handsome man with a line so smooth and corny that I can't believe I forgot it. The gist of it was that he wanted to buy her a drink, which he did, for all of us actually. Later, Nisha walked by him and overheard him say the exact same line to another group of girls.

We rolled our eyes. *Southie guys!*

Nisha had to eventually part ways with us, but Megan and I decided to make moves over to another Southie go-to bar, Capo. I decided to check my Snap and see if any of the Bumble guys had responded to us being out in Southie.

Kyle snapped me back and it looked like he was out in Southie too.

"Where you guys at?" I sent.

"Capo basement."

"What?! We're at Capo! Come up!" *What a coincidence!*

Megan and I were at the upstairs bar and the bartender was loving Megan so he kept making us drinks. The guys said the bouncer wouldn't let them come up from basement to upstairs because of COVID, so our bartender told us a name to say and we had one of our own to try so I told him I'd meet him at the door with names ready to engage. I told the door man the names I was told and he laughed.

"I can't argue with those names! Go on in."

I smirked, feeling cool, guiding the guys in.

"Well, well, well. Look at you Miss Popular!"

"I literally just learned those names," I burst out laughing, trotting over to our spot at the bar, introducing them to Megan.

We all hit it off famously and with another drink in our systems, Kyle and I started kissing and canoodling by the bar top. His friend was actually really cute too, so Megan didn't mind keeping him company while her now infatuated bartender kept the drinks coming for her and her friends.

We moved the party back to my place where we could have some beers and play some drinking games. We put on some music and as soon as Megan went downstairs to grab drinks with Kyle's friend, Kyle and I glanced at each other, knowing it was game time. He picked me up and I wrapped my legs around his waist. He asked "Bedroom?" guiding our way with his free hand back and forth, still kissing me and not looking where he was going.

"Straight ahead."

He slid open my large door and lowered me onto the bed aka mattress, because I was still dealing with no actual bed frame at this point. He went back and slid both doors shut before coming to hover over me. Taking off his shirt, he revealed he was chiseled in all the right places, his pectoral muscles flexing as he scooted me further up the bed. He started pulling off my Stats tank and I made a joke.

"Oh what, you want to take off my Stats tank? I thought it was sexy?" I said laughing.

"Clearly, I thought so!"

He unbuttoned my jeans and I worked them off until I was in my lace thong. Then I pulled him down onto the bed with me and started helping him with his belt and pants. Once exposed and hard as a rock, he lifted my leg to work his way in between my legs. He guided his way into me and I gasped with pleasure as he started thrusting. He felt great and I wanted to moan louder, but I also didn't want Megan or Kyle's friend to know what we were up to, even though I'm sure it was obvious. I tried to be as silent as possible, giggling occasionally and biting his arm or shoulder, whichever was nearest.

He started thrusting faster and I knew he was getting close, so I arched my back and spread my legs a little farther to really feel him deeper into me. That did it for him, as he pulled out just before busting onto my stomach and tits. I smiled, biting my lip, looking up at him, as his face went from strained pleasure to relief to a big grin. *The best looks.*

We both giggled and he grabbed a towel to dry me off. We quickly put our clothes back on hoping the others didn't hear us from the main room. I pushed my hair down laughing, fixed my lipstick—if I even had any on anymore—and adjusted my shirt, which I would later realize was on inside out.

We emerged but they were nowhere to be found. *Huh?* We found them coming out from the downstairs bedroom. *Interesting.* But Megan insisted she was just showing him around the place. We went upstairs to hang out and Kyle's friend was infatuated with Megan, just like the bartender before.

Megan has this effect on men. She has a certain aura to her that naturally makes any and every man fall in love with her when we're out. I can't really describe it, but I swear it's a thing. Eventually, Megan decides to call it a night and the guys decide they should head back too.

The next day I woke up to a snap from Kyle saying that their Uber had been in a gnarly car accident on the way home from my place! They were fine but we both agreed they should've just stayed. Shortly after all that, I was on a flight home for winter break when Kyle texted me a couple times before I told him I was away so we just talked football and occasionally he would snap me. Like this one time...

I went to a wedding over break for a SMU friend, Raquel. The wedding was at Ocean Reef Club in Key Largo, FL, aka super ritzy, and I was excited to see all my friends from college.

I had a pink flowy romper to wear to the first night cocktail party, but it required some help into and out of from my friend Kiki who was also at the wedding. She met me out front of the party to zip me in and we headed in together with her parents and when we got to the bar I had my age-old dilemma of what to drink. *Don't drink wine—not sustainable for the whole night. Vodka—ugh, no. Jameson—perhaps, but it's—like—tropical out?* Kiki's mom ordered a Ranch Water.

"Ranch Water?" I asked.

"Yeah, honey! It's basically Tequila Soda," she responded.

Batter up, tequila! Here we go!

The party took place on this peninsula overlooking the ocean. There was a slight breeze coming off the water and the sun was setting a pink-to-yellow hue in the sky. The open bar was fabulous and the buffet food items were in true Raquel fashion aka the queen of eating off the kid's menu: chicken nuggets, grilled cheese sandwiches, and mini lobster rolls. Her rehearsal dinner party the following day would have a make your own mac-n-cheese bar.

The majority of us closing down the cocktail party walked over to the cigar bar and lounge on the resort and pulled up a few tables. I bopped around saying hi to everyone before sitting down with some close friends from college to catch up and get filled in on the latest gossip. Apparently, this bar was stupidly strict and wouldn't even serve the bride because she didn't have her ID on her. What! It was her damn wedding!

"That's fucking ridiculous," I said. As soon as I did, a woman came up to our table and tapped me on the shoulder, "That's it, you're out of here, you need to leave with me."

"What? Why?" I said nearly in unison with my friends sitting at our table.

"That's the second time you've used profanity and it is not tolerated in the lounge."

These boujee little bitches.

"Oh, I didn't realize. I'm sorry, it won't happen again." She nodded and left.

But when someone told a funny story and I started laughing and said something along the lines of, "Are you fucking kidding me?"

Instantly the woman appears again. "That's it," she said, looking like she was about to lug me out.

"Woah, woah she didn't mean it, she's not leaving," one of my friends said.

"I'm sorry!" I said, gritting my teeth holding my hands up.

"No, she's out."

"Excuse me, let me talk to you," my friend's boyfriend pulled her aside as I sat in my chair awaiting my conviction. Soon Raquel headed over to deal with her, cussing at her saying how out of control this was and then —as if realizing it herself—she made a statement out loud to all of us.

"You know what—we are leaving!" She waved her fingers as if to corral us and we were happy to follow her lead. "We'll go to Moose's boat to hang out there instead," she said glaring at the Ocean Reef Club woman.

With that, we were off to continue our charades on a multimillion-dollar yacht that our SMU friend had brought in for the weekend. *God forbid us heathens take up residence in the elite cigar club of the Ocean Reef Club!* About twenty of us headed onto the boat and I met some new friends of the groom, one being his cute cousin. He was a tall Asian man, with dark hair and somewhat broad shoulders, but more importantly he was pretty funny. We got to talking about me living in Boston and I laughed and said I should've never left the South because all I'm looking for is a guy who hunts and fishes and apparently that's not a thing up there.

"Do you hunt and fish?" I asked jokingly.

"Nope, I'm a California guy actually."

"Damn!" I said sipping my drink, winking.

We decided to make some new drinks on the yacht and then got a wandering tour of the different bedrooms and the upstairs of the boat, while sipping on our too-strong drinks. We wandered past one room where I overheard a girl telling the group that someone had to show her how to golf tomorrow because if she could swing and hit a golf ball better than her boyfriend, he said he would buy her a Birkin, a bag worth one-hundred thousand dollars.

I took another sip of my drink and continued up to the next floor of the yacht with the guys. Here I was on this multimillion-dollar boat, with multiple millionaires, and all I was looking for was someone who liked to hunt and fish. *The irony.*

After sipping drinks and wandering around upstairs, we realized too much time must've passed because there was hardly anyone left on the boat now. I looked around and realized the friends I had planned on leaving with weren't there anymore. *Damn it.* Why do I always allow this to happen to me? My friends Moose and Jedd decided it was probably best if someone walked me back to the hotel, as they were both staying on the yacht. Any volunteers?

"I can take her!" the cute Asian guy accepted the offer.

We headed back to my hotel and got into the elevator up, thinking we'd reached our destination. As soon as the doors shut, it was just like the sexual tension in the movies; he looked my way and I looked his way. We instantly moved toward each other and started making out in the elevator, forgetting to even pick the floor. When the doors reopened again, we realized our mistake and hit the proper floor. I decided to make it more platonic since I was not planning on doing more than just having some innocent teenage-like fun in making out. We got to my room and I offered a "thank you" seltzer so we sat on the balcony and shot the shit and got to know each other more.

"Well, I'm pretty tired, I'm going to call it a night." I said, tipping the remaining drops of my white claw into my mouth and squeezing the can, showing it was empty.

"Alright, do you want me to stay?" he asked.

"Not tonight, but thanks for walking me back!" I walked him to the door and kissed him goodbye before shutting the door behind me.

Immediately I wanted to get out of this romper only to realize it needed a helping hand. *Fuck.*

I opened the door and popped out again before he had even made it to the elevator.

"Wait, can you help me with this? I was supposed to have my friend help me with the zipper!"

He laughed walking back to the room and I turned around and he unzipped me in the doorway.

"Are you sure you don't want me to stay?" he asked, now raising an eyebrow.

"Sorry, I know how this looks, but I'm sure," I said, turning around holding my romper up. "Thank you though!"

"It's because I don't hunt and fish, isn't it?" he asked.

I blurted out into laughter.

"Well, yeah. Obviously," I said with a wink. "Good night!" I shut the door.

I opened my phone revealing texts from my mom and Kassidy, checking in on me concerned they had yet to get updates that I was back in my room, since I was at the wedding essentially alone, after all. I responded back and said I was in my room and all was well and texted Kassidy a little bit more information.

"Made out with my first Asian guy so that was sweet!" I smiled and giggled to myself as I pressed send to Kass, feeling like Vince Vaughn in *Wedding Crashers*.

I noticed I had a Snap response from a few of the usuals but then one from Kyle who I hadn't talked to in about a month. I opened it and it was a response to a selfie I took with one of my friends when we were on Moose's boat.

"You are so beautiful."

Beautiful?! OMG. What a preshy! It was just a normal selfie friend pic!

I sent back "thank yewwww" with a blowing a kiss emoji and heart eyes emoji.

I need to go on another date with that boy when I get back to Boston, I thought to myself before turning out the lights.

12

Marco

Ah, Marco.

The one my friends always referred to as the "Sexy Mexy" because, yes, he was sexy and he was Mexican. We met on my first day at ESPN, my first job right out of college. We were both sitting next to each other at the entrance when we finally started chatting and realized we were both new production assistant hires. I thought he already worked there and he thought the same about me which at least was a good sign heading into our first day. He was super sexy in his suit and tie, let me tell you. He had perfectly tanned skin, a fresh fade haircut, bright white teeth, and a gorgeous smile. Plus, he had broad shoulders and you could see he had nice biceps underneath his button-down. There's something about a man in a suit.

After the usual orientation things, they brought us to a SportsCenter meeting so we could see how they usually ran. I stood in the back with one of my newfound teammates when my phone, which was supposed to be on silent, started blaring out my ringtone: the NFL theme song.

Dah-Dah-Dun-Dun-Nuh-Nuh-BAAH

Of all the days and all the times for my sister to call my phone and it not be on silent... I fumbled to turn it off, but the damage was done. Multiple people were staring at me, and some looking extremely offended. *What? At least it's the NFL theme song*, I thought. If anything, at least these people now know I truly am a die-hard sports girl through and through.

Walking out of the room, I asked one of the veteran employees how embarrassed I should be about my phone, and he told me not to worry about it. So I tried not to. It was mid-August and baseball was in full swing but not quite football yet, so when I walked through the editing studio and heard my same ringtone go off on someone's computer you can imagine my surprise.

No. Why would that song be playing?

I backtracked to look at the computer belting the tune to see a baseball game broadcast by who other than Fox Sports. ESPN's rival. So, apparently the Fox Sports theme song was my ringtone that just went off in the first SportsCenter meeting I had ever been in. No wonder everyone looked at me like I was a traitor. I was like a Russian spy who blew their cover on day one. No one is going to like me now!

Surprisingly, I still managed to make a few friends that day including my now best friend Melanie.

A couple weeks went by and I had made a lot of acquaintances but not too many close friends except for Melanie, some guys in production, and a new friend Hal, who was a Packers fan.

On one of my nights off, I was drinking wine while watching one of my faves, Transformers. Hal had the night off too so we kept texting back and forth that maybe we should hang out despite it being pretty late at that point. Before I knew it our texts began to get very flirty and he insisted on us hanging out.

I took a big swig of my wine and realized it was now empty. I had a decision to make. My glass was empty and could be refilled and continue the night, or I could go to bed.

I mean Hal's cute, right? Right? And he is a Packers fan.

Hal texted again something along the lines of, "Just say the word. If you want me to come over, I'll get in my car right now."

Would he though? Probably not. Wine egged me on. *Let's see if he'll actually come.*

"Fine come over"

Sent.

My phone buzzed immediately. "On my way, send me your address."

Woops. What have I done? I got up to refill my wine glass.

When he came over I noticed he had an overnight bag and joked why he thought he needed that. I barely had poured him some wine before we started making out and made our way to the bedroom. He pulled off my jeans and underwear and immediately started going down on me. I was shocked because I hadn't really let anyone do that in years because guys didn't really do that in college. But I was down.

Apparently, a good bottle of red and a new guy I barely knew from work were the right circumstances for me to be comfortable with it. *Hell, more than comfortable.* I let him go down on me until the cows came home. That's right, I even got an orgasm out of it. Finally. Amen.

Part of the reason I think I was so comfortable about it was because this was truly a moment of *I wanted sex*. No, *I needed sex*. I wasn't attracted to Hal really at all, he had a cute face but wasn't really my type, other than being a Packers fan. So really, I had nothing to lose because I didn't care if he called the next day or not, let alone what he thought of me or my pussy. But I got that answer pretty clearly as soon as I came, he slipped on a condom quickly and went to put his dick into me and barely got through one thrust before stopping.

"What's going on?" I asked, confused.

"I'm so sorry."

"Why?"

He gave me a disappointed look in himself.

Oh... so it's like that.

"Oh... No worries! I was getting tired anyways," I lied about being tired, but not about the no worries part because I had gotten what I needed and that was good enough for me really. With that, he was on his way.

He grabbed his little bag with him but accidentally left one of his damn dress shirts at my house, which I hated. I immediately grabbed it and put it in my car and texted him to meet me in the back of the ESPN parking lot the next day before my shift. I told him no one could ever find out about this. Because, *damn it*, I wasn't going to let my horniness ruin my first job at ESPN!

He thought I was overreacting, but then I became stern and said I didn't even really want to be friends. I was so weirded out by the situation and he didn't help because he would not stop blowing up my phone. Or he'd come up to me in the editing room alone trying to talk about "us." I would just glare at him. *I'm sorry, what is us? What us?* I basically told him he was going to need to fuck off, kindly. Eventually he got the hint and started hitting on every other girl in the office which was totally fine. Just as long as no one found out about whatever "us" meant to him.

A week or two after the Hal drama, Marco and I sat next to each other in the editing room a couple nights in a row and had some playful banter. We should exchange numbers? We should. Once we started texting he asked if he could take me to dinner sometime. Yes, he could take me to dinner. After all, he was the one I had my eyes on since day one. We decided on a cute sushi place by my apartment that week.

Since the restaurant was up the street from my place, we decided we should have some after-dinner cocktails there. Sure. Why not? That would be it. Innocent. *Right, Courtney?*

I slept with him.

Damn it. I know. Apparently, I have a weakness for broad shoulders. And thick biceps. And thick... other things. *Fuck my life.*

I told Marco no one could find out about this, having déjà vu from a couple weeks prior. He said he wouldn't say anything, but he'd like to take me out again. He was adorable with that smile so I said sure. But what I really meant was, YES, honey.

But seriously, no one could find out. This job was important to me. Same with him. So we'd go on dates in secret. What could go wrong? We continued going on one-on-one dates and even went on big ESPN group nights out, one of which we pretended we were just friends even though he would occasionally pinch my butt or slide a hand on my lower back when no one was looking.

Marco and I continued our secret escapades and since he lived so close to the ESPN campus, I would often head over to his place right after my shift and crawl into bed with him or watch the final segments of SportsCenter on LA time to catch the highlights I made.

One night at my place, Marco was fucking me over the side of the couch and flipped me into a crazy angle and popped out my NuvaRing with his dick. The ring was wrapped around his hard dick and he looked at me very confused.

"Sorry, it's my NuvaRing," I said.

"Your what?"

"It's birth control. You've never seen one?"

"No, definitely not."

I pulled it off his dick and pinched it between my fingers, flexing it to show him.

"I'll just put it back in when we're done."

After we finished, I put it back in and Marco looked relieved, but also like he had something to say.

"What is it?" I asked.

"Ok, don't get mad at me, because this will sound bad."

"Marco..."

"So the first time we ever hooked up, I knew you had hooked up with Hal before we went on the date."

"WHAT."

"I said don't get mad!"

I put my hands up to my face. "How embarrassing! You must've thought I was such a hoe! Ah!" I turned around in embarrassment, but turned back to face him. "Hooking up with Hal was a drunken mistake!"

"It's ok!" he reached out and put his hand on my waist. "I didn't judge you, but when we hooked up after our first date, I felt like I could feel something inside of you, but I didn't want to say anything. Because I knew you had sex with Hal, so I figured you probably had a condom stuck up there."

My jaw dropped and I moved my hands back up to cover my face.

"Marco Fucking Correa. You not only knew I had slept with Hal, as if that was bad enough, but you thought I had some nasty condom stuck up in me for a week! And you didn't tell me! And all this month STILL had NOT said anything!" I said horrified, feeling disgusting.

"I just figured it would fall out or you'd figure it out, but now that I know it's your birth control…"

"Oh my God, I could throw up," I said looking at the floor, fingers to my temples, pacing.

"Oh stop, you're fine. I'm still here! I really like you," he said.

And I was starting to really like him too.

Later that month, this different guy Johnny from ESPN asked if I wanted to go to a Boston Celtics game one night. He said it was only about a two-hour drive and the games were really fun. I had never been to Boston so I was down and thought it would be awesome. So he planned the trip. The only problem was, I thought we were going as friends, but I learned pretty quickly he thought it was more of a date. I said thank you when he dropped me off later that night and made sure not to linger so there was no question as to a kiss. As soon as I got into my house, I called Marco to tell him the mix up. Marco started laughing and said he knew Johnny had a crush on me and very much thought we were on a date.

"Why didn't you tell me?" I asked.

"Oh, shit—Johnny is calling me now. Probably to talk about your date," he snickered. "I'll call you back."

He called me back as I changed into pajamas.

"Yeah he's totally trying to figure out what he did wrong and why you guys didn't kiss good night."

"Fuck my life."

Marco kept laughing.

"Shut the fuck up. You should've told me this!"

"I'm sorry. But I will say it's pretty funny both Hal and Johnny are calling me wanting relationship advice with you when I'm the one who's secretly going on dates with you."

We continued hooking up all through the winter. My mom knew about us and got me a gift card to the nicest steakhouse in town so Marco and I could go somewhere nice to celebrate Christmas.

I dressed up in a leather flowy skirt and a tight black sweater. Hidden under the skirt as a surprise for Marco, were some thigh high tights held up by a garter. Marco said he felt out of place at a restaurant so nice when we walked in, but when we were walking to our table I let my skirt swing just high enough to reveal my tight situation underneath to only him.

"What are those?" he whispered into my ear before pulling my seat out to sit down at the table. I winked at him. He bit his lip. That night was a fun one. We barely could keep our hands off each other walking to the car in the snow.

We barhopped the first night it snowed in Connecticut, and I remember I was so excited I ran out of the bar to the sidewalk to catch snowflakes on my tongue. Marco came out too and he kissed me as the snow fell down on both of us.

Our secret relationship even made it all the way to Valentine's Day. We went on a date outside of town at this cute new bar which turned out to be a gay bar. I wore a little black dress and tights with Sorel boots because there was a snowstorm that day. At this point, Melanie and her new boyfriend Mike knew about us, so the four of us went out drinking often, especially on the notorious "train nights."

Oh, train nights. Every Wednesday, this tiny townie bar in Bristol held a "train night" where this little train would drive around the roof of the bar before stopping to land on a number. When you got to the bar you'd receive a ticket and if the train landed on your number you'd win two-hundred dollars. But you had to be quick about it. As soon as the number was announced, you'd have three minutes to give your ticket to the guy announcing to actually win, that way there were no cheating tickets. I thought this was the best thing ever and soon enough made it a regular thing for our ESPN crew. We'd pack that bar even on days we were working by taking our dinner breaks just in time for the train calling. Since Marco and I were going out in public more, I thought it would be ok if people found out about us now, but Marco decided it wasn't a good idea and insisted we keep it under wraps. *Whatever.*

After Valentine's Day the snow didn't let up hardly at all and I was staying over at Marco's pretty frequently so I didn't have to do the thirty-minute drive back to my place.

One morning I was leaving Marco's house and he came down and shoveled my car out before I left.

"Hey I'm working another late shift, so I'm thinking I'll pack a bag and stay here since it's supposed to blizzard again tonight."

"You always do this. You never ask me if you can stay over, you just assume you can."

"Oh? I'm sorry. Did you have a hot date?" I said sarcastically. "Let me rephrase: can I sleep over tonight?" ending with a genuine smile.

"Yes, but ugh, you do this to me! I hate it! You have a hold on me."

"Ok..."

"I just... I hate that I love you."

"That you what now?" I said with a raised eyebrow.

"Woah, woah, that's not what I meant!" he said, laughing holding his hands up.

"Yeah, yeah, I know what you meant," I said, winking and driving away. "See you tonight!"

I drove away and tried not to think about it much but... *Love me, huh?*

We got a new wave of interns added to the bunch, and I got switched to my new shift of Content Screening in the basement, which seemed like a death sentence being taken away from SportsCenter upstairs, but in hindsight, our group was really the bomb.

Why were we so legendary?

I figured out pretty quickly Content Screening is all about time management. If you had a light workload, you literally might have the entire day to sit and mingle with your peeps, twiddling your thumbs. So one light day, I brought in a whole pack of nerf guns and dropped them on each person's desk. It was a newly defined "War Day." There would be points for every time you hit an opponent. Things got so lit, we were crawling under computer editing bays and shooting shots from below desks, diving under desks, rolling across the floor. It was a shitshow. And our boss was loving every bit of it. We were also the crew that would jam out to rap music while we all worked and take bets on all major games going on. So yes, legendary indeed.

Working down in the basement meant me and my group were tight, but I kind of lost connection to the upstairs crew, including missing a new blonde intern from California that had caught Marco's eye. *Real original, Marco.*

The first big blizzard I had to drive into SportsCenter for, my two-wheel drive Jeep was slipping and sliding all over the damn roads and right through stop lights. I joked to my mom the ice was so bad I might as well have been Michelle Quan triple axel-ing out on the roads.

So when the Governor of Connecticut shut down the entire state in a state of emergency for blizzard number two, you bet your damn ass I called out sick the day before in preparation to hunker down and drink a bottle of red wine with my seventy-five-year-old neighbor Eleanor to talk about life and boys.

But with major blizzard number three, I didn't get so lucky. Unfortunately, I had officially wasted my free token on calling out sick after the last big blizzard. Our good old governor called another state of emergency and anyone caught driving on the road would be ticketed. But would *we* have to work? *Yes*, ESPN would pay for your ticket if you were pulled over. And they'd pay for a hotel room across from campus.

I even got a voicemail the night before the storm and my shift.

"Hi Courtney, we noticed you called out sick before the night of the last blizzard and because we didn't want that to occur again, we're calling to get you a hotel room at the Marriott across from ESPN to ensure this won't happen again tonight."

Rats. I was caught. And damn, they were determined. People were rumoring this storm was going to be so bad that they were going to pull out cots on ESPN campus for us to sleep in because we might get snowed in. When I headed into work, it really was dumping snow already. I still hadn't called ESPN back about the hotel room just yet because I figured I could probably stay at Marco's, so I texted him.

"Hey big storm tonight and I'm working late—cool if I come stay over after?"

To my surprise he went off. Like *went off.* Said he was sick of me just coming over like we were dating or something. *Weren't we though?* He was done with me assuming everything without him making decisions. And this was over. WE were DONE.

I was so confused. Everything seemed so abrupt. I tried to call him but he didn't answer. He kept texting me that it was over and there was nothing more to say.

What? There was so much more to say. I had so much more to say. I went to the bathroom and pushed open a stall and sat on the toilet and started crying at work. *Ew, I know.* And then I started panicking about the storm because I hadn't confirmed a hotel room with ESPN because I had assumed I would be staying with Marco. Well, you know what they say about assuming… When you assume, it makes an ASS out of U and ME. And that's certainly how I felt.

I tried to pull it together, but really just cried more in a stall and texted my friend Nicole who also worked at ESPN. She came down to the bathroom to tell me he was a piece of shit anyways. And helped me call ESPN back saying I would need that hotel.

I pulled my shit somewhat together and headed back to my editing bay where I just put on headphones. My group knew something was up though, courtesy of my bloodshot eyes and sniffles and not my usual bubbly, mouthy personality. One friend, who finished ahead of me, said he parked near my Jeep. When I finished my shift and came out to my car, I saw it was shoveled out and remembered my friend. I knew it was him since his spot was empty, and mine was fresher shoveled than anyone else's.

I tried not to cry as I shoveled the rest of my car out and texted him thank you before slowly slipping and sliding in my Jeep, making my way to the hotel. I didn't allow my tears to fully come until I got to my hotel room and heard the door slam behind me. *Quiet. Pain. Loneliness. Ick.* I collapsed on the bed and nearly cried myself to sleep before switching into some sweats and a sweatshirt.

It was storming in more ways than one, clearly.

Now, this next stage of our breakup falls into a more pathetic one really. I try not to judge myself thinking back on it, but hey, live and learn. And dear God, do not go to your ex's house crying.

So, we had another train night. Shocking, I know. But Bristol doesn't have much up its sleeve in terms of going out. Melanie, Mike, and I went but I was really not feeling like my hot self. In fact, after a few drinks apparently I was feeling like a clingy, needy thing. I told Melanie and Mike I wanted to go to Marco's house since he lived down the street. After ensuring them it was a good idea, they obliged.

They dropped me there and I made my way to the second floor and knocked, just in time to realize it was decently late and I was drunk, sad, and stupid.

"Who is it?" he asked.

"It's me."

"Courtney, no. I'm not letting you in."

"Marco, please. I just want to talk."

My mind wandered to him and how he always would smile at me with his perfect teeth.

"Please, Marco."

"No, Courtney. Go home."

I started crying and kept knocking. *Yep, I was that crazy ex*—if you could even call it that. Here I was in a non-relationship, non-break-up, non-ex situation yet again. I kept crying until I fell to the floor, but still kept knocking, begging him to open the door. Another door opened in the hall and I snuffled up my tears and tried to pull it together.

"You need to quiet down," the voice called out as a man appeared out of the door and saw my pathetic self, sitting there with mascara all over my face. His tone softened. "Are you ok?"

"Yes, I'm fine. I'm sorry."

"Did he hurt you?"

"No, I'm ok."

"Ok," he said skeptically, looking at the door. "Do you need help?"

"I'm ok."

Just then Marco's door opened and he popped his head out to apologize to the man and reluctantly let me in, which I don't think the hallway man was too happy about either. The door shut behind us.

"I just wanted to talk," I said, with mascara dripping likely all over my face. I tried to hug him and lean into him, but he held my shoulders away, his arms locked out.

I told him I didn't know why he ended things and I was sorry if I just assumed to come over, which wasn't a solid argument because here I was. My mind wandered again to how when I'd leave his place to go to headquarters, he'd always kiss me goodbye and play with the edge of my skirt and tease his hands up my tights and pull me back into bed on top of him saying he couldn't contain himself when I wore skirts.

I looked down at my skirt now and his hands, holding me out so we couldn't touch. More tears squeezed out.

"I just need a hug," I said, pathetically.

Marco sighed and loosened his arms, allowing me to lean into him. I put my hand on his lower back and cried, but as soon as I moved my hand up his back to pull him in, I was pushed back at arms distance.

"I can't do this. You need to go. Did you drive here? I hope not."

"No, Mike dropped me off."

He called Mike to come pick me up and I cried more and wanted to go into Marco's room but he insisted we stay right where we were standing in the living room until Mike got there. I slept on Mike's couch that night, crying the whole time at what a mess I was. Mike, like the good friend he was, came down once to check on me and reminded me Marco was a douche anyways, which didn't really change my mind at the time but did make me laugh in between crying heaves.

After that night I decided I needed to get back to being a bad bitch. I got back to looking hot—despite it being the coldest winter the east coast had seen in years—and kicking ass at work despite being in the basement. Funny enough, I was actually so sick of being cold at work one day I decided to go to a tanning bed place, which I absolutely don't recommend, because they are straight up cancer in a box, but anyways. I go to a tanning place and get into a bed for as long as I'm allowed just so I could get a little bit of a sunburn and actually be warm. It worked, by the way. Not a sustainable solution, but shit, I finally was warm at work in the basement.

After this was when things really started to fire me up. Like the true stages of a breakup, I had moved from sad to "I'm moving on" to sad and pathetic again, to utterly heated when I found out his real reason for breaking up with me was because he started dating the new blonde intern from California. Marco clearly had a fucking type.

The worst part was they were openly dating! After he had insisted we remain under wraps and a secret, now here he was openly dating the new girl. Naturally, I wanted to know more about her so I stalked her on social media, and wouldn't you know it, she had a boyfriend back in California. Worse, he had just come to visit her in Connecticut! Marco dumped me, well not really because we weren't even technically dating as far as anyone knew, and now he was openly dating this chick as her second boyfriend or side piece.

I found out all of this infuriating information leading up to another train night, which everyone was going to together because most of us were off work and the cash prize had worked its way up to like six-hundred dollars. Melanie and I decided I needed to go out and look hot to get my mind off of Marco, who thankfully wasn't coming with us, but would probably show up. I wore a black leather skater skirt with my thigh high stockings (though the stocking tops were only visible unless I spun around too fast) and a long sleeve blouse and heels. Furthermore, Melanie and I decided it was time people knew about everything that was really going on between Marco and me since a few of them already watched me cry at work with no explanation.

But this telling of the truth might as well have been a déjà vu of a situation. Think my first boyfriend Keagan and my best friend at the time Harley. In other words, I was telling the truth, but also exposing that they were not exactly great people themselves. So, Melanie and I came to the bar and met up with all our friends and I started our exposition. The hidden relationship, Marco wanting to keep it hidden even when we were starting to go on actual dates, him not wanting me to come over anymore, the storm, the breakup, the new girl, and then that the new girl actually had a boyfriend. I mean, is gossiping wrong? Probably. But I wasn't lying, I was just venting, which happened to show people their true colors.

So when Marco showed up to the bar late with her, let's just say it was like Moses parting the Red Sea. Sorry not sorry—well, at least not for Marco.

I was sipping a drink at the bar next to one of the regulars and Melanie when Marco came up and grabbed my arm. I turned around trying not to spill my drink.

"What did you do?" he asked.

"What do you mean, what did I do?"

"Why won't anyone talk to Erica?"

"I don't know. I told the truth about everything to our friends, so maybe because they don't like cheaters?"

"What is wrong with you?" he stormed off.

I took another sip of my drink and rolled my eyes and watched them continue to part the seas all night. Finally, a few people took pity on them and talked with them. They ended up leaving together holding hands, so at least they had each other, I guess.

That week Marco decided to go off on me via text messages. But rather than it firing me up, it just made me more sad. He was defending his new girl fiercely, despite just a month ago accidentally slipping the words "I love you" to me. Even if they did start with "I hate that." He had even gone so far as to block me on every social media platform, something that had never been done to me before and for some reason really hurt.

Naturally, he also had his new girl block me too, as if I had cared about that. He was probably just mad that I had discovered the truth via social media.

Still, I was pretty upset about the whole situation and down in the dumps one day. I was supposed to work that night and so was Melanie, but Melanie was on a SportsCenter shift. I would be going back to the basement where I would probably listen to sad music and walk off to the bathroom to cry. Mike could tell this was my mood and wasn't having it.

"Fuck that. You're not going to work today."

"I have to."

"You're calling out sick and we're playing hooky. It's nice as fuck out and we're going to go to the liquor store and get a bottle and go drink on some patio and drive with the top off your Jeep."

I had to admit, I loved the plan. But I don't ever call out sick, other than that one storm.

"But it's the same day!"

"Just do it. You know you already made your decision," Mike said.

He was right. I called out sick and we went to the liquor store and got a bottle of Jack and some Diet Cokes. We took off the front roof panels of my Jeep and went looking for restaurants with patios, but it was still April and snow was still on the ground so there were none open.

"Fuck it. Let's go to the ski slopes. There's a patio there and we can watch little kids eat shit down the mountain and drink our booze in coffee cups."

If you haven't realized it yet, *Mike is good people*. The kind of person who lifts you up when you're down and grabs a bottle of Jack at the liquor store and suggests watching little kids wiping out to make you feel better.

We went to the ski slopes and sat on the patio in the sun and sipped Jack and Cokes out of coffee cups while twelve-year-old boys attempted the lamest pick-up lines of all time on me while Mike roasted them and they roasted him back. Best of all, I didn't think of Marco once. It was the perfect day, and Mike was right, I needed it.

A few more weeks passed and Marco and his new girl already started seeming to be on the rocks. LOL. Probably because she was balancing two boyfriends and he knew about it now and so did everyone else.

Mike decided he was going to have a big beer pong party at his house. All the crew was going to come, including Marco. I wanted to look hot since it would be the first social situation I had seen him at since train night and had noticed new makeup trends on Pinterest about making your boobs look bigger. So I followed the contouring advice and stuffed a pair of socks under each boob in my already-massive Victoria's Secret leopard push-up bra. I adjusted everything and voilà! I had stage-worthy-looking boobs. The girls were looking great and I was feeling great, too.

The party was fun and I stepped in for beer pong on and off, but really was more there to bop around and talk to all the guys. So when Cole, aka mister all-American-looking, 6'5" jock and one of the totally adorable other production assistants I worked with at ESPN, was hitting me up, I was all about it. In the past, when I found out he had a crush on me, I had blown it off because: 1. I liked Marco, and 2. He was pretty blatantly obvious about liking me which made things just too easy. Goober-like. But tonight, with Marco watching me across the room, Cole would definitely do. Plus, Marco always said this was the one guy he felt like he couldn't beat in a fight at ESPN or the one guy he would be pissed about if he found out we were hooking up. And, Cole towers over Marco too, which he hates. How these things came up in our relationship, I don't know.

When Cole briefly went to go to the bathroom, Marco came up to me. Like clockwork.

"I see you and Cole are talking a lot. Thought you didn't like him?" Marco said sipping his beer, not looking at me.

Mission accomplished.

"Yeah, he's pretty cool actually," I said, smiling at Cole now walking back into the room. Marco's eyes were on me intently as Cole approached.

Marco said hi to Cole and told us he hoped we had a "fun time," then retreated to the other corner of the basement with a different group of guys. *Really, Marco?* There really were hardly any girls at this party so he didn't have options to make me jealous.

I started to get more flirtatious with Cole and he started to get more cuddly with me and suggested we go upstairs to the main room. As we left the basement, Marco glared at us leaving the entire way. No one was up there so when we sat down, we started making out and I felt Cole move on top of me, his hand moving up my side toward my boob and I had a sudden epiphany. *The socks were still in there. Shit!* I slightly pushed Cole up and stopped kissing him and he looked confused.

"Is something wrong?" he asked.

"No! Not at all. I just—could you get me another beer? I just wanted to have another."

"Oh, yeah. No problem. Bud Light?" He got up and headed to the kitchen.

I jammed my hands down my bra and pulled out the pairs of socks and shoved them in the only place I could find, under the couch cushions. He came back with beers for us and we cracked them, taking a sip before making out again. He started reaching his hand up my shirt, *thank God I ditched the socks*, and eventually started pulling at the button on my jeans when I decided we should leave and go back to his place.

I wasn't going to have sex with him, but hey, he really was pretty damn hot and it would so piss off Marco. We didn't have sex, but the next morning Cole tried making me breakfast and started getting all ESPN-boy-clingy on me like Hal and Johnny had, so I pretty much had to quit that cold turkey. Still, having a fun night and feeling wanted helped me get back into my groove again. I started online dating and really truly moved on from Marco, which was great because he had now moved into his pathetic breakup stages with California blondie 2.0 and I was back to being myself and having fun again.

Plus, our PA job time period was coming to an end and they would soon announce who would be staying on board. Melanie, Mike, and I had been discussing who we thought the favorites were and I said them, but they insisted on me, since I had a Highlight of the Month nominee. But I told them I had been stuck in the basement. But they said all the more reason I was "well-rounded." Really, we all didn't want to say it, but we knew Marco was a heavy favorite, since he was the only one with a master's degree.

Sure enough, he got the spot. We were all pissed, but this just made me kick it into high gear. No one is more competitive than me and I got beat out by him. I worked my whole life to get to this opportunity, and I wouldn't just let it float away in the wind. I decided I would go and meet with all the talent producers and broadcast heads at ESPN on the coveted fourth floor before I left. I emailed all of them with a short elevator pitch of why they should meet with me and they all gave me an hour of their time in which I turned it on.

"Hi there! Nice to meet you. I don't want to waste any of your time so I'll get right to the point on why my name is one you are not going to want to forget."

All of the heads seemed impressed with me and I would continue to stay in touch with them for years including one man who said I reminded him of another PA that had come through ESPN. Who was it? Molly McGrath, successful sideline reporter from ESPN on to Fox Sports and beyond. It was a hell of a compliment and I stuck to it to keep moving forward.

But I'll always remember one executive's response to me, that really changed my career goals altogether.

"You say you want to be a sideline reporter? Why are you aiming so low?"

I looked at him so confused since I had given my piece on women being underrepresented in the field already.

"Low?"

"How much air time does a sideline reporter get? Thirty seconds pre-game, thirty seconds halftime with the coaches, and another minute at final score. Two minutes tops, maybe. Is that really what you're fighting to get? Two minutes of time? Aim higher. Aim for the desk."

"An anchor?"

He nodded his head. "Aim for the desk. Where you run the platform and you have the time."

"You're right. I will. The desk it is."

He shook my hand, and when I told him I would be in touch, he laughed.

"I have no doubt you will. I know I'll be seeing you around and hearing your name again, Courtney."

I may not have landed the PA staff position at ESPN, but I felt like big things were coming for me, regardless. I made the connections I needed to and made a lot of friends at ESPN. And so had my counterpart and best friend Melanie, too. When I say I was competitive and would fight for this job, she was right there with me. While I was meeting with the broadcast heads, she was working her connections in the radio department and ended up solidifying a position at ESPN Radio. What a badass. Mike would move back to New York, and I was headed back to California.

I continued sticking with my connections at ESPN, but had to admit I was very sad to leave, even if it was nice to get away from walking past Marco in the halls every day. ESPN was where I wanted to be. So when one of my friends, Andy, asked me for my resume one day and didn't tell me why, I sent it to her immediately.

A few days later, I received a phone call from a random Bristol number and answered it.

"Hi Courtney, I'm a Managing Editor over here at ESPN and I just had a candidate come in to my office for a job interview and turn down the position. She said she couldn't take the position but knew the perfect person to fill the spot and handed me your resume instead. So, how do you feel about becoming a writer at ESPN.com?"

I got the position. And best yet I didn't even have to move to Bristol. My team had remote positions across the country, interacting through Slack and BlueJeans video conferences. And once a year, we would all meet in Bristol. It was a dream job.

I went back to Bristol twice and ran into Marco where we talked normally and I told him I was a writer. He was still a PA, but seemed happy.

I heard he doesn't work at ESPN anymore, and frankly I don't know where he's at now.

The last of our interactions were in Bristol, but when I decided to write this, I checked to see if he still blocks me.

User unavailable.

It made me giggle. He still does. I wonder if he knows that?

13

Jesse

So after not having any luck in the dating department since I had moved to Boston, I actually allowed myself to get excited for my upcoming one. Was I excited because he planned it for us on Valentine's Day? Slightly. But really, I was more excited because this was the oldest guy I had ever gone on a date with. Thirty-nine years old. *Thirty-nine-year-olds had their shit together, right?*

As soon as Jesse and I matched on Bumble, he tried to call me through the app. My phone started ringing in my hand with the app still open and I freaked out and tossed it. *What the fuck?* I let it ring through while lying on the bed.

A message came through on the chat.

"I'm sorry about that. I'm new to this and my sister got overly excited and showed me how to call you."

Aw, he's older and doesn't know what he's doing. Kind of cute.

I replied, "Haha, no worries. I didn't even know you could call people through the app either so I was confused!! But I will call you back."

The conversation was mediocre and the usual blah-blah-blah talk, but no obvious red flags. He called from his mom's house and told me he was drinking wine with his family, including his twin brother I had seen in his Bumble photos. Naturally, we bonded over family and wine. When he made a joke about getting dinner as long as I picked up the tab, he quickly walked it back laughing, "Oh God, if I don't pick up the tab you can call my mother and she will have my head! That's not how we were raised."

We decided on meeting up the following Sunday for dinner. Only thing is, we had both failed to realize that Sunday was also Valentine's Day.

There were no places available in the North End for dinner so how about a lunch? Florentine Café was open for a 3:00 p.m. reservation so I grabbed it for us. I was excited. I even joked to my mom and sister the day before that I had a Valentine's *date*.

"Is wearing a red sweater on Valentine's Day too cliché?" I asked, holding up the red sweater on FaceTime to Kassidy while getting ready.

I had used my new beach waver for my hair and wasn't exactly sure how I felt about it or if my face looked fat, but I decided it was cute enough. I took a selfie. I really didn't have an option since I left my curling iron and my flat iron at my parent's house on winter break, so it was this or straight hair with kinks in it from sleeping.

I decided on my new red sweater with the puff shoulders, high-waisted jeans, thigh-high black flat boots, and waved hair. I decided to step on the scale after getting dressed and looked in the mirror too long.

"Not great," I said to myself. "Monday I'm starting my diet," I now say directed toward Boone, who I seemed to think would somehow keep me to that promise.

I looked in the mirror again. *I look ok. Maybe even good.* I liked this new red sweater. The puff shoulders I felt hid my arms that I'm forever self-conscious of and made them look smaller. Since it was cold out and Jesse had mentioned he wanted to walk around Hanover St., I decided to bring my new leather puffer coat.

I hopped on Uber to check for cars since I was nearing thirty minutes until the date start time. The nearest one was twenty-three minutes away. *Great. I'm going to be late for the sophisticated older guy who's probably always on time for everything.*

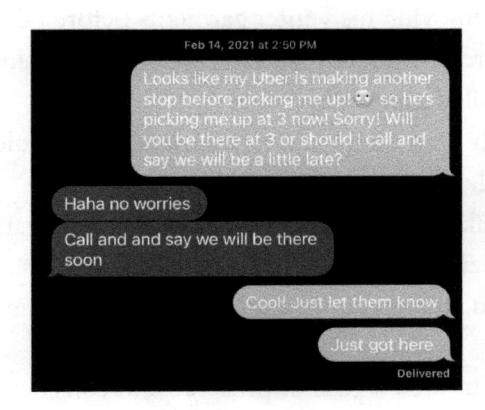

> Feb 14, 2021 at 2:50 PM
>
> Looks like my Uber is making another stop before picking me up! 😅 so he's picking me up at 3 now! Sorry! Will you be there at 3 or should I call and say we will be a little late?
>
> Haha no worries
>
> Call and and say we will be there soon
>
> Cool! Just let them know
>
> Just got here
>
> Delivered

I showed up at 3:15 p.m. for our 3:00 p.m. date, but thankfully they were cool on the phone when I told them I would be running slightly late. I looked around and didn't see him at any of the socially-distanced tables, and I decided I must have beat him there—but *how*? I told the hostess I was there for two people under my name, mask still on, and she led me downstairs to a small table where the walls were dotted with vines and a cute gazebo was fastened over the bar—very Italian vibes. I sat down and took off my mask and called him to tell him where we were seated.

After a strange phone call with Jesse, who was now twenty-five minutes late, I told the waitress I was waiting for someone and waters would be great to start. I eavesdropped to my neighbors' table who seemed to be on a definitely-not-first date discussing a new Candace Owens interview. I decided I didn't want to be on my phone when he arrived so I just sat with my thoughts, their discussion, and my water.

I heard someone coming down the stairs and turned to see who must be my date, but behind the mask you can never be too sure. I delayed standing until I knew it was him close enough and approaching only my table.

He was much slimmer than expected. Like, really slim. Taller too. He had on a black Patagonia jacket zipped up and a small black beanie pulled down over his ears. He approached my table with a slight smile. "Hey! How's it going! You made it," I said, reaching out to give him a hug. He began removing his winter garments before taking a seat across from me, finally removing his mask. He looked a little older looking than I expected, but still decently cute.

"I didn't even know they had a basement. We should be seated upstairs," he scoffed.

I was a little taken aback that his first words were negative, but weirder things have happened.

"I don't mind. It's cute. Look at all the vines," I replied looking up and around.

Jesse ordered us each a glass of prosecco and considered me in silence before asking a seemingly random question.

"So do you have any tattoos?" he asked.

Wait, what?

"Tattoos? No," I replied.

"No tattoos?"

"No, and I probably won't ever get any. I think it's more rare now not to have any."

He lifted his eyebrows surprised.

"Oh, so you're *that* kind of picky. I remember you said on the phone you were picky," I said.

He smiled. "What are you looking for?"

"Well, the last person I dated loved his job, but he wasn't very driven about moving forward. That ended up being a problem for me because I'm a very driven person. Plus, I'm looking for someone who is more of the 'designated adult' if I'm being honest," I laugh, a bit embarrassed admitting it.

Thankfully our prosecco comes, ending the pained silence.

"Cheers!" I said, as we clinked glasses.

After a sip of the bubbly elixir, I decided to continue the conversation since he was just staring at me again.

"What about you? What are you looking for Mr. Picky?"

After a long pause he finally responded.

"Well, after the fourth marriage, I decided I needed to be picky and make sure I get it right."

I was totally taken aback. *This guy has been married four times? How the hell did I miss that?* I try to do quick math in my head on when that would put his first wife.

"So if you don't mind me asking, that means your first wife must have been when you were pretty young? In college?"

"I've never been married," he looked back at me confused.

"You said your fourth marriage?"

"Oh God, no! I meant in my family I've gone through four marriages! My parents are both divorced multiple times, so I don't want to go through that."

"Ohhh," I put my head to my forehead for an "SMH" moment.

"If I was on my fourth marriage, that's when you should get up and walk out of here," he gestured his hands toward the door.

"Don't worry I thought about it, but I just got this perfectly great glass of prosecco and decided I might as well finish it before I go!"

We laughed.

"So are you born and raised in Boston?"

He nodded his head yes.

"That's great. I just moved here from California for grad school and I'm loving it."

Just more staring. I filled the void with some more softball lob questions.

"You said your family is around too? Does your twin brother live here too?"

He nodded again yes. I decided to avoid yes or no questions now since he could avoid speaking if I continued to do so.

"Where do they live?"

He sighed, looking up at the ceiling and readjusting himself in his seat, seeming annoyed that he had to use actual words now.

"Concord. My brother lives in the North End."

"I drove through Concord! It's nice. Did you grow up there?"

Another nod. I decided to shut up and let him ask me a question, thinking of my dad who always jokes to me before going on dates because I'm a talker. *Try not to talk the whole time and let them get a few words in, Courtney!* rings in my head.

Only problem was, he clearly had no intention of getting any words in. I waited just staring back and occasionally making myself laugh or taking sips of my prosecco. NOTHING. I'm not joking. He didn't say a word, just kept staring at me for what was probably forty-five seconds that honestly felt like forty-five minutes of silence.

"I heard Concord has a lot of history. It's old money, right? Kennedy country, or something like that? That's super cool you grew up there! I love history."

He nodded, even though, apparently, my "Kennedy country" assumption wasn't even correct. But I waited for more. Finally he submitted to the silence.

"Yep, Paul Revere."

Words! But they didn't make sense to me.

"What do you mean?" I asked.

He sighed again, rolling his eyes. "It's where he rode."

I tried to put two and two together, finally looking at him confused, saying, "The British are coming?"

He nodded yes.

"I didn't know that he rode that far into Massachusetts! I always thought it happened in the North End where his house is." I go on and on about my love of American history, seeing Boston years ago with my mom and now having toured Paul Revere's house multiple times.

He nodded again. I decided not to talk but, thankfully, the waitress came up and asked us if we'd like anything to eat. We hadn't looked at the menus yet so I quickly grabbed my phone and scanned the COVID-friendly QR code off the table so I could take a look at the menu. I read off a few appetizers to him, and after looking at me disgusted when I mentioned mussels, he decided on the Burrata.

"And do you have any gluten-free bread that can come with it?" he asked.

"Uhm—no we don't have any gluten-free bread," she replied hesitantly.

"Ugh, fine. Whatever. It's fine," he replied rolling his eyes.

She walked away.

"Are you gluten free?" I asked.

"No."

I couldn't help it and I laughed out loud. "Well then why did you ask for it?"

He didn't answer me.

"Man of few words, huh?" I laughed.

Another sigh. "Ugh, I'm sorry. I have to do a lot of talking for work so when I don't have to I take advantage of it. I promise I'll do better," he rolled his eyes.

"I see. What do you do for work?"

"It doesn't matter. It's not important."

Now annoyed, I decided to go back to the question. "Yeah, actually, it kind of does," I scoffed, reminiscing on the conversation we just had at the beginning of the date about working hard at your job.

He smiled, likely surprised I got sassy and then rolled his eyes for the four-hundredth time. "Hah—yes, you are right. It is important." Another sigh. "People give me money and I make it into more money for them," he retorted as if explaining it to a child.

"So you're a financial analyst."

"Yes," he said, pointing at me like I won a prize for my wits. *Now* he wanted to talk. "I work with million-dollar clients and have my own firm I work with. You have to have a minimum of a million dollars to open an account with me."

Oh, so he's one of those. The guys who mention how much money they make or deal with on the first date. I responded the only way I know how in these instances.

"Cool."

At this notion of my now sassiness, he pulled out his phone smiling, "Watch this."

It's a video from *The Wolf of Wall Street*. Oh yes, he is that guy. It's the clip where Matthew McConaughey is explaining to Leonardo DiCaprio what exactly they do as financial brokers. And that, basically, it's all a façade because what they really do is do cocaine, jack off, and get wasted by lunch after closing maybe one deal they can cash in on.

Jesse seemed to be pleased with his video selection for me to watch or maybe more pleased he got to sit and not talk again. I told him I'd seen the scene, but he insisted I watched the whole thing and laughed, because the scene is actually funny.

Our waitress brought out the Burrata and asked if we wanted refills of our prosecco. We said yes. Jesse motioned for me to try the cheese, without saying anything. I pulled a piece to my own plate and tried it and told him it was good. He looked away from the table uninterested.

"Aren't you going to try it?" I asked.

"No, I don't eat things like this."

I laughed again, and it wouldn't be the last time. *This guy was unreal. What the fuck kind of test is this?*

"Then why did you order it?" I asked.

Our waitress delivered our new round of drinks, thank God. After another long pause of his incessant staring, he actually spoke words of his own accord for the first time since asking me about tattoos.

"How much do you weigh?"

I nearly spat out my drink. *Oh, so the Burrata was that kind of a test.*

"That is the most inappropriate question I've ever been asked on a date."

He seemed unfazed. "How much? One-forty? One-thirty? One-twenty? How much do you weigh?"

"I'm not answering that question," I said, taking a gulp of my prosecco thinking there's no way he could ask any worse questions than that. Spoiler alert: I was wrong.

"Fine. I think I know what you want. When was the last time you got laid then?"

With this, my cheeks filled with prosecco and I felt the bubbly sensation start to go up my nose. Thankfully, I got it down before bursting out laughing. I responded back confidently.

"How many inches long is your penis? When was the last time you measured your penis?" I asked.

He looked back at me, eyes wide. And the cocky motherfucker started to respond. "Well actually I—."

I interrupted. "INAPPROPRIATE QUESTIONS. These are inappropriate questions, Jesse."

Our waitress came by again and he ordered the eggplant parmesan for us to split, but once she left, more silence.

"So tell me something about yourself," I urged.

Nothing. More empty eyes just looking at me across the table. I continued.

"I saw on your profile you like the beach. Your photos look like the Bahamas?"

He nodded, so I told him about my family's last trip to the Bahamas. "And I saw you had a photo in Nantucket with your brother? Does your family vacation there?"

He nodded yes.

"I've never been, but I'm going with my mom this year for the Fourth of July."

He just stared.

"I feel like I've done a lot of talking so now you can tell me something. ANYTHING. Here, I'll help you out. Tell me a funny story from Nantucket."

He rolled his eyes, but actually complied and began to tell me a story about being drunk on a Nantucket beach in high school with a girl. She was giving him a hand job in the sand when his dad walked up on them, so she ran away down the beach without her shirt. He slurred his way through the story with eye rolls and avoided eye contact until the end. I had a slight inkling from earlier that this guy might already be drunk or on something, and now I was starting to be reassured. Admittedly, the story was kind of funny, and I was just happy I didn't have to talk for a minute or so, but *really*? That's the story you go with? Ok.

"That's funny," I replied, swigging more prosecco down.

He laughed and also took a sip.

"You want to see something funny?"

At this, he reached in his pocket and pulled out his phone again. Without any words, he handed me his phone again to the same *The Wolf of Wall Street* clip.

"You already showed me this."

"No, shh, shh. Just watch it."

"I already did. It's funny. That movie is hilarious."

He took his phone back and started to watch the rest of the clip, laughing to himself. When he finished, he put his phone back away.

"So you never answered my question?" he smiled.

"What question?"

"How much do you weigh?" he smiled more slyly.

This motherfucker.

"And I'm still not going to."

Our eggplant parm came out and I motioned for him to try first but he refused.

"Ladies first."

I went ahead and reluctantly tried a bite considering he's now asked me twice how much I weigh and hasn't eaten.

"Wow, not going to lie, probably the best eggplant parm I've ever had!" I replied.

"Is it? See. I told you this place is good."

He grabbed a fork and dove in. *God forbid he eat Burrata, but eggplant parm is fine.*

I had a couple more bites, but wasn't really that hungry. Which worked out, I guess, because at this point he was legit shoveling the eggplant parm into his mouth. Now I'm pretty sure he's drunk or on drugs.

I decided to pause and let him take the reins on conversation. Per usual, he just stared at me after eating his food. He reached in his pocket to pull out his phone. I decided maybe I can look at my phone too since the date was straight shit. *Who cares about manners now?*

"How's it going?" a text from Kassidy lingered. I replied.

"Worst date of my life, dude." I sent. "I'll go to the bathroom and call you in a min."

She responded immediately. "No fucking way."

Before I could respond, Jesse held his phone above my phone blocking my vision to my own screen with his screen with *The Wolf of Wall Street* clip playing again.

No, I'm not kidding.

I laughed out loud. "Jesse! You've already showed me this video twice!"

"No just watch it," he slurred, looking away or maybe his eyes were rolling back into his head, who knows at this point anymore.

"No. I already have," I said, handing it back across the table.

He went to take his phone back snorting in disappointment, but before I let go of the phone, I decided it's finally time I can go off.

"Wait, I get it now," I said.

He raised his eyebrows over his droopy eyes.

"You want me to watch this scene because this is you? I get it now. You're a financial advisor. You're Matthew McConaughey. You want me to keep watching this because it's you, right now. You're on drugs. That's it, right?" I said, smiling big and wide, mocking him.

He pulled the phone back from my hand like a child whose toy was insulted.

"Are you kidding me?" he said, not looking up from his phone. "I'm not on drugs. I'm offended you would even say that," he slurred. He lifted his head with his eyes closed, and pulled his arm up dramatically to put under his chin, but instead his elbow went straight into the leftover eggplant parm plate. His fork fell to the floor with a clink causing him to look down in a clearly delayed reaction.

I tried to stifle my laugh.

"I need to use the bathroom." I got up with my phone and retreated.

I called Kassidy in the bathroom and gave her a recap.

"Oh my God, get out of there!" she pleaded.

"I can't."

"Why not?!"

This is the part in the story where I have to admit to you readers that this date came weeks after my realization of writing this book. It's actually the only first date I've gone on since deciding I was going to write this book. Some of you may have been wondering even earlier on why I hadn't just gotten up and left. Really there's a couple of reasons why I hadn't: A. This date was so bad it was borderline theatrical. B. I never leave a good drink behind, especially a full glass of prosecco. C. At least I was still seeing new areas of Boston.

"It's so bad that it's good. We always joke how bad of dates I go on, but this is the worst by far. It just keeps getting worse and worse. Like dude, he just put his elbow in his food plate when I accused him of being on drugs. It's like a movie."

I headed back to our table and was met back with the same deer-in-the-headlights look from Jesse. I attempted to start another conversation but finally couldn't take it and burst into uncontrollable laughter, so loud that the table next to us even glanced over. The laughter bent me over and I literally dropped my forehead to the table I was laughing so hard.

"What's so funny?" broke into my laughing spell and I attempted to compose myself and whipped my head up from the table to see Jesse, with a big drunk smile that seemingly felt like he was missing out on the joke.

I paused and got a breath in so I wouldn't laugh.

"YOU!" I said confidently right to his face.

He continued smiling like he understood the joke, but at this point, he was just a drunk shell of a human being. Our waitress arrived asking if we wanted dessert. I declined for us and she said she would bring out the check. I pulled out my phone to check out the Uber situation so I wouldn't have to wait too long, while, of course, Jesse just sat in silence. After the waitress arrived with our check, Jesse continued gawking at me, so I decided to join in on his stupid staring contest before breaking it with laughter.

"Did you want to split the bill?" I asked, as the bill lied there motionless from him.

He nodded his head no, not breaking eye contact and not reaching for his wallet, either.

I laughed again. "Ok, so what, you want me to get it then?" I said.

He scoffed and threw his head back like I asked the most ridiculous question and then pulled out his card. The awkwardness could not get any worse at this point.

"Our waitress was such a bitch. Should I tip her?" he slurred.

My turn to scoff at him and act like he was ridiculous—because he was.

"Uhm, she was great. She checked on us and answered all your ridiculous requests. Yes, you should tip her. Tip her twenty percent."

He rolled his eyes.

"Anyways," I pulled out my phone. "I'm going to get an Uber."

"Wait, no you can't go yet!" he basically yelled at me, holding his hands out theatrically.

Shocked, I looked up at him. "Why would I want to stay any longer? Literally, give me one good reason."

"I know I wasn't the greatest at conversation. I will do better. But it's not about me. My twin brother is on a first date too and we were planning to meet up with our dates and go out around North End. I told them we would meet them at our apartment overlooking the harbor and he's so much more fun than me!"

The fact that he was selling the brother and the new date over himself was very telling as to how he knew how much he sucked on this date. I paused with my finger hovering over the "Request Uber" button.

"Fine. But only if we're meeting up with them and because I've never been around the North End or the portion by the water." I said, because I actually was down to see a new area even if it's with a complete imbecile.

Thankfully, we had only had two glasses of prosecco so I knew I was chilling, but Jesse was clearly on drugs or wasted. And frankly, really skinny and lanky. I decided I could take his ass out if I wanted to. Hell, in the state he was in, I don't think it would take much more than a good shove off a properly placed curbside.

We put on our winter garments and masks and left the restaurant.

It was cold outside and just barely starting to snow. I texted Kassidy the new developments.

"No! Don't go with him! Who cares how bad it is! Is it worth it?" she replied.

I looked up from my phone at the man walking ahead of me.

"Hey, let's scare these people crossing the street!" he said, turning around, pulling down his mask to reveal a childish grin. Since he basically yelled it, the people crossing heard him too.

"No," I replied back behind my mask to him.

"AGHHHH!" he yelled at the people passing by, turning around and laughing to me like he's the comedian of the fucking century.

I replied back to Kassidy the latest developments and that yes it was most certainly worth it. Jesse interrupted my texting with some more slurs.

"Who are you texting? Your boyfriend?" he said.

"Yes, Jesse. I'm telling him I'm on a date with a complete psychopath," I said, pulling down my mask to reveal my seriousness and, at the same time, sarcasm.

He laughed audibly at this and did a twirl still walking forward the way he was heading.

"Where's your hat?" he said.

I didn't wear a hat and this was a stupid question so I decided to offer him a taste of his own medicine and ignored him even though my ears were actually cold.

"I can't wait to meet my brother's girl. She's such a butterface. I'm going to tell her that when I see her," he slurred.

"No you're not. My God, why can't you just be nice?" I replied back, still looking at my phone texting Kassidy.

We continued walking down Hanover Street toward the water past little restaurants and shops I was not familiar with.

"Wow, that place is so cute," I said out loud, almost forgetting I'm adventuring with the buffoon ahead of me.

He turned around and met my gaze. "You're right! Let's get a drink in there. Go ask if they have a table."

The place was the smallest restaurant I've ever seen, with all four of their tables filled.

"It's Valentine's Day. All these places are booked. And with COVID—we're not getting in anywhere."

"No seriously! Just go ask," he urged.

Annoyed, I opened the door, immediately feeling like I've already invaded this private restaurant space uninvited.

"Can I help you?"

I'm not an idiot, so I ignored Jesse's urges to ask about a table and went with something else to excuse my intrusion and asked if they take reservations online. They do. I retreated out the door.

"You didn't even try! I'm going to ask," Jesse stumbled in.

Embarrassed and knowing his defeat was fast approaching, I continued walking the way we were headed, slowly so I could text Kassidy play-by-play updates.

He popped out and jogged to catch me.

"Oh my God, what a bitch. She said she couldn't seat us. She fucking sucked," he breathed out, taking too much time to spit out his words. He took the lead again with his determined yet shaky swagger, since I didn't know where we were going.

"You realize, not one of the girls you've referenced today as bitches have been bitches."

"Wait until you meet my brother's girl. I can't wait to tell her."

"No, you're not going to. Your brother and his date are at your house, right?"

"They just finished eating too and are walking there."

I texted Kassidy the update.

We finally reached his building, so I let Kassidy know, since she has my location. The building seemed really nice and looked like it did, indeed, overlook the water.

"I've never seen this area. Let me guess, this is where all the cool people live?" I asked.

I can't remember exactly what his slurred reply was, but it was something about how old guys who make too much money and think they're cool all live here. *Seems accurate so far.* We took the elevator to the sixth floor accompanied by silence, our good friend at this point. He opened the door to his place and it was nice, but smaller than I expected—a modern two bedroom with a big living area attached to the kitchen. The living room opened up to a balcony that stretched to both bedrooms as well. The first thing I noticed though, was that it was quiet. Too quiet. *Shit. They aren't here yet. This isn't good.* Now I was in a situation I was not comfortable with.

Jesse headed to the fridge and asked if I wanted a glass of prosecco, revealing an opened bottle of La Marca prosecco, my favorite. I said sure, wondering about it being already opened, and asked where the bathroom was. He directed me with his hand toward what must be his bedroom with an attached bathroom. I went into the bathroom and locked the door behind me and began looking for an Uber. *No way I'm hanging with him alone here.* I finished peeing and re-emerged ready to order my Uber when I heard people coming in.

Appearing from the other side of the door was a tiny twenty-something-year-old, maybe weighing eighty pounds at 4'10", with fake lashes and a big smile. She bounced in with a near-replica of Jesse, his twin brother. They were both laughing and smiling about something and she eagerly said hi to me with open arms and went in for a hug saying her name is Mandy. I liked her immediately and decided to pocket my phone before requesting the Uber.

I asked how their date was and she said it was fine and she asked how ours was. Jesse said nothing in the corner of the kitchen sipping his prosecco, so I decided to carpe the hell out of that moment.

"Oh, you know, your brother barely talked the entire night, asked me how much I weighed three times, when was the last time I got laid, and tried to make me watch a *The Wolf of Wall Street* clip three times before I accused him of being on drugs," I said only half-joking.

Mandy grabbed my arm and looked at me appalled. At this point Jesse was pouring prosecco from the open bottle into all four glasses, including his and his brother's (a good sign), so at least I'd get some more prosecco out of this evening.

"Yeah! She accused me of being on drugs!" he pointed at me and looked to his brother, as if THAT was the biggest offense in the remark I had just made.

The brother laughed and put his hands up in immediate surrender to help his twin out.

"No, no, no! I promise he's not on drugs! Honestly, we were at our mom's house drinking before we came back in to go on our dates, and I drove because Jesse had too much red wine there."

"Oh, great. So you were just plastered for our first date then. Much better," I took a swig from my glass with my new sidekick Mandy at my side.

To change the subject, Jesse's twin decided we should listen to some music and tried to get the portable Bluetooth speaker going. Jesse decided to join in on the socialization and slurred out loudly from his corner against the kitchen cabinets.

"You girls should arm wrestle," he blurted out, his eyes wildly excited at his thought. "Mandy, I will give you one-thousand bucks right now if you can beat Courtney in an arm wrestle. Oh, it will be so great. Don't you think?"

Mandy tried to laugh it off giving a shrug and I laughed too saying nothing, getting the idea of where this was going.

"Yes! You have to do it. One-thousand bucks cash right now, Mandy. And Courtney, you get five-hundred bucks if you win."

I immediately realized what was happening and felt my gut turn. I am as confident as they come, but there was that one self-conscious thing—*my arms*. My arms must be so big to him, that he is looking at me like some show horse. *An oddity. A party favor. A use of entertainment.* He was using me as his cash cow for entertainment like his prize-winning boxer or fighting dog. I tried to hide my blow to the heart by acting semi-compliant and not completely dismissing his ridiculous notion.

"You realize what he's doing? He's already betting against you!" I said to Mandy.

Mandy turned to face me, but clearly she could tell I was jabbed by the comments.

"No, that's stupid we're not doing it!" Mandy replied.

By this point, Jesse's twin had got the music going and a ten if not fifteen-year-old club song blared to life through the portable speaker.

Don't you worry, don't you worry, child! See heaven's got a plan for you!

"Isn't this song great?" the other twin remarked, bouncing next to us smiling.

Mandy and I looked back and forth to each other and giggled and she pulled me aside for a whisper. "These guys are, like, really old."

"Yeah, I know. Oldest guy I've gone on a date with. I'm twenty-eight, so he's eleven years older."

"What! I thought they were thirty-six! I'm twenty-four!"

"Yeah, thirty-nine. They're older. But I don't plan on seeing this guy ever again."

"Yeah, your twin kinda sucks."

"Totally."

We laughed and came back into the kitchen conversation of nothingness between with the club music still going.

"Who wants to smoke weed? Mandy, you said you like to smoke, are you down?"

"I'm in!" Mandy hopped off her barstool with a big smile on her face, pulling my arm to come with her so I wasn't stuck in the kitchen with Jesse. I followed along, but not really interested in smoking. But hey, maybe weed would make me feel a little bit better after the arm wrestling comments.

"I just got this medical grade stuff so it should be good!" the twin said, trying to keep our spirits up, despite Mandy and I clearly disliking his other half in the kitchen.

Mandy took a hit from the piece. "Actually it's not that bad! Try it!" she said holding it out to me.

The thought of COVID popped in my brain with the piece outstretched to me, so I wiped off the mouth portion with my sleeve (like that would somehow destroy COVID) and decided, *why not?*

I lit up the small piece and watched the bowl get bright, inhaling a good amount of smoke, reminiscing on the last time I had smoked.

Probably close to a year or more now. I exhaled. We went back into the kitchen and Mandy and I took our seats at the barstools.

"Who here needs to lose weight? Raise your hand!" Jesse blurted out from the corner upon our arrival.

Mandy and the brother recognized what Jesse was doing so they immediately shot up their hands without hesitation. I didn't want to, but Jesse had raised his hand too and I knew I couldn't be singled out, so I raised mine as well.

"Ok!" he yelled. "Well then let's all agree to lose five pounds!"

My heart sank again. Mandy glared at him.

"I don't fuck with you!" Mandy said directly at him and pointed at him.

I realized with this remark that everyone knew it was about me. I felt tears start to burn the back of my eyes, but I wouldn't dare let them make an appearance. Not here. I have seriously tough skin, but damn, a girl can only take so much.

Desperate to turn the tables and mood altogether, the other twin urged us to pick new music and our new songs.

"Courtney, you pick something!" he said.

"I don't care. Anything country." I said, opening the Uber app, trying to harness my feelings.

"I love country too! Who's your favorite?" Mandy said to me.

"Anyone." I said, defeated. "I need to pee."

I retreated to the bathroom, yet again, and allowed a couple of tears to fall from my eyes, without making my eyes red or ruining my makeup. I dabbed my eyes with a piece of toilet paper and told myself to pull it together. *So much for having a fun high to make me feel better about the first comments.* I check the Uber app and the nearest one is twenty-six minutes away. *Damn it. Not again.* And I know it's snowing outside. What a nightmare. I request it. *I got twenty-six minutes to kill with these clowns and little Mandy at my side. I got this.*

I checked myself in the mirror briefly and re-emerged to the kitchen.

All three faces turned abruptly to look at me with overly happy expressions announcing my arrival, clearly trying to cover up the fact they were just talking about me or the fact that I am clearly the wounded animal here. I went to take a sip of my prosecco to stifle the awkwardness only to realize it wasn't in my hand.

"Oh shit, I left my drink in the bathroom." I turned to head back for the bathroom. I saw my glass sitting on the back top of the toilet and grabbed it only to hear Jesse's voice from the kitchen.

"Get back in here, fatty!" he yelled, laughing.

I stopped dead in my tracks, thankfully still in the bathroom where they couldn't see me. Did he really just call me a fucking *fatty*? Now, I was pissed. And thankfully, it sounded like I wasn't alone in my reaction. I heard Mandy scream back at him immediately.

"Fuck you! You're a fucking piece of shit!" Mandy yelled, followed by interjections from his brother.

Thank God I got an Uber. I lingered a bit, but eventually came back into all their yelling, pretending I heard nothing. At this point, it was easier that way and I needed to be smart. After all, we were still in their house and standing up for myself would probably lead to tears he didn't deserve. *Just—what—twenty-two or so minutes left at this point?*

I took a seat next to Mandy again at the barstools. She grabbed me and whispered she doesn't like my twin at all and he's not a good guy. I told her not to worry, I already knew and had called my Uber. She grabbed my hand and squeezed it. We decided we should exchange numbers since we're fun and our dates suck, saying we would totally have to go out together soon.

Jesse decided to cut in again.

"I have a fun topic. When was the last time you guys got laid? I'll go first. It's been a year for me and two years for my brother! Can you believe that?"

His brother tried to hide the embarrassment on his face. Mandy and I laughed before retreating to our own conversation about what the hell we were doing here. The other twin tried to join in by bringing up the music again, but eventually realized we weren't interested, so he decided we should all dance to his throwback tunes. He playfully enticed Mandy off her barstool who rolled her eyes, but seemed like she didn't mind. After all, it was my twin who was the asswipe.

Jesse tried to join in on the festivities just mimicking his brother and came up behind me trying to put his hand on my waist. I immediately moved his disgusting hand and he tried to play it off. He tried again, this time trying to kiss my neck while his hand grabbed for my waist, likely trying to feel some rolls or something. I flinched in revulsion from his face near me and basically slapped away his hand this time, saying "don't" with a very serious expression right into his eyes. He got the picture and didn't try to touch me again, but he still lingered, dancing near me. The dance party lasted about ten minutes maybe, so I figured now I'm in the final stretch with probably another ten minutes to go. The twin brother dancing with Mandy asked if she wanted to see his room.

Uh oh, time's up for me. I need to get out of here.

She accepted in a "show me around" kind of way, but eventually the door shut behind them. *Shit. What do I have now—eight minutes to go? It's not too bad to wait outside in the snow. I'm out of here.*

Jesse came over to try and mimic his brother's ways, but before he even could, I got up from my barstool, saying I had to head out.

"My Uber is arriving," I held up my phone.

"No! Cancel it," he said, irritated.

"I have to meet my friends for our 6:30 p.m. reservation downtown. They already know I'm on my way," I said, putting my coat on.

Ooo, yeah. Good one, Courtney.

"What? What! No! UGH! No, no, no. UGHHHHH!" he started throwing a full-blown temper tantrum.

Rather than watch the show, I decided to bail quick. Like, *now*.

"Ok, well, I'll just show myself out. Bye!"

I walked out the door and as soon as it closed, I broke into a sprint to the elevator clicking the button incessantly. It arrived and I pressed the close-elevator-door button behind me, still hearing his tantrum from his apartment and thankful he didn't follow. I got downstairs and went outside to wait for my Uber and started to feel tears coming again.

Thankfully, my Uber pulled up just a couple of minutes later and I hopped in and immediately started to cry, tears pouring from my eyes.

The driver repeated my name and the inputted address to me and I said "Yes, thank you," still crying.

"Are you sure you want to go there?" She turned around with a look of genuine concern.

I looked back at her with confidence and a little giggle came out regarding her confusion. "Oh, yes please! That address is my house. Get me away from here."

"Oh, ok, good. Just wanted to make sure. Let's go," she replied, putting the car into drive.

"Sorry for the tears, just had the worst date of my life," I admitted and gave her a brief rundown ending with the part about him calling me a fatty.

"Well, he sounds like a real piece of shit. And he'll get what's coming to him. They always do. You don't deserve that. And... you're not fat."

She drove me home and I tried to compose myself, coming into my house to see my dog overjoyed at the sight of my presence. I tried to smile at his adorable face, but just kept crying and knew this date had penetrated a hole in that thick skin of mine—even if it was just a small hole.

I barely made it inside and decided to lean against my fireplace and call Kassidy, rather than go flop in bed and cry. But she didn't answer, so I called my local friend, who didn't answer either. *Where are they?* I remembered it was Valentine's Day evening and they were probably out with their boyfriends, so I called and cried to my mom. Obviously, she was furious about the guy, but she was also full of "mom" questions too, asking me why I would even go that long into the date and drink prosecco at his house. I left out the weed details, too. She would've had a heart attack if she knew those. Still, I told her what I had told Kassidy— the date was so bad it was borderline comical.

"Well enough of that bullshit," she said.

The next morning she called me to check in and tell me she and my sister had found a service that could deliver human shit to his door. Was

I interested? I laughed and told them it's fine. They still schemed in the background of the phone call anyway.

"You need to report him, Courtney. What if he had said that to someone who doesn't have as thick of skin as you and was suicidal over it? Hailey said you can do that. I'm serious," my mom said.

"I'll report Jesse on the app today."

"Jesse? No, Courtney. That's not his name. His name is Satan," my mom interjected.

"Ok, Mom."

I went to report him on the app and the little fuck had already deleted me off the app, so I couldn't report him. *That motherfucker.* Thankfully, one of my friends had dealt with something similar so she gave me the email to reach out to Bumble with and said I could send the screenshots I had of his profile to them and they would handle it. As promised, they responded quickly and said they take the safety of their users very seriously. Surprisingly, I didn't have to say what he said, besides checking the box for "verbally abusive."

I kind of felt like a pussy filling it out or maybe that it was a waste of time, but the voices of my family and friends who reacted to the story resonated in my head. "Yeah, you had tough skin, but what if the next girl doesn't." ... "What if he said that to someone who is suicidal about the things he says." ...*What if it breaks her.* I think of my cousin. The thought was enough. *It's not about me or my feelings. What if he does it again.* I finished the form and I gave them his information, or the screenshots I had of his profile, which I had thankfully taken right when we matched to show Kassidy the new prospect.

Thankfully, I haven't run into "Satan" at all in Boston since, but I'd be lying if I said I was totally ok after it. After all, I didn't go on a date for nearly six months afterward. As much as I hate to admit it, I haven't worn that red sweater since either.

14

Tanner

"...and at the end of the night he called me a fatty! Can you believe that? I can't make this shit up."

"So did you punch him in the face?" Tanner asked.

"No."

"Well, you should've. I would've. Want me to come beat him up?"

I laughed at this. Despite being 6'3", Tanner was far from the fighter type and much closer seated to the lover position.

Fun fact: Whoever said you can't still be best friends with your ex was wrong.

Tanner and I haven't been a couple in over two years and live across the country from each other, but we still talk nearly every month. Hell, we've even taken to sharing shitty dating stories with each other.

But I should really start from the beginning.

I met Tanner in high school because he and Kassidy were good friends. Tanner was the total star volleyball player of his school and had a crush on me. Tanner and I would always flirt if we were at parties or on each other's Facebook walls. Anyone who had a Facebook from 2004-2013 knows what I'm talking about here. How were we so shamelessly shooting our shots on our public pages? You have to love it. Years passed, and we pretty much stayed in touch by just hitting each other up on social media about our golf videos or fishing photos.

After I decided to reenter the dating world post breakup with Matt, I went on Instagram to do some scouting. What did my scouting consist of? Looking at my last six Instagram posts to see who had liked all six. The reoccurring names that I was potentially interested in would be the scouted. I'm not sure why this was my process, but I guess to me it meant these people were somewhat interested if they always liked my posts.

This led me to another pretty boy jock from my high school and Tanner.

So I sent them both a text and said something like... "Yo, I'm thinking of grabbing some beers and maybe mix in some Jameson to watch the Thursday Night Football game in Newps—wanna come?"

Newport Beach or Costa Mesa was always the place to go out and tonight was going to be a good game—Minnesota Vikings and Los Angeles Rams. I figured one would be in and the other would be out but, lucky me, they both said they were in. *Woops.* I had overbooked. Thankfully, the other didn't end up following up after the gym so I was meeting Tanner out with one of his friends.

I remember exactly what I was wearing and how nervous I was. I had a black tank top tie-up bodysuit, a flannel tied around my waist, black jeans, and a pair of wedges, which felt weird because I hardly wore wedges. I also felt a little self-conscious because the last time I wore an outfit like this Matt made me feel like a piece of shit. But, I decided *no thinking like that*. It was game time. Literally.

I walked into the bar Tanner picked, Black Knight, and it was poppin'. I spotted him at the bar, where he turned around and smiled so big and got up to give me a hug. It had been years since we had seen each other in person. Like YEARS. The last time I saw him, we were in Vegas with his friends and I had a major POTS attack. Remember those autoimmune problems I had mentioned earlier? Postural Orthostatic Tachycardia Syndrome aka POTS is a fun one—let me tell you. Not great. Anyways, back to Tanner.

When he stood up, I forgot just how tall he was, and the electricity between us was immediately the same as it always had been.

"I just ordered you a Coors Light. Figured I'd wait for you to get the shots going," he said.

"Perfect! Oh shit I need to check my fantasy lineup before kickoff," I said.

I whipped out my phone to make sure I had put Rams wide receiver Cooper Kupp back in, but as soon as I went to do it, the kickoff was underway.

"Who you got?" he asked.

"I was going to put Cooper Kupp back in my starters. Whatever. I'll put him in next week. Jameson shots, anyone?" I asked.

We took shots, Jameson for me and tequila—Cazadores reposado, specifically—for Tanner. These wouldn't be the only shots we'd take considering Kupp would have a record-breaking game and he was on my bench. I was standing on the barstool yelling at the screen, Tanner was clapping and laughing at me, we were placing sports bets on the side. With every time I stood up and then sat back down in my barstool I found myself wanting to sit closer and closer to Tanner and so I did. And his hand would find its way over my shoulders or on my lower back until finally we were tipsy and laughing after a play, and he leaned in and grabbed the back of my head to kiss me. *It was like fucking fireworks.*

He wasn't the first person I had kissed since Matt, but it was the first time I was feeling something when someone kissed me. Honestly, it was probably not even halftime before we gave into kissing each other. After that, we were chugging beers and yelling at the game and I was having an existential crisis on whether to pout or cheer when Cooper Kupp would score. Ultimately I decided to cheer, because, fuck the Vikings all day. #GoPackGo, you already know.

We ended up running into one of Tanner's friends from high school who updated us on one of Tanner's ex-girlfriends who was now a lesbian.

"Damn I knew I was bad in bed, but I didn't think I was that bad!" he joked.

"Shit, you really turned her, Tanner," I said, joking back.

"Trust me, I'll prove that wrong to you tonight," he whispered in my ear.

I looked up at him and he winked at me.

I kept teasing him the rest of the night about his ex going lesbian, implying his sex game or maybe his dick was not up to par. This joke continued as we left the bar and walked to our Uber.

"You think you're really funny don't you?" he said, tickling me and making me laugh, pulling me in to kiss me.

He ran his fingers over my lips and used his thumb to pull down my lower lip.

"God, I love these lips."

He leaned in and kissed me again until our Uber pulled up.

We hopped in and I immediately got on top of him and started making out with him and kissing down his neck. He started laughing and pretended he wanted me to get off, but held me on top of him.

"Courtney! I'm trying to get 5 stars!" he laughed out over my shoulder to the driver who laughed back.

We pulled up to his house, and I whispered in his ear as we got out of the car. "Let's see what you got. Although, my hopes aren't high with what I've heard," I said joking again.

Just then I realized I was missing something—my purse.

"Shit! We gotta go back," I said.

He rolled his eyes back into his head and put his fist up to his mouth since he was clearly ready to do other activities. What can I say—I am who I am and whether that's predictable or unpredictable in this way, I'll let you decide.

We swung back to the bar and I ran in and sure enough they had my purse. We got back into the same Uber and reconvened with what we were doing before. When we got to his place we barely made it up his apartment stairs without ripping each other's clothes off.

"Fuck, I've wanted to do this for a while," he said into my mouth.

"I know," I breathed back.

He pulled himself out, rock hard and way bigger than I expected.

He tried to get into me, but I hadn't had sex in quite a while, so this was going to need some leverage. He fingered me to get things going and then I told him to get it in.

"I don't want to hurt you."

"Just fuck me, Tanner."

With that he thrust hard and slid into me and I lost my breath. He grunted and hunkered over the top of me and slid his arms underneath mine and began thrusting into me harder and harder.

"Fuck," I said, biting my lip so hard it almost bled.

I decided to take control and flipped him over to ride him like the cowgirl I am, riding him forward and then switching my saddle up and riding him backwards so he could watch my ass. He grabbed my ass with both hands. He flipped me back over and then fucked me with one leg up over his shoulder until he told me he was going to cum. He pulled out his dick and came on my stomach and boobs and then grabbed my hip for stability.

Fireworks.

The next morning we woke up and I was ready for round two. I rolled over on top of him and started kissing his chest and worked my way down to his cock which instantly started getting hard recognizing my presence kissing over the top of his boxer briefs.

"Well good morning to you too," he said from above the sheets.

I poked my head out from under.

"Hi," I replied, then poked back under and pulled down his boxer briefs and started sucking on the tip of his dick which led him to sigh out.

"Well aren't you just a little nympho."

After sucking on him, feeling him getting harder and longer, I came out from under the sheets and got back on top and rode him again until he came.

"Fuck, you trying to kill me girl," he smiled.

He rolled over and cuddled me like a giant monkey, looping his arms around my neck and his legs around my waist. It felt good to be held, but this was Tanner. *Was I even into this?* I knew he always liked me but having him cling to me was almost making me want to run. I looked around his room and saw a whiteboard on his wall with some writing on it. I couldn't quite make out the shitty boyish writing until I squinted better to see.

"YOU CAN ONLY SLEEP HERE IF ASKED."

What... the... hell...

"Uh, what the fuck is that?" I pointed to the whiteboard. "You wrote that for girls didn't you? You're such an ass!"

"Oh God," he threw his head back into the pillow. "No, it's not like that! Ughhh, I was hooking up with this chick that I didn't even really like beyond just sex—but anyways she would always come over unannounced, and then she would never fucking leave! So I wrote that on the whiteboard because I didn't want to have to keep asking her. It was awkward."

"Well, shit! I'm so sorry I didn't ask if I could stay! I should probably get going!" I got up to leave and he pulled me back down into the bed.

"Trust me when I say, you never have to ask."

I started to get into my feelings with that comment so naturally I told him I should get going. Since my car was parked at a friend's house nearby, Tanner decided to walk with me so I could drive him to pick up his car that he had left at the bar. We got dressed and I realized I couldn't find the flannel I wore the night before that I had borrowed from my friend. We gave up looking and walked out of Tanner's place to see the flannel strung across a bush.

"What the fuck!"

Tanner started dying laughing, bending over to brace hands to his knees.

"What did I just fling my flannel off into the bushes? We start stripping in the driveway or what?" I said.

"Apparently."

We started our lengthy walk of shame through the main streets in Costa Mesa until we got to my car, mainly talking about work. He said he was working at his dad's bar as a bartender, a bar he would likely take over one day. Once in my car, and thoroughly hungover, we headed to Goat Hill Tavern where he had left his car parked. At one point, we somehow got into the conversation of another girl we knew and then birthdays.

"Well yeah, that's because it's in March right around your birthday."

I froze, confused. "Wait? What? How do you know my birthday, Tanner?"

He looked embarrassed. "I don't know. It's like March sixth or something."

I raised my eyebrow at him. "I knew you had a crush on me, but damn, I didn't know you stalked me too."

"HAH—Shut the fuck up! It's just because mine is the next day."

"Mhmm," I said, smirking.

"Well, I had a fun time. Maybe we can do it again?" he said, getting out at his car.

"I'd like that," I said as he walked to my driver's side window.

He kissed me through the window. But before I drove off I yelled one more remark.

"Can't believe you know my birthday, bro. So weird." I smiled in my side mirror at him and he threw his hands up like whatever.

I called my friend and told her about our phenomenal sex, and she instantly said she had a mega-vibe about it, insisting I liked him.

We went on another date and, after the first date, he said he knew he wanted to date me and he wanted me to be his girlfriend. He was a guy who knew what he wanted, but I wasn't so sure yet. I tried to play it cool when I was with Tanner around my friends and family because I felt like they were still getting over Matt. Still, I was falling for Tanner.

I was that carefree girl that was just wandering the world in rose-colored glasses and I didn't even care. I was finally so happy.

At the time I was in the interview process at Washington State University for their new Social Media Head for the sports department which would have been a dream job. One week during the interview process I stayed with my relatives to go deer hunting for my first time ever and I'll always remember talking to my aunt when she picked me up from the airport.

"Are you excited about WSU? How have the interviews been going?" she asked.

"Really good."

"You don't seem so excited?"

"I am, really. It's just—I hate to even admit it—and don't tell my mom, but I am really liking the guy I am talking to. And it feels... I don't know... real. So I'd love to get this job and he even said he would make it work if it happens, but yeah. I guess I'll be happy either way."

When I came home from Washington, we went on several dates, whether it was just us two or out drinking with his buddies at their frat house of an apartment or going out in Newport. Finally, he even started coming down to my neck of the woods in Aliso Viejo to go on dates. We were inseparable. Even if he had to work, I'd meet him at the bar, have a couple beers and close up with him. We would go to the brewery down the street from my house and would barely make it to my car before he'd push me up against it and start kissing my neck. *Every time.* We were so hot and heavy, it felt like high school and it was really fucking fun. Within three weeks of hanging out, Tanner accidentally let an "I love you" slip while we were making out that stopped me in my tracks.

"Tanner!"

"Fuck, I just do. I don't even care if you say it back. I just do. Fuck it," he said, throwing his hands up theatrically.

One day I was feeling pretty POTS-y and my vertigo was raging, so I took an Uber down to my doctor's office to get an IV. Tanner said he would pick me up from the appointment since it was by my parent's house and then he could re-meet them.

My mom totally remembered Tanner, saying he was always the nice one asking "Mr. and Mrs. Schellin" if they needed any help at any of our high school and college parties. That Sunday we came back over to watch football with them too, and my dad and Tanner spent the whole day chitchatting, laughing, and drinking Coors Lights.

"Nice guy. I like that Tanner," my dad said.

Two family members down, one to go. And the last would be the most important critic—my sister. Hailey and I are best friends if you haven't already noticed. Like two peas in a pod. People call us "The Blondes" now. Or in high school "the surfer girls" since our Range Rover's license plate was SRFGRLS even though only one of us still hit the waves after middle school. We are opposites in terms of left brain, right brain. I'm the creative, all over the place one. Hailey is the organized, type A, has her shit together one. We're a great balance, but also can go full crazy on each other. Actually, one of my friends described our relationship perfectly in a text recently.

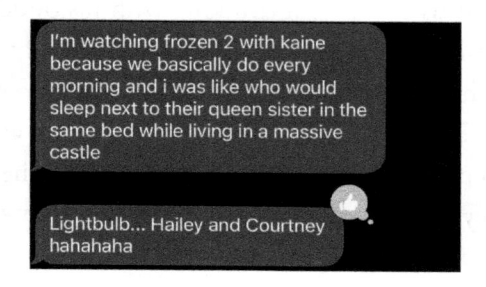

> I'm watching frozen 2 with kaine because we basically do every morning and i was like who would sleep next to their queen sister in the same bed while living in a massive castle
>
> Lightbulb... Hailey and Courtney hahahaha

Needless to say, I wanted her to like Tanner. The only problem was, Tanner was already starting off on a terrible note in her mind due to a trip to Vegas I took with Tanner and his friends years back. To sum up what happened—I ended up having one of my first full-blown POTS attacks, and had to call Hailey to leave her friends and come meet me in the lobby so I could go get an IV. Then we moved all my things over to her room because she was so mad that the group I was hanging with were bad apples and didn't care that I nearly "died." But really, they had no idea, so her anger was slightly misguided.

Well, let me just tell the story...

So Tanner invited me to Vegas as his date, but I thought of us as friends and had no intention of hooking up with him. But I wanted to go because it was Memorial Day weekend and my sister and all her friends were already going too. The first day I partied hard with a group of girlfriends also in Vegas, having probably ten drinks at a pool party. Coming back up to the room we ran into Tanner and the guys heading back as well from the casino. I was so drunk I slammed right into a wall. *Yep, that kind of drunk.* So Tanner laughed and picked me up over his shoulder, putting me to bed when we got to the room. Later that night, I woke up to the group telling me it was time to wake up and get ready and rally. We were going to a club.

"Ugh, I don't know if I can do it," I sighed.

"Here, this will help." One of the guys motioned to a table with white strips laid out on it.

I wasn't exactly a "drug-user" per say, but I definitely dabbled in giving everything a good ole college try in my frat hard days. I actually thought cocaine was pointless. The first time I did it off of a key with a girl in the Barley House bathroom, she was so amped on it.

"See! Don't you just feel invincible?" she asked.

"No, not really," I laughed.

I realized after years of being prescribed Adderall, cocaine probably wasn't the drug for me. Coke didn't make me feel invincible, just awake. Although, one time I did too much at a frat boat party and felt like I was going to have a heart attack, so that wasn't fun. With that said, I am one-hundred percent responsible for why my health problems haven't exactly gotten better. Then again, when my doctor told me to go on a "no gluten, dairy, sugar, alcohol, or soy" diet when I was nineteen years old and freshly going to college... I hope she didn't hold her breath. Technically she didn't say anything about no drugs though?

Well, so much for keeping promises.

I got up and snorted a thin white line.

"How do you feel?" the guy looked at me all excited like the college girl had.

"Meh. Do we have any energy drinks?"

Tanner split a red bull vodka with me and we walked arm-in-arm down to the club. Once in the club they gave us a table and I made the huge mistake of not switching from my original drink of choice. I probably sipped down fourteen red bull vodkas at our table, including sips of my friend's drink without realizing it had Molly in it.

We had a hell of a time. But that next morning when Tanner tried waking me up to go down and get breakfast with them I said I couldn't. Tanner asked what he could do to help but I said I would be fine and just needed to sleep. I tried getting up to take a shower and felt like I was going to have a heart attack. I called one friend and she tried to convince me I was just "coming down" and to take a shower and listen to happy music. Little did she realize, a shower for a POTS person is literally the worst advice. So that didn't work. I went to lay on the bed and started thinking, *What if I just lay down and have a heart attack and die up here and no one would know.* With that, I called Hailey, reluctantly, because a lecture would likely ensue. Hailey is straight as an arrow and has never dabbled in drugs. She parties and gets drunk, but even then she's usually the one in control. I told her my dilemma and she was pissed to say the least, not only because now she would miss a pool party, but also because I did drugs. Still, she said she would meet me in the lobby of my hotel.

Low and behold, once in the lobby, we saw a giant billboard for IV therapy in my own hotel. *Thank God.* We went and I lied on every checkbox about how I was feeling because I didn't want them to send me to ER or something instead. Thankfully, they walked me in so I could get my damn IV. The IV was freezing, but not nearly as cold as the death stare my sister kept giving me. I finally couldn't take it anymore and started busting up laughing. I usually start laughing at all the wrong moments because I can't handle being in fights or people being mad at me or even being sad for that matter. It's not a great trait, but apparently it's common. Like when my mom caught Hailey and I for having forbidden MySpace pages, I couldn't stop laughing even though our parents had us sitting in the middle of the room in kitchen chairs like we were criminals under interrogation.

So of course I started laughing at Hailey trying to be so mad at me while I was getting my IV, causing her to laugh before stopping to be serious again.

"Idiot," she said.

And then she took out her phone and took a photo of me getting the IV and looked at it and laughed and when she saw me smiling too she composed herself again.

"Idiot."

Fast forward a few years to me telling my sister I was going on dates with Tanner.

"Ew, I hate that guy," she said immediately.

"What? Why?"

"Courtney, he left you in Vegas when you were sick. I hate that guy."

This is not how it happened, as you're aware, but she didn't want to hear it. So when it was time to go Sunday Funday with Tanner, I invited Hailey and her friend Meg and I warned Tanner of this despite me telling Hailey literally one-thousand times that Tanner didn't even know about the situation. We ended up having a good time and Tanner even brought up Vegas and Hailey tried not to smirk about it.

"I had no idea, Hailey! I would've been up there in a heartbeat for Courtney."

"Yeah," Hailey said, sipping her drink. "I know that now," she said with a smile, apparently just giving him a hard time.

But I knew she was warming up to him. Especially when Tanner went to the bathroom and Meg said, "Do you see the way he looks at her and how he's always looking for her hand? So damn cute. He really likes her."

Yeah, he really did like me.

The weekend before Halloween we went on a date to Opah in Aliso Viejo and he kept doing his thing where he'd just smile, look down, and shake his head.

"What is it now, Tanner?" I smiled back at him before looking down and stabbing at some lettuce on my plate.

"I want you to be my girlfriend, Courtney."

I started laughing.

"I'm serious, Courtney. I want you to be my girlfriend so badly. Why won't you just say yes?"

"Because, it's so soon. Why do you need me to be your girlfriend so badly? It's just a label."

"Because you're the coolest, most beautiful, super fun, beer-drinking, sports-loving girl and because I just love you."

I looked up and set my fork down. "Tanner! Again! You have got to stop saying that!"

"I'm sorry!"

I looked at my food and then up through my lashes at him.

"Ok, Tanner. I'll be your girlfriend."

"Finally!" he said, rolling his eyes and reaching across the table to hold my hands. Then we kissed over the top of the table like the goobers we were. We got back to my place, aka my sister's townhouse where I rented a room, and I introduced Tanner as my boyfriend to my sister's friend visiting and they both lifted eyebrows and said "Wow." Tanner and I both blushed.

The next night we all went out for Halloween, and Tanner was open to taking all the photos with me, which was such a stretch from any of my previous boyfriends. The following morning we were up bright and early to board a party bus to a giant tailgate for the Rams vs. Packers game for my sister's birthday party. I showed up to the bus with an Aaron Rodgers jersey on, a cold Keystone Light in hand, and Tanner at my side. Tanner was one of the stars of the show. He was my sister's stabilizer and dance buddy on the bus when she wanted to dance on the seats. He was my beer pong partner. And he was the guy who lifted me and Hailey off the ground when we tipped over drunk taking a photo.

It wasn't long after this I started getting all googly-eyed for him like he was for me. He wanted me to meet his mom, so we went to a swanky place called Nick's in downtown Laguna Beach and she was adorable. I loved her. She ordered Cakebread chardonnay and I followed suit because, Cakebread—hell yeah.

Tanner tried to pick up the tab for "his ladies" but his mom beat him to the punch. We said goodbye to her and walked down the street to a whiskey bar called Marine Room. I pulled up a barstool and sat down and Tanner came up behind me and snuggled me, wrapping his arms around me and kissing the top of my head.

"What would you like my dear?" he asked.

"I don't know yet."

"Alright, I'm going to go to the bathroom while you decide."

He walked to the bathroom and I just felt so happy in that moment. Everything was finally coming together in my life even though there were still a ton of question marks. I didn't have a job yet, I was still on unemployment from the ESPN layoff and hadn't heard back from WSU, but I had him. And that really was starting to mean something to me. He walked out of the bathroom and just as he did "Tennessee Whiskey" by Chris Stapleton started playing. He was in a blue flannel that was making his eyes pop and his scruff was on point and I swear this moment dropped into slow motion as he walked over to me and started smiling.

Holy shit. Feelings came over me like a waterfall of ecstasy in slow motion.

Ugh, God! *F E E L I N G S.*

Worst of all, *that* feeling. I know that feeling.

Did I really? It had been what? Two months! No. Could I? The answer is yes. Yeah I did.

I fucking loved him.

He came up to me with a sly look and leaned one hand on the bar and the other on my chair as I just sat there with a stupid grin on my face.

"So, you love me or what?" he asked with an eyebrow raise.

My stupid grin must've said it all. Was I drooling too? Jesus. I'm not saying it now.

"Are you fucking kidding me!" I said pushing his chest away.

"What!" he said laughing and pulling my bar stool into him.

"I was literally just going to say it but apparently my face said it all! I was so excited to finally tell you I loved you back but you said that. And now it's ruined!" I pretended to pout.

"Aww! You can still say it. C'mon!" He got more serious and pulled me in and whispered to me. "You know how long I've been saying it to you and how I feel. I would love to hear you say it."

I looked up at him and his eyes were so green and genuine, and damn he was so handsome. How did it take me this long to realize it and to try things out with us?

Just say it to him. You know you mean it.

I blinked hard and bit my lip before meeting his eyes again.

"I love you, Tanner. I really do."

He broke out into a big smile and grabbed my face to kiss me, and it felt like no one else was in the room again.

"Let's get a drink to celebrate, shall we?" He moved around to the back of my barstool and held me in his arms while he tried to flag down a bartender.

"Ok but first take a selfie with me. I want to remember this night and how happy I am in this moment."

He smiled and kissed my head and I pulled out my phone to take it and had that same stupid revealing grin in it while he leaned his cheek into the top of my head and smiled. We looked so cuddly. And damn, were we so in love, whether I wanted to admit it or not.

Everything escalated from here. We would hang out whenever we could and every time we did we couldn't keep our hands off each other. He was so kind to me, and adored me. We'd go out with friends to parties, bars, or concerts and at some point in the night he'd always snap a photo of me when I was laughing or not paying attention and post it to his story with just the heart eyes emoji or "dead" with a heart.

Tanner taught me what it should be like to feel loved and is one of the best guys I've ever dated. I mean, Keagan was on the same level, but we were just kids when we dated. Tanner and I were adults—well, not really with our personalities—but you know what I mean. It felt like that drunken high school love where you're so into each other but more grown up.

Until, one day, it didn't feel as grown up and those pesky feelings of doubt and judgment started kicking in. Tanner loved video games and chewing tobacco and getting drunk at his bar after work with the locals and at first I was totally fine with all those things, until I realized—maybe I wasn't.

The first time I had a "doubt" was we went up to Lake Tahoe for Christmas, and even though Tanner grew up skiing, he decided he didn't want to do it anymore. This was a big red flag to my mom and sister for God knows what reason but more of a pink flag for me. I ended up having to text Matt about my ski gear because I thought it might still be at his ski house, and I knew they were up here too. He ended up calling me while he was digging around and said he couldn't find it. That still didn't change the fact that Matt and his whole family would be in Tahoe at the same time as Tanner and me so we might run into him. Tanner wasn't thrilled about this especially when I told him he would have to play it cool.

"You're asking me to be ok and chill with someone who hit you? Fuck that."

"He didn't hit me per say."

"Why the fuck do you still defend him like that?"

"I don't! He's a piece of shit. But my family doesn't know that stuff really and his family are still good people so can you just promise to be cool."

"Whatever you want babe, but don't make me say hi to him because I'll have some things to fucking say."

We didn't run into Matt or his family, thank God, and Tahoe ended up being a great time. Tanner even wore a Santa onesie on Christmas day. We'd even sneak off to the bedroom to have sex, and I told Tanner I really wanted him to get me off. We'd wake up in the morning and I'd try and shove his head down there, but he never wanted to and would always end up watching Fortnite videos on his phone on my chest. At first I thought how he watched videos was cute, but him not getting me off was killing me. Tanner was so cute and cuddly but never as sex-driven as I was. He was always making me feel tingly down there and yet every time I'd try to jump his bones he wasn't into it.

"You're so horny all the time. All you want to do is have sex," he'd say.

"Is that a bad thing?"

This, coupled with my mom and sister being weird about Tanner not skiing, was getting under my skin. It was like everyone was making their comparisons to my ex who was right across the mountain. I didn't realize it was getting to me, but it was. I think it somewhat had to do with the fact it was Christmas and Tanner and I were splitting Christmas with my parents and his. He came up to Tahoe with me for a few days and

Christmas Eve, and then we'd be spending Christmas Day with his folks since they always had a huge party.

Driving home, we started getting closer his parents' house in Newport and I started freaking out.

It was Christmas day and I left my family to go to my boyfriend's parents' house after just a few months? Matt and I dated a few years before we did shit like that. And we'd been broken up for what? Less than a year. *What was I doing?* How did I even know if this was real? What was I thinking saying I love you to someone after a couple months of dating?

I was about to lose it. I felt tears pulling at my eyes as soon as we exited the freeway into Newport and I knew I wasn't ready. But how could I tell Tanner that? It would break his heart. The whole car ride he was talking about the party and how happy he was I was coming and got to meet all of his family and their close friends.

I kept my gaze out the window and felt his hand reach over for mine, which I purposely had tucked all the way to the other side of the car.

"Court? You ok?"

"No. I don't have a bottle of wine. I wanted to bring a bottle."

"Oh, it's fine. You don't need one, really."

"Tanner pull into this store now. I need one. And I need to pee and pull myself together and look presentable." I was full-blown hyperventilating now, unbuckling my seat belt and rolling down the window to get space and air. The car felt tight.

"Ok, ok. I'm pulling in. Court, what's wrong? Talk to me."

"Nothing, I—I'm fine. I'll be right back," I said, barely getting the words out before pushing open the car door barely in park and running into the store.

I went straight to the bathroom and had a full-blown crying panic attack. I stared in the mirror and tried to rest my heart rate and pull myself together.

Stop. He loves you. Just fucking stop. What's wrong with you?

I looked down at my feet and clicked my heels together in my converse like I was Dorothy trying to transport home and squeezed my eyes shut to stop tears from coming.

Breathe. You're ok. He's a great guy. He cares about you. He wants you to meet his family. He loves you. Stop.

But every time I thought of him loving me it made me feel sick, because did I even feel the same way back? He was so sure and here I was having a panic attack in a Whole Foods bathroom about it. *God, I suck.*

I texted my best friend Briana my crisis at hand which made me feel better that someone knew. Then I cleaned up my eyes and went to grab a couple bottles of wine. I breathed through what Pinterest articles and exercises had told me to do when my heart got crazy and focused on the positives to stop my brain from going down the dark, fucked-up rabbit hole.

By the time I got to the car I told Tanner I was doing much better, but he looked so sad and I could feel the weight of all his emotions on me. It was almost like he could read my mind, but I couldn't coddle him or overdo it. I needed to keep myself stable right now so I could do this.

When we got to his parents' house, my plan was to grab my bags and beeline to the bathroom but we were bombarded by his sweet mom as soon as we pulled up.

I didn't deserve this. I didn't deserve him. *Stop.*

Tanner knew I was still uneasy and told his mom the drive was long and I probably wanted to get ready, so she led us down to the guest bedroom. A wooden plaque hung over the bed with "Love" written largely in cursive with a quote defining what love was.

Now God was just laughing in my face at this point. *You're a fraud. You shouldn't be here.* I felt my hands start to shake and I tried to take another deep breath.

Tanner didn't linger when he put my bags down which I appreciated and I lied on the bed and closed my eyes but everything was spinning as soon as I did. I opened them when I heard someone coming in. It was Tanner with his family cat. He knocked once on the open door and I rolled over to let him know I saw him and smiled a sheepish, embarrassed smile.

"I brought you someone to keep you company while you relax."

This made me smile bigger because he was such a good guy, but led me right back to my feeling that I didn't deserve him. He didn't deserve someone who was unsure.

"Thank you. I'm sorry."

He sat the cat down next to me on the bed and he walked by me and flicked his tail up past my face. Then Tanner told me I didn't need to apologize and brought me a Coors Light.

Once I showered, drank my Coors Light, and listened to some country music I was feeling much better and ready to take on the party. Which ended up being a hell of a time. The next morning we woke up and I opened presents with Tanner's family, and boy did his mom spoil me. She got me a Rebecca Minkoff purse, a Barefoot Dreams sweater, and so much more.

"Kelly! This is way too much."

"Oh, stop! Just let me! I always wanted a daughter and didn't get anything but boys so this was so fun for me," she said.

That sort of killed me.

The new year came in hot and the first few months breezed by, but I realized Tanner and I were creating a trend with our date nights. Tanner usually had to work every weekend, so we were going out during the week for our date nights, but we'd always end up getting really wasted at them. And then we'd come back, I'd want to have sex, and Tanner would want to for a little, but then as soon as he came, he wanted to throw a lip (aka chew some tobacco) and play Fortnite.

And as much as I hated to admit it, getting wasted and not getting off was a midweek combo that did not feel right to me. But then there were the times of watching him dance at his family parties and always running up to me like a school boy wanting to dance with his crush or introduce me to someone, or me watching him coach kids in volleyball, so date nights and getting off made me feel like I was asking too much. He was balancing two jobs after all, running his longtime family bar in Newport Beach, and coaching club volleyball. But still, there was always this way about Tanner that he was always complacent. I was always pushing myself and challenging myself but even when business was tight, it was always enough for him and that was starting to weigh in my thoughts too.

When we went to our high school rival volleyball game, one of his old colleagues and coaches of the team told him to reach out because they were looking for a new assistant coach.

I kept reminding Tanner to reach out because it seemed like a great opportunity, but he put it off, saying it was a ton of work and not a lot of pay. Or at least it was when he was coaching previously for Dana Hills high school. This struck another nerve with me because I'm the type of person who is constantly pushing and motivated to get more and gain more and keep moving up. But Tanner seemed pretty complacent with where he was. In his career. In his relationship. In his life, really.

I wanted him to want to reach like I always did, which seemed hypocritical because I was still looking for a job, but I wasn't giving up and was adapting to new roles I thought I could take on. And I was still really sexually frustrated with Tanner. I kept telling him how much I like sex and if he would just go down on me then I wouldn't be so horny all the time, but he said he never really did that. *Well, you're going to have to start figuring it out.*

I was getting sick of doing our same old get drunk at Buffalo Wild Wings or the brewery on our midweek dates or getting drunk with friends in Newport on the weekends and decided we should go on a trip. Thankfully, he was unlike Matt in not wanting to travel and was way down. He even requested the time off which was a big deal.

We decided on Portland since neither one of us had ever been there. We went to a Trail Blazers game with Tanner's friend who lived there and my friend Melanie from ESPN was working the game and was able to meet up with us after, too.

The trip was so fun, but because Tanner and I had our own private room I had bought some new lingerie to surprise him in. I woke up earlier than him and stole away to the bathroom to put on my incredibly sexy red set: a lace see-through bra, matching thong, red lace garter belt, and red stockings. I came back to the bed and hopped under the covers and slid over to him and started kissing his chest. But he wasn't having it.

"Not right now, Court."

I moved my way down and tried to give him head only for him to grab his dick and block my face.

"So tired babe."

I grabbed his hand to feel what I was wearing but he still didn't seem interested. Now I was annoyed.

"You don't even want to see my new outfit I got for you?"

He still didn't roll over which made tears start to come to my eyes. *Fuck me.* Maybe I was just being dramatic.

"Please look," I said, likely before a large voice crack looming ahead.

He lifted his head off the pillow and opened his eyes to a squint.

"Very nice." And flopped his head back down on the pillow.

"C'mon babe!" I shoved him trying to wake him up.

"Babe, I'm so tired!" he tried pulling me in backwards as a little spoon into him. I let him and then tears started dripping sideways down my face, but I wasn't facing him so it was fine. I lied there letting him sleep longer until finally I checked the clock again and it was nearly 10:30 a.m. I tried nudging my butt into him to try to get him to want to and eventually tried flipping over again onto him, but it was no use.

"I literally buy sexy lingerie for you Tanner and you can't even open your eyes for it. I mean, it's 11 a.m. C'mon. Fuck me, babe."

He tried rolling over underneath me between my legs and groaned. I finally gave up and released my leg off of him rolling myself off.

"You know sometimes I think we're more like best friends than we are boyfriend and girlfriend."

I got up and walked to the bathroom to take a shower and start the day. I didn't know it then, but later Tanner would tell me that those words were the hardest thing he had ever heard me say to him. Maybe they hurt so bad because, deep down, we both knew they were true.

Months went by and we kept dating and honestly things stayed relatively the same. We went to concerts, sporting events, birthday parties, and golfing. We really were having a hell of a time despite me bitching about him only going down on me maybe once a month and him not wanting to have sex all the time like I did. He even planned a trip up to his house in Mammoth for our birthdays because he knew I liked to ski on my birthday, even if he didn't want to. He loved the mountains and would drink beers on the porch and take Boone on walks.

I ended up taking a job for a friend's company running social media for their business and would have to start working in the office which meant no more late night weekday dates.

Stagecoach, this crazy country music festival that literally every single one of our friends goes to, rolled around and we got into one of our first big fights. The second day we were there, I noticed Tanner was drinking Jameson which was a "hell yes" for me drinking and an "absolutely NO" for him drinking unless it was a one and done situation. Tanner is a tequila guy and Jameson just really fucks him up.

So when I saw him touting around the bottle I warned him he was going to get fucked up. As soon as we walked into the concert he could barely even stand, and propping up someone who is 6'3" and potentially going to puke on you is not great. I brought him to the food stand and got him some water, but I really needed to pee. We walked to the bathrooms and had to split ways for the women's and men's but before I relayed a message.

"Listen to me, Tanner. This orange trash can. Meet here as soon as you're done. Ok?"

"Yep, I got it," he slurred.

Spoiler alert: *he didn't got it.*

I walked out and waited. Ten minutes. Twenty minutes. I asked people in the bathroom if he was in there, he wasn't. *Jesus, Tanner.* I tried calling him and he didn't answer. Fuck this, I was going to find one of my friends or the group at least. I was about to miss one of the sets I came to see, too. I texted one of my friends to meet at the beer tent nearby and he said he would. As soon as I did, Tanner started calling me. I answered it and he was belligerent and inaudible.

"Tanner, I can't hear you or understand you, text me where you are."

But he kept calling. So I started rejecting his calls. Now I was irritated. *Why the fuck did I have to deal with this shit?* I ended up pocketing my phone and chugging my beer with my friend before I said I should go back to my group and find him. We made way for our group and thankfully

Tanner was with them, but he was shirtless, could barely stand, and his bros were propping him up while he tried to dance to the music in his cowboy boots. His whole family was now in our crew and his mom was furious at him and trying to tell him to pull his shit together. Even then, in that moment when I was so irritated at him, he still made me smile.

Big idiot.

He saw me and immediately stumbled over to me.

"Babe! I lost you! But y-you were ignoring my calls."

"No I wasn't! I couldn't understand you," I lied, partially.

"Y-yes you were. That was b-bad. Mean." And he pointed at me serious and then started smiling. "But I still love you. So much. So, so much baby."

"I know, babe. I love you too."

Getting him home was a mess in itself too, and I was frustrated that I wandered around for nearly two hours by myself while he kept trying to call me while inaudible and drunk and was trying to blame me for it.

So the next morning when he woke up I told him I wasn't mad, I was just—*ugh, I don't know.* Frustrated? Disappointed? Annoyed? We had talked about how we had to cut back on drinking so much and getting so fucked up and yesterday was like everything the opposite of that. I understood wanting to let loose at Stagecoach, but not at the expense of me having a fun time and being alone. Him barely being able to stand or talk wasn't cute or fun, it was just a hassle. I wanted to have fun too. So I told him to just reign it in and don't drink Jameson today. We could talk about it more when we got home after the weekend was over.

He said he was embarrassed and thought everyone was mad at him. I told him they were just annoyed and I was going to go out to the pool and he should come out to. He came out and announced his apology to everyone and everyone forgave him. And his mom told him the real apology he owed was to me and he told her I was the first person he apologized to. We still had one more day and night of Stagecoach to go though, so he said his apologies and it was time for Day Three shenanigans. It ended up being my favorite day because: A. Tanner wasn't blacked out, but also B. The music and the vibes, because everything was just so laid-back and fun. Tanner and I danced to some of our favorite songs and he kissed me on all the lyrics that reminded him of me.

But even heading back driving with my sister, I could just feel this pit in my stomach that Tanner and I maybe weren't meant to be. Probably because she kept saying that to me and my mom wasn't sure about him working at a bar. They really were getting into my head about it, but there were other red flags. At this point my sister and I were butting heads so badly about it I knew I needed some space with her or we might ruin our friendship with one another. I decided in late June I was moving out to a beach bungalow in Laguna Beach.

I started looking secretly and found a place I really liked just before boarding my flight to Las Vegas to meet up with Tanner for the annual volleyball tournament he was coaching his usual team in. I showed up to the hotel room and he was sleeping, and so was his fellow coaching friend Brick. But Brick's girlfriend was also awake so we decided to go down and get bottomless mimosas while they slept. Since the guys had to coach anyway, we headed down to the pool next and took Jell-O shots. We were pretty fucked up when the guys got done coaching so we rallied and got ready to go out with them. But I knew I mixed way too many things and was going to be feeling it tomorrow.

I woke up and got a Bloody Mary to go and went to Tanner's last games. We came back up to the room and all decided to nap but as soon as I went to get ready to go out for the last night I was feeling mega POTS-y and knew I wouldn't make it. I felt like a piece of shit for it. They went down without me and I cried in the hotel room alone for being such a fuck up. They ended up coming back to the room since they didn't really feel like going out either which made me feel somewhat better. But it didn't change the fact that Tanner and I were in this cycle of getting fucked up and being imbeciles and all we did was fuel each other. I didn't know how to say no and neither did he because we were both always the fun ones. No wonder our birthdays were only one day apart; we were essentially the same person.

Needless to say, you know how I keep saying I need a partner who will be the designated adult? Bingo. Here was my first realization of that. I need them to be the one to tell me, eh, maybe we don't need another one. Instead of, you won't pussy! But that was so us. And it was not an easy habit to pull out of. I was a train going full steam ahead always with no one telling me to slow down. Instead, Tanner was steaming along right next to me.

We got in a big fight one night about me wanting to stay in for once and Tanner wanting to go out after I had just hosted my first event for my company and why didn't he get that? He said he was sorry and asked why couldn't I just tell him that, and I told him I wanted him to recognize it without me having to say it. I argued that maybe I just wanted to stay in and him just have sex with me and please me for once since I had a long ass day at work.

"It's always about sex with you."

"No it's not! That's not even what I'm saying. You're not listening to anything I'm saying. Fuck! I don't know if I can do this anymore."

"You're going to break up with me because I won't go down on you. Wow."

"That's not what I'm saying at all, but yeah that does piss me off. I'm just saying you work at a bar and I worked my ass off today and for once I don't want to go out and get drunk. Like I'm working hard to become something and you're just—"

I stopped before I could say anymore but I had already said too much.

"Oh so that's how you feel? Damn, ok. Let's just go home. We can talk about this in the morning or I can get you an Uber home if you want."

This same fight happened every month, like clockwork. I started realizing this fight always landed on the week I had my period. And honestly, wasn't I being kind of judgmental to Tanner? He loved what he did. I used to not care that he was a bartender, so why did I care now? I realized he didn't have the same motivation as me in his career and it bugged me. I really had nothing against him being a bartender or managing the bar. It was just his lack of drive doing it that I didn't understand. But I loved how he loved me—shouldn't that be enough?

I also realized at this time that I started taking out all my life frustrations on him. I wasn't in sports anymore and felt like I was losing myself and who I was as a person. Without my career in sports, I felt like I wasn't good enough anymore. I didn't feel like Court Does Sports at all. I decided to start seeing a therapist to talk everything over. I even started reading a book about how to embrace my feminine side with my partner and not take out things on them or cling to them over it all. And everything helped, but it was simply putting Band-Aids on things that couldn't be fixed. I finally decided I needed to write again in order to function as my truest self. So, I started writing my first novel, which brought back the motivation I needed, but wasn't exactly fixing anything between Tanner and me.

Throughout our relationship, Tanner often sent me songs that made him think of me randomly throughout the day and I loved them. Always country and always sappy.

One time we ended up going to a Chase Rice concert the same night and didn't realize it, because I was going for a birthday and he was going with friends. The girl's birthday I was going for was being all crazy since she just got dumped and said no boyfriends could go to the concert with us. So when she found out Tanner was going, she wouldn't even tell me where our seats were so he wouldn't know. Joke was on her though because our seats ended up being three rows apart. We stayed in our separate rows to appease her, but when the song "Eyes on You" came on, one of our songs, I turned around to look at him and to my surprise he was walking into our row.

"Sorry, but I gotta be with my girl on this one," he said, coming up behind me wrapping his arms around me and tipping my cowboy hat as he leaned in to kiss my cheek.

My friend tried to hide her annoyance when our group started aww-ing.

Tanner was always like that though. Drawn to me. *Damn, we really did love each other.* I wanted it to be him so bad, but I was forcing a square piece into a circle hole. And it sucked.

Whenever we went to concerts together we were always swaying together in sequence, but when reality set in it wasn't the same.

As we started drifting apart, I started getting less songs texted to me and I took it personally. *Fuck, I was taking everything personally.*

I was a walking ball of emotions. Every time Tanner tried to be supportive, he would say, "I just want us to be like we used to be. I just want the old Courtney back," which would send me into a tailspin. I finally snapped at him and told him I wasn't the same Courtney and I was never going to be. I had probably broken up with Tanner three times that month and always called him crying the next day saying sorry I didn't mean it and he'd always say I know, but this isn't right Courtney.

We couldn't let each other go.

I finally told him I thought we should take a break while I went to visit my friend Melanie in Atlanta before her wedding and *it was just a break.* Then the following week we would go to West Virginia for Melanie's wedding like we had already planned. Everything would be fine.

After visiting Melanie, I started to feel myself again and really get a grasp of who I was as a person. *I was a writer.* I didn't have to work at ESPN to be considered one. It was who I was as a person and would always be, and she helped remind me of that. Beyond that, I wasn't meant to stay in California. I needed to leave. Get out. I decided I should go to grad school.

All these epiphanies made me realize things about Tanner and our relationship. It wasn't the bar that bugged me. It was the feeling of being stuck in life and being stuck in a routine and being stuck in Orange County. I never pictured my life being in Orange County and I realized, Tanner was never going to leave. Don't get me wrong, it's a great place to grow up and raise your kids, it's just not the life I see for myself.

I came back feeling better about who I was and where I was going, but still had some unanswered questions about Tanner and me. I still loved him, but maybe I wasn't *in love* with him. I didn't tell Tanner this, but I did explain to him that I was a career-driven person and not having my career was messing with me, so I still needed time to figure out who I was. He said he was there for me one-hundred percent and just wanted me to be happy again, even if it wasn't with him, but he hoped it would be.

Tanner and I decided to continue with our plans to go to West Virginia together anyways as whatever we were, and it ended up being a great trip.

We explored new bars, hit up a national park before the wedding day, and barely made it in time for the ceremony start like idiots because we were chugging drinks at the bar and didn't calculate properly how long an Uber would take in the mountains of West Virginia. Again, we both clearly need designated adults in our lives.

After the wedding we were told we were going to a bar that was essentially built into an old gas station. Needless to say, I was stoked. If you know me, you know I am the perfect amount of hick and boujee, and hole-in-the-wall, local bars are my shit. *This is the West Virginia I wanted to see.* When we go to the place, Kay's, there was a tiny door through the gas station with a big lit up sign above it. When we walked in, everyone turned and ogled at us like a scene out of a movie, but when they recognized we were with a one of Melanie's friends, a former alum about our parents' age, they were in an uproar and held up their beers.

It was unreal. People were buying us beers, singing "Country Roads," making out, and I'm pretty sure at one point there was a dog and someone got on the stage and took off their shirt. All this was going on as we were all packed in together tighter than freaking sardines in a can. It was so West-Virginia-good-time I can't even begin to tell you.

The next morning, I was thanking my lucky stars that I bought a giant Michelada can on our drive in because man were we hungover. We rallied and I threw on a West Virginia tie-dyed shirt Melanie was letting me borrow with my raccoon hat and headed down to our giant tailgate right in the parking lot of our hotel.

God, Melanie and her husband did it right.

As usual, Tanner and I made ourselves at home, making friends left and right. I stuffed my jean shorts with beers and Tanner took shots with the guys. I even helped Melanie cut her long overalls into cut-off overalls when she decided it was too damn hot for them. She was rocking the bridal raccoon hat I made for her for the tailgate, too. We walked into the stadium with beers in our hands, plus one in my back pocket, no questions asked. I turned to look at Tanner.

"Can you believe this?" I held up my beer so stoked.

Just then a guy working the gate asked me if I could "kindly chug my beer."

"Yes, sir, I absolutely can. And I tipped my can back and chugged it until it was empty and handed it back to him.

I ran over to Tanner, grabbed his hand and showed him a big toothy grin. "I love it here!"

If I was already loving it then, imagine how I felt when we got to our section. Our group ruled the section and every time we scored we would toss Melanie's sister into the air for however many points we scored. Tanner and the boys kept coming back with IPAs for our group because we all needed to hydrate with something since it was so bloody hot.

We won the game and all sang "Country Roads" together, swaying with our sweaty arms interlocked, and I made sure my raccoon hat was on and proud. Tanner said he would never be caught dead in one, but by the end of the day when we went to the hotel bar to have a drink, I tossed it on his head and he didn't even fight it. Instead, he rocked it.

We went up to our rooms and decided to order room service and just pass out. Naturally I wanted to have sex, and Tanner was down too, but we just didn't feel like us. It felt fake. *It was fake.* As soon as Tanner came, I thought, maybe, just once he'd want to make sure I got off, but he rolled over. I knew. And I think he did too. I rolled over and let my tears roll across my nose and face like they had months ago.

Tanner and I really were just friends.

The next day we made way to Pittsburgh, where we had flown into originally, and checked into our new hotel just for Sunday night. We went down to the hotel bar before we decided on our plans and I ordered a Bloody Mary while Tanner just leaned his head on my shoulder while he watched a Fortnite video.

I overheard the person next to me talking fantasy football and started listening in. He was asking the guy next to him a certain player's name but couldn't think of it so I chimed in.

"Oh shit, dude. You just got schooled by a girl."

"Yeah, well she knows her shit, let me tell you," Tanner chimed in clicking his phone off and joining the conversation.

We ended up making friends with these guys who were going to go to the game, but decided to party around the stadium instead. They were going to take a ferry across the harbor and asked us to come, saying they'd show us a locals day.

Tanner and I looked to each other and basically simultaneously said "hell yeah." Like I said, two steam trains, baby.

We explored all around Pittsburgh, partied outside the stadium, and made a bunch of friends. I even rode a mechanical bull at one bar and am pretty sure we danced on a table.

We left feeling so satisfied with the trip, but didn't say anything about what we were. I think it was just known, and maybe that was ok. As soon as we got back, I tried not to hit up Tanner, especially not to drunkenly have sex or anything, because it would complicate things. At first, it was hard for us, since it was like losing your best friend. Finally, we both decided we should probably take a break from talking to each other every day.

Thankfully when we stopped talking it was right before I had a big party bus day for DeeDee's game. DeeDee, aka my basically little brother was playing in the NFL and had an away game in LA. So naturally, my family, DeeDee's family and friends had planned to go watch him with all our friends and family on a party bus. Ironically, this felt like things coming full circle, since a year earlier we were going to another game for DeeDee when things initially started between Tanner and I.

Everything was fine and hunky-dory until I opened my Instagram to see a photo of Tanner out with his big group of friends. The friends we used to go out with. It hurt. Not that it should, but it just did. *I missed him. I missed us.* But there wasn't an us anymore. I teared up at the game, but decided to suck it up and move on. At this point in the game, I had already stubbed my toe through my sneakers courtesy of their decorative spikes and had felt my toenail lift. Not great. On top of that, since I was limping, I rolled my ankle leaving the stadium.

Like I said, I'm clearly not the designated adult.

The next day I had a message from a guy from college I hadn't spoken to in a couple years asking about my ankle, since I had posted a photo of the swollen monstrosity on my story. I ignored it and went back to watching Tanner's story, but then he texted me again asking about it.

Rob Bridger. Wow, TBT. He was kind of a nerd, but always so nice and adorable. *Eh, why not.* I responded. And damn did he pick the right time to text me, right when I was fresh off a breakup. But isn't that how boys always do it? I swear they have radar for it or something.

Fast forward a month, and Rob was keeping my mind off of Tanner. I decided to have a Halloween party at my house since I hadn't even had a welcome party yet. And yes, of course, I would invite Tanner even if we weren't really talking and I was keeping my mind preoccupied elsewhere. It's not like I was physically hooking up with anyone else.

Everyone started showing up to the party and I couldn't help but keep looking to the door to see if it was Tanner. Finally he showed up with some friends and I nearly held my breath when he walked in. Sure, I was having fun talking to Rob, but I still had feelings I couldn't ignore for Tanner even if I knew I didn't want to be with him.

So what did these nerves lead to? Shots. Lots of them. And beers. And White Claws.

Thankfully I was surrounded by all my best friends. From my new Laguna Beach bungalow, we walked down to the Dirty Bird, a notoriously fun bar that's always jam-packed. It's really a "blackout bar" per say, because half of us never remember the night by the time you end up there. Per it's notorious ways, I woke up with not much recollection of getting home, thankfully only walking distance away and I came back with some friends who slept over as well in my bed and on the couch. I woke up with some texts from Rob, but texted Tanner to say I'm glad he came and it was good to see him.

He replied something like, "Yeah, whatever" or something totally unbecoming of him.

Uh oh. My missing memories. *Something for sure must've happened.*

"What's with the 'tude?" I bravely texted back.

"Dude, you invited me to your party saying you wanted to see me and as soon as we got to the bar you hit the dance floor and started dancing and making out with this older black guy right in front of me."

"What! I wouldn't do that to you!" I replied immediately and then called him.

Tanner told me everything kind of laughing despite being irritated, since we were best friends and the night was a shitshow for everyone.

"Dude everyone was trashed and making out with everyone. I think I'm the only person who didn't. And when you were making out with some old black dude on the dance floor, I wanted to leave, but all my bros were making out with chicks too. It was wild. Crazy night."

"Well, I'm sorry I did that. I'm sure it wasn't intentional."

"It's fine. I'm not mad. I was just confused, but I'm over it now."

The next couple months went by and eventually we started talking again and decided we should meet up one night in December. I had finally realized what I wanted and I was going to apply to grad school and leave California for good. I was finally feeling like me again. I was going for my dreams and I didn't feel stuck. But when I invited him over to talk he said he wanted to start.

"I just want to say I'm glad you asked me to come over because, well, I've always known it was you. You're the one. And, Court, it's always going to be y—"

I cut him off before he went any further.

"Tanner, that's not why I wanted to talk actually. I should've been more clear. I wanted you to come over so I could tell you huge news I haven't told a lot of people yet."

I went on to tell him I was going back to school and the schools I was applying to and exactly what I told my mom when she started crying asking why I was applying so far away from her.

"I told her: Mom, I see myself in ten years, with a family of my own and a couple kids and a house with a bunch of land and animals where the dogs run loose and my husband will be teaching our kids how to hunt and fish. And when they get a good kill they're going to bring it home to me and I'm going to help them cook it up. Now, can you honestly tell me you see that for me in California?"

Tanner started laughing and smiled a little uneasily.

"You know what Court, I'm just so proud of you. What makes me even more happy is seeing you here happy. You seem so much more like yourself again."

"Thanks. I feel more like myself again now that I'm back on track with figuring out what I want to do."

"So, I guess that means we're not gonna fuck then?" he asked, laughing.

"Who said that?" I said with a smirk and we instantly jumped on each other.

"Not in the front room!" I squealed as he pulled me on to him. "People can see us! Plus the Ring doorbell! My mom will get notified."

I ran into the other room, and Tanner chased after me, flipping me around and pulling down my pants. We started having sex right then and there. We poured a glass of wine after and cheers-ed it before heading back into the front room to watch whatever football game was on. After laying and snuggling together we tried to go at it again, but I fell off the couch and when Tanner tried to catch me from falling, he started to slip himself.

Next thing I knew, the glass started to slip off the table and, just like in a movie, it felt like slow motion. It slipped off the edges of rod iron holding it up and landed wedged between the carpet and fireplace, but it didn't break.

We both looked at each other relieved and immediately burst into laughter. But the joke was on us, because as soon as we laughed the glass shattered into pieces landing all on the ground.

"Oh, shit."

"Fuck."

We looked to each other with both our mouths open, but then immediately started laughing. *Steam trains need designated adults.*

"Damn it, Tanner."

"Oh c'mon. That's not only on me."

"You're going to pay for a new one."

"Ok, fine."

"Now I'm going to have to Google this," I said. "What do I even search?"

Honestly, it's pretty damn fitting that this is how Tanner and my last serious relationship talk went down. Getting drunk, watching football, hooking up around the house, and breaking my parents' glass table. Oh, and then me blaming it on Boone bumping the table. *Sorry, Boone! You'll be exonerated shortly as soon as your Mimi reads this page. Woops!*

Anyways, Tanner and I are still friends. How could we not be? I made it clear I wanted him in my life and he wanted me to still be in his. We said fuck the rules about not being friends with your ex. Occasionally we will get horny and send each other a sexy snap. I mean, c'mon! Who doesn't? Or he'll send me an old sex video of us he still has on his phone that he said was too good to delete. By the way—he wasn't wrong. It was too good to delete. Or maybe I show up to his bar the first visit I get home from Boston and get a little too drunk with the girls and tell him I think I still love him. The best part of that accident was that he knew exactly what I meant. He looked at me and said, "Court, you know I love you too. I'm always going to love you and care about you. We're still best friends."

See? He gets it even when I'm not sure I get it.

And you know, maybe occasionally I come home and go to his bar to have a burger and a beer just because I do miss him and want to see him. Even if he did bleach his damn hair for fun. Honestly, he actually pulls it off.

Ironically, the other night I watched an episode of *The Vampire Diaries* (shocking, I know) and it was the episode where Elena had just broken up with Damon because they weren't good together. She wanted to be friends with Damon, but he was like—uh, yeah—fuck that.

Elena asked his brother Stefan if he ever thought that Damon and her could be friends like how she and Stefan are, and Stefan's response was so perfect and so fitting for how Tanner and I are.

"I don't think you can be best friends with someone and in love with them. You can only be one or the other. So, no. I don't think Damon and you will ever be like us because we're best friends."

Should Tanner and I cool it on sexting each other? Maybe. Should I stop getting wasted at his bar? Perhaps. Should I stop looking up photos of us when I hear "Eyes on You"? Probably. But I honestly think those things will start changing with time and as we're both getting older. I won't say maturing, because, who knows if that'll ever happen. *Do steam trains mature?*

And, hey, if we're both still single and just messing around on the phone with each other occasionally when we're bored and lonely—no harm, no foul, right? Like I said, we'll probably grow out of that eventually or stop once one of us gets hitched up. That's just the kind of people we are.

Listen, all I know is this: Tanner taught me how a woman should be treated and how she should feel in a relationship. There were things he didn't give me that I want in a relationship, but he's still an amazing person. And at the end of the day, we are so alike it's insane. There's a reason to this day every one of my friends says they loved Tanner. Hell, I still love Tanner! Tanner and I sure as shit make a hell of a team together and are the life of the party. But we're not the match for each other. *That match. The one.*

But the girl who does get to be his match, that one, will be one hell of a lucky girl. And, honestly, I might even be invited to that wedding.

We'll see.

15

Rob

Is saving the best for last still a thing? Hah, well best in what regard, I guess.

Rob.

I really put off writing this chapter because for some reason it's the most confusing one. I never dated Rob. I never was even interested in Rob when we first met and knew each other from college. He wasn't in a frat, and I was very clearly a Beta Beta Beta girl. It's not that being a GDI (aka God Damn Independent) was bad or anything, I was just into the douchey California guys in Beta Beta Beta with the exception of some frat-hard Pike guys aka the guys who spent most of their time chugging pre-workout and vodka.

Still, that's not how Rob and I met. As you know, I worked for the football team as the assistant video coordinator for my four years at SMU and Rob played for the team. In my second year, I was on the field filming the offensive line like I always did, when he came up to talk to me.

Admittingly, I don't remember this story to the T, but he does. He said I was wearing a Kappa T-shirt and jean shorts and vans with white high socks. His conversation starter?

"So you're a Kappa? That's cool."

He said I didn't take my face away from behind the camera and I just made the noise "mhmm."

This is not out of the ordinary as I didn't like talking to any of the guys on the field while I was working for obvious reasons. I was there for a job, not to be some piece of eye candy for them.

Still, Rob and I became friends and would have more conversations, but if I'm being honest, in college I didn't really notice him. Apparently my type is guys who used to have crushes on me that I didn't give a chance to. Seems to be a reoccurring theme here I'm just now realizing. *That's weird, right? Why is that?* Maybe I finally want something real and not a fuck boy? But can I go from being a fuck girl to wanting feelings reflected back after so many years of wanting someone who doesn't want you back? *Huh... I don't know.* But clearly, I'm trying... or changing... or—dare I say it—could this be growing up?

Anyways, Rob hit me up via texts a year or so after college and we started talking briefly but nothing monumental. We would like each other's pictures on Instagram, I had new boyfriends and he had a girlfriend of what seemed to be a couple years. You know the drill. But one random night late he texted me "Go to sleep already."

Odd, to say the least, but whatever. I just figured he was drunk. But then again, why text me? Didn't he still have a girlfriend?

After some digging, which we will get to, it turns out he did at that time and she was out of town that weekend for a bachelorette weekend.

About six months after his unexpected text, my boyfriend Tanner and I had broken up, and I was on a party bus to LA with friends and family to watch DeeDee, now a wide receiver for a new team, play an away game against the Rams. We blasted "All I Do is Win" and obligatory game day songs on the way up while handing around a fifth of Fireball while ripping shots.

I was wearing leopard bike shorts, a "Dee Freaking Dee" red tee, a red

Gucci belt, and gold studded sneakers. You might remember this is the game where I would then stub my toe through my spiked sneakers and roll my ankle.

Naturally, my ankle was swollen three sheets to the wind and the toenail was already purpling underneath my pink polish, with blood seeping from underneath it. I posted a photo of my ankle to my story and said "game day aftermath," or something like that, thankfully my polish covering anything too gruesome.

Some direct messages off the photo came in, but one name stood out: Rob.

"Damn! That looks like it hurt," he said or some variation of that but I didn't open it because I didn't really care that much.

The next day I got an actual text message from him though.

"Hey Courtney, it's Rob Bridger! I wanted to text you and check in on your ankle! That looked like it hurt but you guys had a good time!"

I remember laughing when I saw the message because of the way he started it, as if I didn't know who he was. I thought to myself, I am single now... And bored... And he was always cute... *Eh, fuck it.* I replied.

And the rest was history. We started texting and everything started flowing. Like so naturally.

At this point I was now living in California working as a social media manager for local businesses and I remember we were texting so furiously it was hard for me to get any work done. We'd finish each other's sentences, talk about our dreams, what's next even. It was honestly a little weird how fast we clicked into place. And yes, I was fresh out of a breakup and having someone talk to me the way he did was so exciting and new.

He had just graduated from Duke's MBA program and was about to move from Durham, NC to New York City. He would text me how much he wanted to show me Cameron Indoor stadium and watch a Duke basketball game, how much he wanted to show me New York City, take me to my first ball, since I said I had never been to one. He reminisced on the first time he saw me and how he remembered our first conversation perfectly. He even brought up one conversation I didn't even remember occurring at Milo's the night of a date dash my senior year that I went with Bradley to. He said he said hi but I ran past him crying to get a cab. To this day he always wondered if he had said something wrong to make me upset and wished it wasn't about him. *Stupid Bradley always ruining things. If only I had known.*

Still, he didn't hold back in our talking to each other. He wanted to know even more about me moving forward. Like *everything*. What were my hopes and dreams? Goals? How many kids did I want? What kind of houses did I like? Where did I see myself settling down? What did I see for my life? He wanted to know it all and I did something I likely wouldn't have done otherwise: I let him in.

I freaking let all of him in on all of it.

He even started sending me sexy snaps in the bathroom mirror just not showing everything. And I'd do the same, sending back kind of teasing photos with foggy mirrors covering everything perfectly.

It was right around Halloween and I was hosting my first housewarming party and a Halloween party at my new place in Laguna Beach, as you remember. It was a beach bungalow a couple blocks from the water with a big front yard and back yard with a small living space, but enough for me and my dog Boone. I was dressing as a fortune teller and doing epic makeup, which I had already practiced once before and sent Rob pictures of.

We were still talking back-to-back about anything and everything from football to traveling to our parents to our siblings. We even talked about a random funny story of how one time I got mistaken as a porn star "Misty" at a porn convention by a Terry Crews look-alike in Vegas. Later, Ron Jeremy bought my sister and I a drink when we were like eighteen years old in Vegas. It really is a wild story. Anyways, I told Rob this story and he immediately told me my name was being changed to Misty in his phone. I laughed and asked him if he'd seen any of my work, which he probably had, to let me know, but he disliked the comment. Said he didn't watch porn really. Instantly that made me surprised, but then again, he was kind of nerdy so maybe not.

The more we talked I started getting a sense maybe it was more than that. He grew up Southern Baptist, which to my knowledge was as strict as it gets. So I started having some lingering questions. If you're catching my drift, I was starting to think he might be a virgin. Sure, he had sent me a dick pic, but there was this weird feeling I was getting that he might be one and I needed confirmation.

So I asked around, starting with my friend Bobby at my Halloween party and confirmed my suspicions weren't entirely wrong.

"Hey I have a random question for you—did you know a guy from SMU named Rob Bridger? He was on the football team but he was in your year."

"Oh you mean the virgin guy?" Bobby laughed.

Shut up. He did not just say that.

He went on to elaborate that he didn't know if he was still a virgin, but freshman year Bobby was dating a girl named Grace, and Grace's best friend was dating Rob so they would double date. Grace had said her best friend and Rob were both dating each other because they were both virgins or something like that. Thankfully, this conversation happened early in the night, because you already know it goes from here to the Dirty Bird courtesy of the Tanner chapter.

Just so you know, this series of weeks was literally jam-packed in true Schellin fashion. I hosted the Halloween party and then two days later we were off to the airport to see the Houston Astros in the World Series. Our best family friend was one of the coaches, so we were definitely going to go and support!

We were flying out for the games in Houston and Rob and I kept up talking incessantly. I decided I wanted to see more of him though and decided we should FaceTime. And why not make it a memorable one and facetime him at the game? It would be loud and I could just show him the scene and not talk much. He answered and the conversation was brief, but basically have fun and crush some beers for me. Which I most certainly did.

We continued texting, which to my dismay led to drunk texting on my end, where I called him "babay" too many times and said in all caps, "WHEN ARE PLANNING A TRIP YO."

We kept up our texting and then he started sending me some snaps.

But I felt like they may have been sexy because of how the conversation was progressing.

Walking on the plane at 5:00 a.m. with my gay best friend Alec, I filled him in on all the deets and how this was likely going to be a dick pic. So naturally he was in on watching. We opened the pic and sure enough it was but it wasn't your normal dick pic per say. Not that I've received a lot, since Tanner opened that door for me, but it seemed kind of amateur. *Not his penis! The photo.* The dick was actually great, Alec and I both agreed, but the photo made us kind of tilt our heads like huh? It was like a faraway selfie style photo, no face, in the shower, and his dick was hard. Again, not complaining but it further made me question and discuss with Alec the likelihood he might be a virgin. Regardless, not enough to deter me. Since I knew he was kind of nerdy in college so whatever if he wasn't as experienced? Right?

We landed in LAX and I got home just in time to hand out candy at my new place in Laguna Beach, because I found out our street, Catalina, would be a shitshow full of kids and adults. Like people drove in from various places in the state to come to Catalina Street. Needless to say, I didn't want to miss it and so I called in backup and had Kassidy come down in costume to help me hand out candy and drink wine with me in the front yard with my neighbors.

I dressed as a dead cheerleader—think Megan Fox in *Jennifer's Body*, white contacts and all. Kassidy dressed as a pineapple aka a "fine-apple" as we called her despite the oversized yellow rotund suit. She got there and I told her about Rob and how things were progressing and she urged me to FaceTime him, so I did. He was at a pregame dressed up as Scooby-Doo. I could barely hear him but I said "What do you think of the costume?" showing him the cheerleader look with blood down my face and my contacts in, and he smiled tipsily and said, "You look beautiful." Which threw me off big time since he was at a pregame and I had fake blood down my face. But I smiled and laughed and said he looked good too and we'd talk later.

Beautiful. Is it just me or does that word not get used very often?

But clearly at this point I was hanging on every word whether I knew it or not.

A few days later I got up to drive to work and witnessed a gnarly car accident in Laguna Canyon. The car slammed into a tree in the center divider and I immediately pulled over and ran out to help. To my shock, no one else was pulling over except for one other car. There was a small dog that was ejected from the car and running in the street scared so I ran over and picked him up and calmed him and then headed back for the car. Running over to the car, I saw the worst thing I could have seen. Kids.

There was a girl who looked to be a teenager in the back seat and she was hanging out over the mangled door unconscious, but she looked more than unconscious. Her face was smashed in and I saw her small red converse on her feet. There was a younger blonde girl in the front and the front of the car was squished down onto her like a blanket and she was screaming. I instantly felt like I didn't belong. *How could I help?* I didn't know what I could touch without doing more damage. I just said "It's going to be ok," as a nurse ran up and yelled "I'm a nurse!" *Thank God.* I was frozen. I watched the nurse go immediately up to the girl in the back and check her wrist for vitals and she immediately went to the front to check on the little girl screaming. I knew that wasn't good.

More people had gathered and someone had called 911. I could hear the sirens and I just continued petting the dog's head that was panting in my arms. The man in the front seat was now yelling asking about the girl in the back, and no one was saying anything. I wanted to go up and hold her hand, but I was too scared. The nurse finally ran back there to the girl again and said that she was alright. She was going to be alright. I wanted to believe her so badly.

I gave the dog to animal services who had gotten ahold of the family and told them the dog needed comfort. The cops also asked me what I had seen and then I headed to work. But that night I couldn't stop thinking about it. Especially when I drove past the scene in the canyon and it looked like nothing had happened, despite some messed up dirt in the center divider by the tree. I told my neighbor about what had happened since she was a nurse and maybe she had gotten an update. She hadn't.

The next day I walked out and the paper next to my car revealed the worst. The teenager in the converse had died. I felt helpless. And I felt like I should've done more. I should've went up to her. I shouldn't have been scared of her. It sounds weird, but I felt guilty.

That night my neighbor Lynn invited me over when she heard me crying and we sat on her deck and talked about what had happened. She had heard some updates at the hospital and explained seeing something like that never gets easier. Apparently the man driving them to school was a family friend doing a favor by driving the kids to school and he had a heart attack while driving them that morning. It was horrible.

Lynn and I were both crying and she handed me a glass with water in it.

"Drink this, it will help."

I took a sip only to feel an intense burn in the back of my throat and I swallowed painfully looking at her through tears.

"It's tequila," she said.

"Oh," I said the words barely coming out.

I thanked Lynn for her help and the tequila and started texting Rob. Finally, I just called him and cried. He listened and even calmed me down and explained that she probably was dead on scene and there really wasn't anything I could've done. Even if I had gone up and held her hand and talked to her, she probably would not have heard me since she was probably brain-dead. Rob talked to me in medical lingo too since his dad was a doctor.

The next morning I was embarrassed I called him crying and blamed it on the tequila courtesy of my neighbor, but he told me not to worry about it and he was happy to talk me through it. I told him I really didn't cry in front of a lot of people or do that kind of thing though and he said it was fine. But I knew, I was letting him in *deeper and deeper*.

One day when we were talking, he told me about how cute he thought I was in college but was too shy to ask me out.

"Well, I wish you had."

He said we could make up for it now, now that he had become a much more confident man and not a boy. We started talking about how talking to each other was making us feel. And that I hadn't felt this excited and tingly about someone in a while. He said "Same." And we both laughed and made nerdy jokes about *Star Wars* and *Transformers* which somehow led to wanting to see each other in *that* way. Like what kind of people bring up robots and *Star Wars* mid-sexting? Me apparently.

He wanted me to send a photo. I said I really didn't do that, because at this point in my life, I really didn't! He said I didn't have to. But still, I got up and took a selfie in the mirror in a sweatshirt and a Calvin Klein thong. Surely, this wasn't breaking any of my on-camera rules. Hell, I posted more revealing photos in swimsuits. But this was personal. I was sending it to *him*. After that one, I decided to up the ante and sent a photo with my shirt pulled up so he could see my boobs even. Like, what! I put heart emojis over my face so you couldn't tell it was me though.

Alas, my first tit pic was sent. Who knew it'd be the first of many in my lifetime...

This led to a flurry of dick pics from him. After that, coming to visit started getting brought up again. I told him I'd look up some fun concerts and saw Luke Combs was playing. He responded with heart eyes emojis. I started telling my friends about what was going on but promised I wouldn't get my hopes up. Watching football one Sunday, Rob and I kept snapping back and forth and apparently he was dying of some sickness, but was loving our fun snaps. He finally said, "Damn, I need to be in Laguna."

At this point I decided, fuck it. I'm going to pick a damn date. I responded and said "I'm just tryna get to Nashville." And I sent the Ticketmaster link for the Luke Combs concert I had mentioned before. I dropped an eyeball emoji after the link. A few minutes went by and he hadn't responded which was already weird. The kid was non-stop on his phone when we were texting. Hours went by and I opened it to now see his read receipt reflecting back to me as "Read." *What the hell?* The next day I decided maybe I freaked him out, even though he's the one who kept saying to visit. Maybe a concrete date was too forward? So I decided to make lightly of it and joke around.

"Not a Luke Combs guy, that's cool." I sent with a laughing emoji face.

Minutes later: "Read."

What the actual! Maybe he thought the link was me asking him to pay for the tickets? *Shit*. So I explained.

"I wasn't saying for you to buy the tickets, you know. I'll pay for my own and my flight and hotel and everything I just thought it might be fun!"

And nothing. Again.

The worst part? I could see he had now turned off his read receipts to me too.

At this point I was baffled and just plain hurt. But mainly confused. I had really allowed him to get to me and let his way inside and now I felt disgusting and empty and used. But I knew he meant all the things he said. *Right?* The stories he had said were all spot on and not made up. So what the fuck happened? Plain and simple: I got my hopes up. Really far up.

I decided not to let myself be consumed by it entirely if I could manage, and cried for a couple days before I all the sudden got deathly sick. Like knock-out flu kind of sick. I went into urgent care to get some help and they came out, asked my symptoms, and then came back with multiple nurses and asked me to go to a back room. They apologized for wearing masks and said they weren't trying to be rude and that there was a "strange Chinese virus" that was going around and they wanted to make sure it wasn't what I had. Had I been to China? No. Other questions like this.

I spent the next few days dying in bed or my couch where my family quarantined me before quarantining was cool. I ended up tweaking my neck during this lovely spell of sickness and had to get a steroid shot just so I could move it back to normal, which I then caved and texted Rob one more time just telling him I was sick now too and hopped up on painkillers and now got a steroid shot in my neck since I tweaked it.

No response.

My final text I sent dealt with him and the coaching job he almost took with University of Arkansas's football team before he decided to go to grad school. The Arkansas's football team was struggle city under the former SMU coach and announced soon he was getting fired. I sent him a screenshot and said something like, "Good thing you didn't take the Arkansas job after all!"

Still, no text back.

WHY? Seriously. What had changed? New girlfriend? Like why ghost me entirely.

But still, I wouldn't give him the satisfaction of another text. I was heartbroken and, admittingly, naively so, because I had let him so easily and quickly in, but regardless, it didn't change the pain I was feeling. A month had gone by and we hadn't spoken at all when Rob posted a throwback photo. I noticed the photo is flooded with girls comments, many from SMU I knew. And one girl even comments "Wait, we all know Rob?!" so I decided to play a game on the post. I liked the girl's comment, and apparently so had a couple other girls. *The little shit. Could we all really be being played by the virgin nerd?* I was so mad. Like, I had managed to not get played by the biggest of the players and then this fucking guy comes along and plays me? C'mon man. Where's ESPN's Chris Berman when you need him? I decided I was going to comment on the photo but only if Grant would like my comment too. Of course, in true bestie fashion, he said he would. "Looks like the shy guy from filming days." As soon as I comment it, Grant likes it. And you know what, Rob does? He likes that damn comment of mine.

Ok. SO YOU CAN'T TEXT ME OR TALK TO ME BUT YOU CAN LIKE MY COMMENT? I was livid. *You roped me in into your mind games for God knows what reason and then just stop talking to me for no reason or no explanation given?* At this point I knew I had to move on and got back on dating apps.

But rumors started going around about this new virus the nurses had told me about at urgent care, and it looked like New York was getting hit pretty bad aka where Rob would be moving soon. But whatever, fuck him. Why should I care? Even though I still watched his stupid name pop up on my story every time I posted and he even had the nerve to like all my damn photos.

I'd still see Rob's stupid stories and him watching mine all the time which was annoying but one day something weird stood out on Instagram. His name popped up he had liked a photo posted by a wedding ring designer. Like my favorite wedding ring designer because they are vintage inspired. And it wasn't just one photo liked it was multiple. And he followed her. *How weird is that?*

Still, I stayed strong and didn't text him no matter how many weird coincidences would happen. But by February, Rob started sending me memes on Instagram. Like stupid memes. About margarita machines in showers and shit. Like what the fuck. I didn't respond. Well, not yet anyways. I wouldn't cave and text him until March, when quarantine officially began and COVID was officially something people we're worrying about. I was bored and ended up texting him saying that when he was super sick in November it was probably COVID.

"Damn! Probably!" he responded *immediately*. I rolled my eyes and tossed my phone. I left it on read and then we'd play this game of texting each other and me leaving him on read for a while. Back and forth throughout quarantine. I had gotten into a rhythm bouncing between him, a fuck boy Cole, and Tanner whenever I would get bored.

Finally, mid-quarantine I told Rob we should have a FaceTime date so we can play drinking games like Never Have I Ever, etc. The only problem was, I had already had three FaceTime hangouts prior to this one playing drinking games so by the time I got on with him I was hammered. I barely remember the questions we did and think I may have whipped out a boob and my phone died right when that happened. Plus I remember bringing up the wedding ring thing too and I remember he didn't give an answer just kind of laughed. *Damn.* Why'd my uncle have to pop in on my cousin Sidney and my FaceTime and insist we all take whiskey shots! We all know by now I can't say no to that!

From this point on we continued our texting for a couple days, then stop texting for a couple weeks trend, which was fine because I was distracted with plenty of fuck boys at this point via Snapchat thanks to quarantine.

I had tried to keep swearing off Rob, but sure enough by the end of summer and at my going away party, I was hosting a clambake and my mom and I were freaking out since we had never hosted one before. So, I caved and texted him about the clambake and said tell me all your knowledge since, as a southern boy, he was bound to have it all. And he did. He texted me ingredients, secret tips, good apps to make, everything. It was actually really helpful. So we started talking again just before I would hit the road with my cousin to drive across country.

By the time we got to Colorado there were two hurricanes aiming to hit his hometown at the same time and I decided in our joking text to bring some more seriousness to the situation since Rob would likely be moving to New York in the Fall.

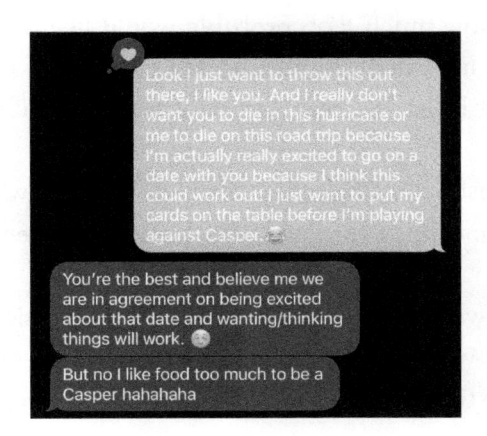

> Look I just want to throw this out there, I like you. And I really don't want you to die in this hurricane or me to die on this road trip because I'm actually really excited to go on a date with you because I think this could work out! I just want to put my cards on the table before I'm playing against Casper. 👻

> You're the best and believe me we are in agreement on being excited about that date and wanting/thinking things will work. 😊

> But no I like food too much to be a Casper hahahaha

And we kept talking and texting but even after saying we would go on a date, no real plans were ever really made. And I was always the one starting the conversations. *Why did he say these things when he didn't mean it?* One weeknight in the fall I decided to just call him. He didn't answer at first, but then he immediately called me back and we talked on the phone for three hours. THREE HOURS. I told him I didn't believe him or trust him. He said he didn't get that because he was so into me and started laughing thinking it was comical that I thought he wasn't into me. But I told him, how would I know, Rob? You don't show it? You don't tell me you are so how would I know? He said he would try and be better about it then.

He didn't though. So I stuck with the dating apps while Rob and I were forever locked in this stupid texting back and forth bullshit.

December rolled around and I was already back home from school, and I decided to do another one of my "tests" on Rob because I was getting confused again. Every person had told me my own advice back to me—*if a guy wants to make it happen, he's going to make it happen.* Like this is my golden rule in dating I tell everyone. So, if Rob wasn't texting me first, he wasn't interested.

But there kept being weird signs. I was driving to my hair appointment and the song "Saltwater Gospel" came on. I sang the lyrics and thought about how much I loved the song. But then my mind wandered and I thought about how much Rob probably would like that song. Weirdly enough, I got to my hair appointment and saw he had a new story up. I clicked it and saw he had posted it ten minutes ago and it nearly made me drop my phone.

It was screenshot of "Saltwater Gospel" playing with the caption "This Song!" I messaged him and said I was just listening to it and I loved it too.

But that was weird. My hairstylist believes in all the signs too, so when I brought it up with her she played devil's advocate saying maybe he just sucked at texting and liked me starting all the conversations since he always responded.

Alas, I came up with my test. As cringe as it made me feel, I would text Rob every single day for a week, responses or not, and the next week I wouldn't text him once. I would wait until he texted me first. So I texted him every day for a week. And he responded every day except for one. Some conversations were football, some were more serious like his family member having an abnormal cancer screening and then more serious talk about them potentially having to put down the family dog. Pretty heavy stuff toward the end of the week. So I decided to extend said test when he didn't respond to my last one and said at the beginning of the following test week, "Thinking of you, know you had a rough couple days this week."

And then I waited. And I didn't get a text for a week. Didn't get any texts for two weeks. No texts for three weeks. And I decided, you know what. Fuck you, Rob. (So I thought.) But once a fuck boy collector, always a collector, I suppose.

February came and it was NFL Playoffs and the Packers were in. I remember standing at our bar cracking a Keystone Light and my phone lit up with his name with a long-ass message. He sent me this elaborate text about what football plays and routes he thought the Packers would run and if he was right he got to call what type of shot I would take. Insert the famous Elle Woods quote—"I'm sorry I just hallucinated." WHAT? *Like, WHAT THE ACTUAL.* I don't hear from you and you send me this? The audacity! I happily opened the text and left it on read.

I stayed strong and didn't message him for a while. Like two months. But March Madness came and I was bored in Boston especially since I had not gone on any dates since Jesse, and wanted to talk basketball with someone. I texted Rob about his bracket. That was it. At least, it was supposed to be for me... Just an innocent texting about basketball.

But then he started snapping me that PBR (Professional Bull Riders) was in town. I said I loved PBR, and joked "BRB, coming down now." He replied, "PBR and chill? And then beach day after." I said yes. And he said, and I quote...

"I would die to be on a beach with you right now."

Oh no. *Nonononono.* Did my insides immediately fall back into fuck-me-up mode? Yes. But I decided to go the bitchy route.

"Don't fuck with me Rob. Because a bitch just might," I sent with a plane emoji.

He said he wasn't. I decided to call him out. Megan was sitting on my porch drinking ciders with me, soaking up the rare heat wave that was hitting Boston in March, and she decided she wanted to go to Florida. So fuck it. *Let's do it.* The things northerners do for sun, let me tell you.

"Fine, how about May twenty-first weekend?" I asked.

As soon as I pressed send I took another sip of my cider and put my camo ball cap over my face.

"Watch. The minute dates and actual plans get mentioned this guy runs," I said.

But he didn't. My phone buzzed.

"Can't that weekend I have a wedding."

"Ok fine how about first weekend in May?"

"That one works for me," he sent with the eyeball emoji.

No way. I told Megan no way he follows through, but she could already see the stupid smirk on my face.

"Don't get your hopes up, ok? You said this guy bails."

"I'm not."

Oh, I was.

I text him some more follow up questions to see if he's serious and two days go by of no response. *There's the Rob I know!* Finally he texts me back the most vague text of all time about the beach being nice and some other incredibly vague details. I called my trusty and true best guy friend Grant to get input since he knows all the ways of the Rob Bridger fuckery.

"Call him out."

"What do you mean?"

"That's the most vague fucking text ever. Like you're trying to plan a trip. Call him the fuck out."

"Ok fine, I'll draft something up and send to you to proof."

I decided on a lengthy text telling him he always does this and the minute things get real he bails. And I wasn't looking for a relationship, I was looking for a good time. It was freezing in Boston, I was down to go to the beach, but also, if I was going to go to Pensacola, the real reason I was going was because I wanted to see him.

I sent it to Grant.

"It's perfect. Send it."

A few hours went by and then my phone buzzed while I was bitching on the phone with Grant while I was walking Boone.

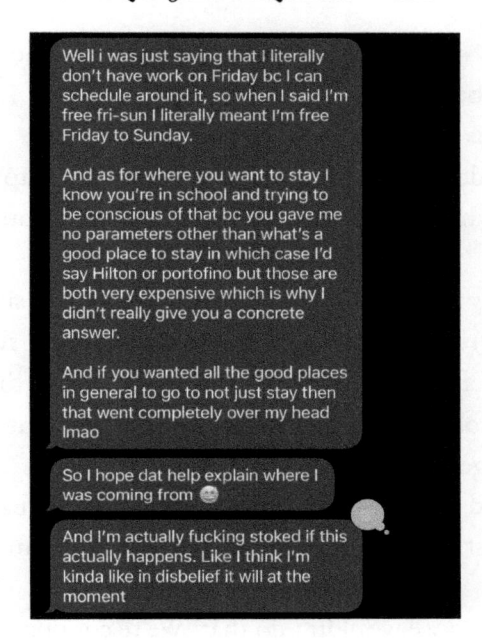

> Well i was just saying that I literally don't have work on Friday bc I can schedule around it, so when I said I'm free fri-sun I literally meant I'm free Friday to Sunday.
>
> And as for where you want to stay I know you're in school and trying to be conscious of that bc you gave me no parameters other than what's a good place to stay in which case I'd say Hilton or portofino but those are both very expensive which is why I didn't really give you a concrete answer.
>
> And if you wanted all the good places in general to go to not just stay then that went completely over my head lmao
>
> So I hope dat help explain where I was coming from 😄
>
> And I'm actually fucking stoked if this actually happens. Like I think I'm kinda like in disbelief it will at the moment

I read the text out loud to Grant on the phone while standing by the U.S.S. Constitution in Charlestown Harbor.

"Wait, did I just get called out?" I asked.

"Ask him to split the Airbnb with you."

"What! No! Why? I don't want to do that."

"No, seriously do it. It will make him more responsible about actually doing this. If he says no, you have your answer. And if he says yes, well, I think you gotta go."

Another text buzzes in.

"Oh my God, he said 'sounds good send it over to me when you want' with a smiley face! Now what? Oh God. What have I done?"

Laughing came over the other end of the phone. "No way you back out now. Just do it. Go to Pensacola."

And just like that, in the next couple days, an Airbnb was booked and the flights were booked. Megan and I were going to Pensacola, Florida.

When was the last time I had even seen Rob in person? I nearly fell over when I did the math in my head. SEVEN YEARS. *What the fuck was I doing?* Like what the actual fuck was I thinking booking this trip? Naturally I started panicking. But only behind closed doors or via FaceTime to my best friends.

The consensus was clear from the majority of them.

"Honestly, I don't like him but I think you've got to go down there and figure out what the hell this is. There's no way you'll know unless you just do it."

I would've usually had a drink on the plane but since I had been cracked out on Adderall for the end of the semester, I realized I hadn't eaten in days so, for once, I thought better on it and didn't drink. We landed in Pensacola and hit the bathroom to freshen up, except Megan took forever to get ready in the bathroom. Finally he called me and I answered and said sorry, we're about to walk out of the bathroom.

"It's fine, I just wasn't sure if you guys got an Uber and ditched me or anything!"

"What! Omg no we wouldn't do that! We're coming out now," I said, as we popped out of the bathroom, and to my surprise he was just around the corner. This was it.

He smiled when he saw us and I tried to take in who was standing in front of me. He was way taller than I remembered. But still totally cute. And his hair was short, despite some of his recent snaps showing he had longer locks.

"Hey! How was y'all's flight?" he said, still having that little twang in his voice I remembered. Just slightly.

I gave him a hug and Megan introduced herself and he took my bags from me.

We headed to his car and he drove a truck, which you'd think I would've known, but I didn't. It only added to the appeal. He helped us load everything in and we were off. I told him I got an interview for a position as a student professor at Emerson and he was so stoked for me. He even said he's proud of me, which even seemed like much for him to say to me after the times he had ghosted me in the past. We drove past what's probably the third plastic surgery sign and Megan brings it up.

"A lot of plastic surgeons here," Megan said.

"Megan's a nurse," I said.

Without a beat he jumped right into it and even went into O.R. terminology talk with her and she was visibly impressed.

"Rob's dad is a doctor."

"Well, and I kind of work in the field now too," he interjected.

He explained a little more of how he knows so much and explained what he did in finance was actually work with small and large hospitals when they want to buy each other out. So he was still connected to the medical world.

Rob decided to take us to a restaurant on the water and as we parked I realized I didn't grab my sunglasses. He without hesitation takes his off and hands them to me, after already coming around to my door to hold it open for me.

"Here you can wear mine. I'll be fine."

"Oh, it's ok."

"No seriously." I took them and it instantly reminded me of my dad, which I realize sounds weird, but my dad always gave us his sunglasses if we forget ours, despite my dad's sunglasses looking much more like something a baseball coach would wear. At least Rob's were Ray Bans and might not be that noticeable.

The place was right on the water and awesome despite the humidity. Megan and I were trying to adjust, and thankfully had changed into jean shorts and light tops. We grabbed seats at the bar while we waited for our table. Megan and Rob ordered cocktails and I ordered my usual Coors Light. Once seated, we went through the motions of normal talk until Megan got up to go to the bathroom.

"I'm seriously so excited to see you, Rob! It's been so long!" I reached across the table and gave his forearm a little squeeze.

"I know it's crazy. I really didn't think you guys would end up coming! I'm so glad you're here though."

I decided to switch the topic into how things were in Pensacola. Last time he was saying he was sick of it. How was he feeling now?

"Yeah. My plan is to be out of here in July or August and move to a bigger city just because I can with my job right now and I want to spend the rest of my twenties and early thirties somewhere new and then come back to the South to settle down later on."

"Nice. What cities do you like?"

"Well, any of the big ones really. I could go back to Nashville. Or Dallas, but probably not Dallas. I loved New York and I'd be down to go back. Chicago, Boston. Just not Atlanta. I don't like Atlanta."

After lunch, Rob drove us around Pensacola and showed us where he went to high school and I made some jokes about him making homecoming court which he laughed and said yeah right, which was odd to me since he had told me that before but I guess he was being modest now or something. We drove through some rough parts of the neighborhood too and then this song came on about exes and Rob asked if we had heard it. And naturally exes came up. We listened and I said I didn't have any crazy exes, just one I didn't like. Otherwise, I was still friends with mine. Rob laughed.

"Yeah, I'm not friends with any of my exes and I don't like any of them really" he said. "I mean there was one who was a really nice girl but the other ones were, yeah, just no."

He told us one story of his ex who accused him of flirting with a girl she didn't recognize at his going away party for grad school to move to Nashville, and he told her he didn't know what she was talking about and she threw a frying pan at his head. A frying pan!

"She had trust issues, clearly. The next day at 5 a.m., I brought a box of her things to her house and left it at her front door and that was that."

Soon we were approaching a fish market and he said that was where he would come to in a day or two to pick up fish for us to have a big cookout the last night featuring Chef Rob.

"Why don't we just do it now? Besides it looks cool!" I said.

"Seriously? Ok! We can do it now!" he said, pulling into the parking lot.

Joe Patti's aka the fish market was poppin' and was, indeed, so cool. I looked at him wide-eyed as soon as we walked in.

"Uhm! You almost had us miss this!"

He laughed and shrugged. "I didn't think you guys would be so into it!"

"Think again, bro."

Rob got a ticket and started scouting what ingredients he needed and Megan went searching for snacks and wine. I followed her, letting her pick the snacks since we knew I wasn't big on snacking anyway. I did find a sweet T-shirt to buy for my Dad, so I carried that along with me. We found a wine store at the back and Megan got to talking with the girl at the register. I saw Rob get in line and the line was moving quick, so I decided I should bail so I could go help him and so he didn't think we ditched him again. I caught him right at check out.

"Oh, there you are! I was nervous because this is gonna be a lot of food."

"Oh, yeah, we're here!" Suddenly Megan popped up with the wine too, and Rob was already paying the tab for the fish. *Wait— did he mean he wanted to split?* It was hectic so I checked out with my shirt and Megan with the wine.

"Just tell us what we owe you, Rob, and we can Venmo."

"No worries."

While waiting for our shrimp to be cooked, Megan went to the bathroom and Rob put his arm around my shoulders and squeezed me into him.

"I'm so happy you're here," he said, now smiling looking down at me.

"Me too," I said, smiling up, but looking away, fearful I might start blushing.

He kept his arm over my shoulder and asked me about school and wanted to know what I ended up writing for a story assignment I had told him about a few weeks earlier. I nearly forgot I told him about it and was shocked he even remembered but told him I wrote about a pirate and an escaped slave and a jewel they were hunting. Since he was a history nerd, I knew he would appreciate how I laid it out in historical context with real history and historical artifacts.

"I want to read it. Well, if you'll let me. I know writers are particular about that kind of stuff and who can read their work."

"You can read the pirate story," I said, choosing my words carefully. God forbid, he knew about the "dating piece" I was working on.

We left Joe Patti's only to realize now it was pouring down rain. Like torrential downpouring.

"I'll grab the car and pull it up for you girls!"

The whole parking lot was already flooded with about four inches of water. Rob ran out in the rain and pulled the truck up as close as he could to the exit we were using. We still all got soaked. And just as soon as the rain started, it stopped in true southern fashion. Since the bridge was broken from a previous hurricane, we were set to hit major traffic heading to the beach so we hit a gas station and I picked up some beer for us. From there our playlist goes from Megan's TikTok hits, including Olivia Rodrigo's "déjà vu" and a song called "Drugs," and her and Rob bonded over their unhealthy addiction to TikTok. Megan shoved her camera to the outside of my rolled down window.

"Smile, you two!"

Unable to object on short notice, I smiled but my face felt like it was all up in the camera. Rob smiled too.

"Oh my God, Megan! That photo was like so close up of my face!"

Rob butts in immediately with, "Well you know what, Courtney, it's a really pretty face."

I smiled and looked away trying not to blush.

Then somehow the music ventures to us listening to emo hits from our middle school days like Taking Back Sunday, Good Charlotte and all the likes. The traffic was horrible because of an accident too, so Rob took us on some back roads and we ended up seeing some really cool waterfront homes, an airfield where drugs used to be smuggled in, and some fish camps tucked away. I let my hand ride the wind from outside the window.

"Do people hunt around here?"

"Yep, they do. Just about anything really."

I asked him if he hunted and where he would go and he told me pretty much everything and told me some of the places he goes.

"What kind of guns do you own?" I asked.

I saw Megan in the side mirror roll her eyes at me. He listed an impressive list of artillery.

"You have an AR? That's so cool," I responded, trying not to smile.

But Megan was smirking at me in the rearview and knew exactly what I meant by "that's so cool." More like *that's so hot*. I grabbed Rob's phone to switch up the music and put on "Saltwater Gospel" and Megan laughed out loud.

"Oh, this song! Courtney loves this song."

I wondered if he remembered the back context on the song and our conversation a while ago. Probably not. Actually, *hopefully not*. That might be embarrassing.

"Same here. Actually, I always save it and play it as soon as I cross the bridge because it means I'm almost home."

We decided to save it for the bridge then and crossing over it with the windows down was pure bliss. Once we got to the Airbnb, Rob unloaded the majority of everything and Megan and I decided we would start getting ready.

"I'm excited. And I'm liking him. Is that bad?" I asked Megan.

"Ok that's fine, but don't sleep with him on the first night. That way you have something to look forward to."

She was right. I should wait. We ended up walking to a bar called Peg Leg Pete's and grabbed some barstools and ordered some oysters. The NFL draft was on and the Packers were about to pick so, me being me, soon I was talking all things Packers with the rest of the bar. Rob's friend Steven, a Navy pilot and so *Top Gun*-esque, walked in and our oysters came out. Rob showed us how he eats oysters his way, on a saltine with Crystal hot sauce. The four of us decided to head to the next bar—a total beach bar with live music and cabana-like hut structures. I ordered my usual Coors Light and Megan got her usual margarita while the boys ordered other drinks.

"What'd you get?" I asked Rob.

"Oh, this?" he pointed to his drink and took a sip. "I chose violence. Vodka Red Bull."

After finishing our drinks, I decided to up the ante.

"Let's take a shot, hmm?" I said like an excited little kid. "Tequila? Or picklebacks? I'm doing Tequila."

"Me too," Megan chimed in.

Steven opted for pickleback and Rob said he will go pickleback too.

I headed over to the bar to order and Rob popped up next to me.

"Hey you—uh—I just wanted to say you look really beautiful tonight. I mean, I'm sure you know that, but I wanted you to hear it from me."

There's that word again.

"Thanks Rob," I said smiling and likely blushing so I looked away.

Eventually we left that bar and Rob said we're going to the original place of the Bushwacker drink. You know, that chocolate banana kind of drink that really tastes like a milkshake even though it's basically all alcohol?

We got to the Sandshaker, and there was live music so it was packed. Way more packed than the beach bar. As we walked in, Rob walked ahead of me and ordered us all Bushwackers.

Leaving the inside to go to the packed outside section I grabbed Rob's hand in front of me and he squeezed it to make sure we didn't lose each other. But once the first touch was initiated, it was almost like we were like magnets. If I let go of his hand, I felt his hand go to my waist or my lower back just keeping close to me, which was comforting. If we were on the move, he'd reach and grab my hand, even in the not so crowded parts. After dancing and having a fun time we decided it's on to the next and left to go to a bar right next door but when we get there we realize it's closed.

I'm definitely getting drunk at this point, courtesy of the Bushwacker and I'm genuinely confused how none of my companions are because they've all been drinking hard drinks and I've been drinking beer (besides the shot and Bushwacker). While I'm thinking this, I realized Megan and Steven are now up ahead in the parking lot walking back to the truck. I decided to ask Rob if he's drunk but right before I started to ask he stopped me, slightly holding my arm. I turned to see what's up.

He cupped his hand on my cheek and leaned down to my face and pulled me up to his face and kissed me. It totally took me off guard. If

I was feeling dizzy before, now I was hopeless. I had a delayed reaction when he pulled away to smile and I leaned back in and kissed him again. I smiled and looked away.

"I've been waiting a long time for that Rob," I said, reaching up and touching my lips.

I could see he was looking down at his feet smiling and he grabbed my hand and we ran to catch up with Megan and Steven.

"Also, are you drunk?" I asked. "Because I'm, like, very drunk and I'm only drinking beers, so I don't get how you guys aren't."

"Oh, yes, I'm drunk. Like very drunk, too."

Rob, Megan, Steven and I headed back to the house and I went out on the patio because it was pretty out. Rob came up behind me and started kissing my neck.

"I can't believe how pretty you looked tonight just pulling something together that quickly. You came out and I was just—uh, yeah, blew my mind."

"What? This little dress?" I said looking down at my six dollar neon orange tube dress.

He flipped me around to face him and had me pinned up to the balcony. "Uh, yeah. That little dress. God, I was so nervous at the airport to see you, Courtney. But I'm so happy you came because now this is something."

"I was so nervous at the airport too. What? It's been like seven years? Trust me, I was nervous." I put my arms around his neck and ran my fingers through his hair.

He started kissing me and wrapping his arms all the way around me pulling me in closer. Suddenly I got self-conscious that we were still on the balcony and Megan and Steven were probably inside watching us awkwardly. I pulled back and laughed as he started kissing my neck now moving his hands up my body.

"We should go in."

"Oh, yeah. Probably."

We went in and decided to play the game Never Have I Ever. I decided to test the waters and use this opportunity to get answers and see if Rob was actually a virgin.

"I'll start. Never have I ever had anal," an aggressive starter, sure, but whatever. Rob gets up to get a drink right after I said mine and Megan and Steven laugh, saying they're surprised, and put down a finger.

Rob came back to share the small couch with me and had me drape my legs across him. He kept his hands on my legs and played with my feet massaging them softly, while everyone went. But usually it was just Megan telling Steven he was playing the game wrong, because he kept saying things he had done.

"Never have I ever had sex on the beach," Steven said, still playing the game wrong.

Rob took a sip of his drink and put a finger down. *Ah-hah!* I had my answer. Even though, sneaking suspicions were leading to this answer.

"Alright, well, I'm falling asleep. I'm going to bed. I'll see y'all in the morning," Rob said, getting up.

"Me too." I got up and followed suit, thank God, because I didn't even realize how late it actually was. We got back to the bed and Rob rolled over on top of me and kissed my neck and dry humped me. But even though I wanted to have sex, I knew Megan was right and I shouldn't, especially since I was fucked up. I kissed him back but eventually I couldn't do it anymore.

"Nooo, Rob." He kept kissing my neck. "Not yet."

He kept kissing me… "I want to wait a little, Rob."

"Ok, ok," he said, kissing my lips one more time with a tipsy smile and rolled off of me and pulled me in as a little spoon and fell asleep almost instantly.

We continued spooning into the morning and every time he woke up and readjusted, he pulled me in and he was constantly hard, which was honestly impressive. But I didn't want to have sex now either—hungover and sober. For our first time too? Yeah, no. But before I got up I decided to say something.

"I'm pretty damn impressed you've been hard this entire time." He sleepily laughed and pulled me in close and pushed his hard groin against me and I heard him fall back asleep again.

Rob and I got up to get subs from Publix and coffee from Starbucks to cure everyone's hangover.

"Do I have to put a bra on?" I asked Rob.

"If you ever hear me answer that question with a yes, then you should just slap me right then and there."

We drove through a Starbucks and ordered. A woman, with a mask on that reads "happy" with a bumblebee on it, is working the window. And apparently really talkative and about to make me feel awkward as hell.

"So are you guys visiting Pensacola?"

"Uh, I live here, but she's visiting," Rob replied.

"Wow! That's awesome. Why'd you come here? What are you visiting?"

"Uh, him" I said, pointing to Rob.

"Oh that's fun! So are you guys dating?"

Oh no. Why. Whywhywhywhy.

There was a long awkward pause and Rob didn't turn to look at me. He just stayed facing the girl in her bumblebee mask at the window. I decided someone had to speak before I broke into a thousand pieces over the awkwardness.

"No," I said.

She raised her eyebrows. The awkward pause continued. So I tried again.

"Maybe," I said.

Now her eyebrows really raised. *Oh God, no one is speaking again.* Try again.

"I don't know," I said.

At this point, I don't even know what is said after this, because I turned to the opposite window and basically black out from embarrassment. Rob held up whatever the conversation was and grabbed our coffees.

I finally turned to face him to grab the coffees.

"Oh my God, I'm so sorry, Rob. I didn't know what to say and I just wanted to fill the silence and it was so awkward and—uh—I'm sorry," I sputtered out, putting my hands up to my face.

He started laughing. "Don't worry about it. All that went through my head as she asked the question and you kept answering was ERROR, ERROR, ERROR!"

"Same! Ah!" I kept my hands up to my face.

"Like Jesus lady! I haven't even had my fucking caffeine for the day how the fuck am I supposed to know!" Rob said, shaking his coffee in the air.

We hit the store and got Megan a sandwich and grabbed some Bloody Mary ingredients, despite forgetting the horseradish.

"My family is kinda like the kings and queens of good Bloody Marys, so we will see what you got!" I told Rob before he started making one for me and him.

I joined Megan on the porch and, before I knew it, I had a Bloody Mary being delivered to me by Rob. I took my first sip and Megan started laughing and I turned around to see she's laughing at Rob who was eagerly awaiting my reaction.

"Wow, ok. It's really good."

"Yes!" he said with a little fist bump. "Got the Schellin Bloody Mary seal of approval!"

After a couple sips I felt like I was already tipsy and started laughing hysterically. "Shampoo effect, y'all!"

They both looked at me like I'm crazy.

"What?! You guys don't know the shampoo effect?! It's after you've been drinking all night and you have a couple sips of your first drink and you feel like you are already drunk again."

"That's not a real thing," Megan laughed.

"I swear! One of my best guy friends who was like a little brother told me it in high school and it's the shampoo effect because of when you wash your hair with too much shampoo and you keep trying to rinse it out but your hair is still too soft."

They both started laughing at me and with that we packed up and headed to the beach with Bloody Marys in tow. On our way out the door,

Rob and I were alone and he said he wanted to show me something. He had me walk down the front deck and pointed to a brown roof of a home on the other side of this condo building next door.

"That's my childhood home. That's where I grew up all of high school," he said, adding his parents had moved out just a couple years ago.

"Ahh, so when you said I did good at picking a spot, you meant I did *really* good on picking our spot."

"Yes," he laughed. We all headed down to the car where he, yet again, opened the door for me. The beach was hot and the sun was divine hanging in a perfectly blue sky. As soon as I laid down, I could feel the sun baking me into my towel in the best way. I said I would definitely be wanting to go in the water soon.

I got up and took the first steps down to the water and Rob followed shortly after. Rob said it was cold and I said it didn't have anything on the Pacific and waded in, joking at him not to be a pussy. Naturally, he dove in after I said that.

"So my friend told me Portuguese man-of-wars are in Florida and to watch out for them and I was like no they're not but then I realized I think she's right?" I asked.

"Yeah, we have them here."

"Have you ever been stung?"

"Actually, if I'm being honest, I can't think of one part of my body that hasn't been stung by a jellyfish."

"Oh really? I feel like there's a story here."

"So usually everyone here knows when jellyfish season is but usually those are the best swells for surfing so—"

"I'm sorry, you surf? And, there's waves here?"

"Yeah! And double overhead sometimes."

"What! You're blowing my mind right now."

"We do!" he said, laughing. "Anyways, when it's jellyfish season and we want to surf, me and my friends will wear pantyhose so that the barbs and stingers don't get you as bad. So one day, I put on pantyhose covering my arms and my legs because I was in a spring suit. The only problem was, my face wasn't covered."

"Oh no."

"Yep. I went to go over a wave and I didn't want to duck dive under it because it was jellyfish season, so I went to go over the wave and right in the crest of the wave right in front of my face is this big blue blob."

"NO!"

"Completely just slapped me across the face, instantly started hurting, but the waves were super good so I still paddled out and surfed for an hour before I got out."

"You got slapped in the face with a Portuguese man-of-war, and you kept surfing because the waves were good…"

"They were double overhead! I told you."

"Oh, right. Ok," I said, rolling my eyes and dipping my head back into the water to add emphasis.

"My face blew up like I had a peanut allergy and I had black lines going across my face for over a week."

"That's seriously insane. That reminds me of in the Caribbean we were diving in little spring suits and there's always these tiny little jellies that will get you, but they never do anything too bad except leave a little mark and sting at first."

"You dive? I didn't realize that. Did I ever tell you I'm a divemaster?"

At this I turned around to face him and started dying laughing, and allowed myself to fall into the water and just float.

"What?" he asked, smiling at me.

I lifted my head from the water while I floated. "Are you Superman, too?"

He started laughing and suddenly seemed slightly embarrassed. "No, definitely not."

"Well, I'm not so sure. You surf, you're a divemaster, you've been slapped in the face with a Portuguese man-of-war, what else?" I asked, jokingly. "You know what—from now on, I'm no longer believing a word you say."

I was floating in waves and he was right nearby, slowly but surely edging closer to me, so I decided to cut the awkward tension and literal distance.

"Come over here and be my anchor?" I asked, lifting my head out of the water, still floating.

When he came over, I was thinking he would just hold my arm or something, or put an arm under me, but instead he full blown picked me up like a princess or a bride being hauled to her room with his arm behind my back and the other under my knees holding me closely and with a good grip. Now we were practically face-to-face and I was somewhat out of the water. I realized now it's probably super obvious how touchy we were and didn't want that PDA.

"Let's go a little deeper," I said. He walked us out deeper so at least I was submerged.

"Tell me some things you're bad at Superman?"

"Well, I'm really bad at basketball. My nickname is Frankenstein because of how stiff and bad I am at dribbling."

I tried not to laugh. "Ok, that's a start."

I tried to adjust myself out of the princess position, but he held on to me tighter like he didn't want me to get down. So instead I said fuck it, and readjusted myself so my legs were around him as if he were picking me up to have sex with me.

As soon as I did this, he smiled at me but now I felt even more awkward because our faces were practically centimeters apart and I didn't want to kiss him. So I tucked my head beside his to avoid direct eye contact, and looked over his shoulder.

"So what else, Rob?"

"Things I'm bad at, huh? Uhm, horseback riding?" he pondered. "I didn't grow up around horses so I'm probably bad at that."

"Hey! Well, I got you there at least," I said, leaning my chin on his shoulder.

Rob started to walk us deeper into the water and he kept his hands holding me against him and I realized he was pretty hard against my pelvis this entire time since I flipped around, and now he was only getting harder.

"Well... I can tell you're not cold anymore," I said over his shoulder, him still carrying me, so he doesn't have to face me saying it.

At this he started dying laughing and I pulled back to see his face.

"I don't think it's any secret that I'm very attracted to you, Courtney."

I smiled and put my head back over his shoulder.

"Alright, I actually am getting cold though, now," he laughed. "Let's go in."

Little did I realize, while we were out there Megan took a snap and sent it to my best friend Kassidy of me and Rob canoodling in the water. She zooms in on us in the water and then flips the camera back around to her shoving potato chips in her face. It's actually hilarious. If I could attach a video to these pages, trust me I would.

Once back on the beach, Rob pulled out a book called *1776* he was reading. *Ugh, as if he couldn't get any better.* History buff, and reading about one of my favorite topics: our country. But I didn't say anything. Ironically, he told Megan and I the chapter he's on is the battle of Bunker Hill.

"Where are you guys in relation to that?"

We both started laughing.

"We literally live on top of it and Courtney's place overlooks the monument. You'll have to come see it in person. And if you're going to come visit, let me know so I make sure I have it off!" Megan said.

He shut his book. "Oh it's not an 'if' I come visit, Megan. It's a 'when' I come visit. My cousin lives in Boston and they just had a baby I need to meet, so I need to get out there. But let's be real, the main reason I'll be coming is to see Courtney and stay with her. So I'll make sure I pick a good weekend for you guys."

He said it so matter of factly, no hesitation. I was shocked, but didn't show it, and continued laying on my towel in the hot sand just kind of taking in the fact of what was actually happening.

I was in Pensacola to see Rob. And now he wanted to see me in Boston.

At that, I cracked a White Claw from the cooler and enjoyed some more sunshine.

Eventually Steven met up with us all and we got some food at the little beach bar above us. I realized sitting there I was getting so tired and fading fast. *Damn, I knew the previous night would catch up to me eventually.*

"I think I should take half an Adderall before we go out," I said to Megan.

"Courtney. No. Don't." Megan didn't do drugs of any kind, and really, I didn't either anymore, but I was obviously still prescribed my Adderall.

"I take them all the time! Plus I did it all last weekend with Melanie in Charleston! I'd just split one. I'll be chillin'. Promise."

We packed up all our beach bags and headed back to the house, but I couldn't help but feel a little guilty Steven had come for the boring part of the day/night because of the traffic. Steven asked what I was in school for and I told him creative writing. Rob told him I used to be a writer at ESPN, but now I was in school to write books. Megan chimed in.

"Uh, yeah and she's writing the funniest book ever right now. It's about her dating life because she's gone on such shit dates."

At this they both immediately perked up and looked up wide-eyed at me. Rob had no idea about this book, on purpose, but Megan and I both discussed it was bound to come out sooner or later so I guess now was that time.

"Well how bad are these dates we're talking about?" Steven asked me.

I gave them some highlights from my Valentine's date with Jesse and then my date with Dirty Don to highlight what dating in Boston was like and they got the idea.

"Welcome to Boston!" I said, lifting my palms up in surrender.

Steven lit up. "Oh my, you have to write one on Rob now!"

Rob, who I had been avoiding eye contact with, immediately fired back. "What! What would she have to write about me? One page? 10/10 would not recommend?"

Oh, if only he knew. Rob already had a small chapter in progress and was even mentioned in the damn intro. I tried not to laugh.

We started getting ready and I asked Rob if he wanted to split an Adderall with me and he said sure.

"Ok, but are you sure? They're XR. And I know sometimes people freak out and aren't used to it."

He laughed. "I'll be fine, Courtney. I have ADD, too."

"Ok." I carefully pinched the pill to open the capsule and poured half of it into the other half of the capsule making sure it was even. One side had a little more than the other, but whatever. I tossed it back like a shot and swallowed it back with my Michelob Ultra. I put the pill back together and give him the actual pill to take. I hopped in the shower with my beer only to realize afterward I had forgotten to pack a hairbrush somehow.

So I went to borrow Megan's but it was stuck in the bathroom Rob was showering in. Steven and Megan decided to start heckling me.

"Just go in there," they said, raising their eyebrows and nodding their heads. "Go in there. Why not?"

"No! Stop!" I said laughing. My heart started racing and I started getting nervous.

"Courtney, we're all adults here. Just knock and go in there."

I'm really nervous or something all the sudden. *Wait, no.* Not nerves. My heart starts racing harder. Shit. *Not now, POTS.* I felt like I was going to pass out and realized I needed to lay down stat. I don't even respond to Megan asking if I'm okay and just head to my room, flopping onto the bed leaving the door open. My vision stays somewhat stagnant just starry but my heart pounds like I just ran a five-minute mile.

Shitshitshitshitshit. A POTS attack now? Really. More like a self-induced POTS attack. *Idiot.* What water did I have to drink today? *And no, light beer doesn't count, Courtney.* What had I had to eat in the past, I don't know—few days? As someone with POTS, I'm supposed to drink triple what other people drink—water, not booze, Courtney. *God, I suck at being an adult or self-care even.* This is last night's hangover, today's dehydration, not eating, POTS, and a sprinkle of Adderall all arriving at the same train station ready to fucking blow up my heart.

"Hi," a voice called me from my inner meltdown and I heard the door shut. It's Rob entering the room fresh out of the shower, smiling, interrupting my tailspin. I don't say anything because I can't.

"Are you ok?" he asked, wondering why I was silent.

"I'm dying," I managed to get out, me now laying on my side in fetal position.

"I have to say I didn't expect you to want to take a nap after taking the Adderall."

"I'm not napping. I'm having a heart attack."

"Ah, I see," he said, now laying himself next to me so we were facing each other. He reached his arm over me to hold me. "What can I do to help? Tell me and I'll do it."

"Support me and tell me I'm going to be ok," I said, starting to laugh, but really trying not to cry.

His face turned into a pity pout. He started to rub my back with one hand and held my other hand. "You're going to be ok. And you don't need to worry. We still have so much time. So just take all the time you need and lay here until you feel better. And relax. No one goes out until later like eight-thirty or nine-thirty so you have a lot of time, ok?" He squeezed my arm reassuringly and kissed my forehead.

"Ok," I squeaked.

Rob actually knew I had a bunch of autoimmune problems and had POTS, so I felt like I could trust him with this information. Plus he had dealt with it because his mom and brother also have autoimmune issues. Megan came in shortly after Rob left to check on me.

"My heart is fucked up," I told her.

Funny enough, she understood too because she actually just got diagnosed with POTS after getting COVID in the fall.

"Well, I guess I won't gloat and say I told you so about taking the Adderall since you feel like shit, but I'm going to get you a water. You're dehydrated. You need to drink it and then you can keep lying here."

"Ok, I'm going to take turmeric too so I can take down any inflammation likely in my damn liver."

I lied in bed and had more convulsions of chills and kept trying to sip down as much water as I could, no matter how much my hand shook. But I knew we were running out of time on going out. I had to make a decision. Megan came in and told me we needed to make a decision.

Shit. I was screwed. What if we went out and I really felt like shit? I wouldn't even be able to leave. It was all or nothing. And we both decided there was no way Rob would go out without me. Time to buck up.

Megan blow dried my hair, and thank God for turmeric, because I was starting to feel alive again. I did my makeup pretty quickly, added my finishing touches, and slipped on my wedges and looked in the mirror. Short scrunch dress was on point, makeup was looking fine, hair was blah, but damn, shoes were fire. Thank you, SHEIN! Yep, I was ready. I emerged from the bedroom with my opening line ready to rock, because—*writer*—and the guys turned to me looking shocked that I'm ready to go and making it out.

"I may not be Jesus, but I just rose from the dead, bitches!" I said, smiling and holding my arms up.

We hopped in the car and I brought a raspberry White Claw so that when I was up to it, I could try and get back in the game. I didn't plan on getting messed up though because Rob was DD-ing and I didn't want to be drunk if he was sober. The only problem was, everyone was pretty tired and poor Rob was still talkative as fuck, likely courtesy of the Adderall I split with him. I wanted to be peppy but I literally couldn't. Steven for the most part tried to keep up with Rob's conversation when he could, and about forty minutes out, I decided to come back to life and crack the White Claw. The crack resonated through the truck cab.

"It's go time now baby!" I said turning to everyone with a little hoot and holler and a fist pump, yet again rising from the dead. "Can I pick a song?" I asked.

"Ya-ya-yeahhhhhhh" blares out on the radio, the intro to "Party Like a Rock Star" and I turn it up louder even.

Megan started laughing immediately. "You would."

I turn around and cock my head confidently. "What can I say? I'm a spectator sport."

Rob started slapping the steering wheel he's laughing so hard at this one. "I love it."

I turned the volume down for a new important announcement that would not be welcomed. "So I know I'm not everyone's favorite since I delayed us but—I need to pee."

Groans started erupting from the back.

"It's no big deal. I should strap that lawn chair flopping in the truck bed," Rob said.

Megan and Steven groaned again at this and Rob pulled off at the next gas station.

"Hustle," Steven said.

Oh, and I did. I jumped back in the truck and smiled to Rob.

"Thank you," I said, reaching over and tapping his hand on the center counsel.

"Of course. Anytime," he smiled back.

He really was just a nice guy, wasn't he?

We got downtown and parked the car. It was Fiesta Weekend, which is a big weekend in Pensacola for debutante kinds of balls and history apparently. We grabbed a margarita at the back end of this brewery and then made our way inside to meet Steven's flying buddies. Rob was talking up a storm with Steven's roommate so I hung back with Steven and Megan.

"You guys want to go to the lobby?" I asked.

Megan smiled, having heard my joke dozens of times, and Steven rolled his eyes.

I point to the top of my drink and drag my finger from the top to the bottom.

"Lobby."

Steven laughed and we "lobby-ed" our drinks and headed out to hit a couple more bars when finally Rob looked at Steven mischievously.

"Since we're deciding where to go next we should probably show them it," Rob said.

"Seville?" Steven asked.

Seville has old ceiling tiles making it feel old-school New Orleans-like. Better yet, it's like ten bars in one, all different styles. Rob told me all this while walking just ahead of me like a tour guide leading us down the first hallway. Lemme give you a brief breakdown of this place, for those of you who don't know it. As soon as you walk in to the left there is the "skank tank" as the guys call it. It's a giant dance floor filled with people grinding to Ying Yang Twins and Cardi B with a big screen projector playing '90s rap music videos and even has multiple levels overlooking the dance floor. Walking down the hallway you pass by a billiards bar with biker-esque vibes. Next is another thin hall with what appears to be a karaoke bar. Past that there's a bar with a live band playing on a stage and then a courtyard with an outdoor bar with music playing outside. Needless to say, I was in heaven.

Rob continued ahead of me leading us outside and I saw he had his hand outreached behind him, clearly wanting me to grab it. But I decided I was feeling like I wanted to play hard to get, so I decided not to grab it and see if he noticed. His hand kept hanging at his side facing back to me awkwardly and I started to giggle. Finally he looked down at his hand and then to me, but I pretended not to notice, taking in the scenery around. I even put my hands behind my back, like the child I am. Finally, Rob, sick of holding his hand out behind him, just reaches to my side and slides his fingers into mine and pulls me along. My stupid smirk only grew bigger with this.

While outside I noticed something about the courtyard. "This patio looks just like—"

"Pat O'Brien's in New Orleans?" Rob answered.

"Yes! They copied it?"

"Well technically Pat O's probably copied them since this bar has been around longer. Pensacola has been around since 1550."

"I had no idea there was so much history here."

I was probably drooling at this point. But when Rob had us follow him back to the last and final room, we entered through two large antique double doors into what I will call the crown jewel—a giant dueling piano bar. *Yep, I was definitely in heaven.*

The piano bar was packed, but we managed to grab one barstool and then eventually a table. If you've been to piano bars, you know how hard that can be! As soon as we got a table Rob leaned to my ear.

"I'm going to do a quick round to see if I know anyone. I already saw a couple of familiar faces, since it's Fiesta Weekend."

With all the debutante festivities, I was sure he probably knew a ton of people here who were likely part of the ones dressed to the nines in tuxes and nice dresses. *So southern.*

Rob came back and Megan and Steven decided they wanted to go explore the other bars, but I wanted to stay at the piano bar, so Rob and I stayed. The piano bar was electric and I think the guys playing were nearly as drunk as the bachelorette girls dancing on the stage courtesy of all the drinks the crowd was buying them.

We decided to check on Megan and Steven, who were content people-watching in the skank tank. While walking back to the piano bar, we passed one of the side bars with a bunch of little unique flags with specific symbols on them. I pointed to them and said they looked like pirate flags.

"Actually they are the symbols they use on the undersides of plane wings. So like in WWI and WWII they could distinguish different country's planes." From there he goes down the hung up flags pointing out each symbol and their countries. "That's Taiwan, Japan, America, they got rid of the red dot though so it wasn't too similar to Japan..."

At this point I basically stopped hearing him because I was kind of in awe. I finally burst out laughing.

He smiled back at me confused.

"You take fun facts to a new level. You have background and context and you just know so much. Like, about everything. You can talk pilot-talk to Steven and medical-O.R.-talk with Megan and then random stuff like this."

He just smiled back in response.

We headed back to the piano bar and somehow got into the topic of relationships after talking about Steven and Megan and their past relationships. Both had been in relationships where cheating was involved and I told Rob that I had never done that, and probably never would in my life.

"When I'm dating someone, it's them and no one else. Like I don't even have eyes for other people. But that's just how I am. For me, you're either all in or you're out. Otherwise, what's the point?"

Rob smiled and agreed. "Yeah, when I'm with a girl and I like her, I straight up get tunnel vision."

I smiled at this comment. The bars were about to close so we decided to head back.

We got back to the house and basically all passed out, since we're all so tired.

I hopped into bed with Rob once I put on my pjs and instantly Rob slid over to me and started cuddling me. He pushed himself up to get on top of me and I don't fight it and just let him kiss me, but I turned my head so I could fall asleep and he could just kiss my neck. Plus if I'm being honest, I was still processing and considering everything that had gone on between us and how it may make sense. Could I be with someone who was as bad of a communicator as me if not worse? Like he straight up ghosted me. For months. I told him I'm so tired and we can pick this up in the morning and he retreated and instead pulled me in front of him to spoon.

Right before I was about to fall asleep, I had a realization. *We didn't have sex... again.* Meaning, now I was down to one more day/night. And we had to get up at like 4:30 AM in the morning the last day so there was no way I was drinking much the last day. In other words, I was going to have to do this soberly. And, likely, he was going to be sober, too. Hell, the sun might even be freaking up while we do it.

I woke up that morning and remembered the night and still felt POTS-y and, yet again, started overthinking everything. So I had an internal debate with myself.

Shit. Why don't I want to have sex with him? Wait—no. That's not it. What am I talking about! I want to have sex with Rob. I have for a while. Brain shut up. I am Courtney Fucking Schellin and I want to have sex, damn it. I'm doing this. I've waited way too damn long to do this. Especially with him.

Rob is oblivious to my inner turmoil, obviously, and was still spooning me with his arm laying over my arm. But that's not where I wanted his hand to be. It was go time, baby.

I gently lifted his wrist and he started moving like he was waking up. I slowly slipped his hand up my tank top onto my right boob.

Naturally, this got his attention immediately and I felt him start to grow behind me where it counts. My face might as well have turned into the little purple devil emoji. *Court, you mischievous little minx, you.*

He started to slide his fingers over my nipples, circling them to get them harder. *Yep, he was ready to rock, too.* I slightly sighed at this and he started kissing the back of my shoulder and then the side of my neck. I rolled over to face him. With this, he pulled down my shirt, spilling out my boobs one by one, then lifted himself up and pulled himself on top of me. He started grinding his hard penis through his boxers against me, and I could feel how big he was. This was going to be fun.

Feeling his erection on me told me how much he wanted me, which just built me up and edged me even more. I breathed out his name. He pulled down his boxers and revealed his stiff penis. He spread my legs with his hands and went to slide himself into me but it wouldn't go in. *Typical.* He kept pressing himself slowly as not to hurt me and I started giggling. He looked up at my eyes.

"I didn't realize you were so big," I said, smirking.

He smiled and said, "Well you're also very tight."

With that, Rob slides a finger into me and clearly wetness wasn't the issue. Rob just needed to get that first slide in and we'd be golden. He finally got his tip in and started rocking to get it in farther without hurting me. But I was edging for his dick now and patiently anticipating him entering me, sitting my head up watching him tease me. He finally slipped himself past my so-called threshold and I gasped, throwing my head back into the mattress, still holding eye contact with him. This made him smile, proudly almost, but that look quickly transitioned into a man who's about to get to work. He laid his upper body on top of me and started thrusting deeper into me, starting out slow and then going faster. I hung onto his shoulders from the back whimpering with pleasure and trying not to dig my nails into his back too deeply as I hung on for dear life.

Unfortunately, right as I was getting more and more turned on, I started feeling POTS-y and uncomfortable. Probably because my heart was racing and I was dehydrated, but I didn't want to stop. But Rob noticed something had changed with me because he slowed down and lifted himself to face me and stopped. My face must've said it all.

"Are you ok? Do you need me to stop?"

"Yeah just for a second," I said sheepishly, annoyed at myself that I was the way I was.

"It's totally ok," he said sympathetically as he pulled out of me. He plopped on the bed next to me. I lied there for a second but decided there were other things I could do... I rolled over to get on top of him and started giving him head. I wanted to please him now. I worked my mouth around the top of his penis going as deep as I could until I would gag. The first time I looked up at him he just lied there with his mouth wide open in a smile. Which made me want to burst out laughing, but I kept to it. *Maybe not a virgin, but maybe not all that experienced either,* I thought smiling. I started sucking up and down slower with my hand in unison then stopping to see where he was at.

"Get on top of me," he said with his big open-mouth grin.

So I hopped on top and rode him like a cowgirl. I switched from bouncing up and down sighing every time he got too deep and then embracing the pain and twerking myself faster up and down. This led to more open mouth gaping from him, which made me happy to know he was loving it, but still kind of made me want to start laughing. I decided to keep up the momentum and flipped to reverse cowgirl making sure to keep him inside of me as I switched. I started bouncing my ass up and down while riding his now incredibly hard dick, my ass in his face exposing all of me to him. He started audibly moaning at this. Before I know it, he completely surprised me. He sat up, picking me up by my hips and flipped me from reverse cowgirl straight into doggy style. Somehow he stayed inside of me throughout this act and he thrust himself into me deeper.

WOW. OK, ROB. Maybe he was experienced after all.

I moaned loudly in pleasure arching my back deep which clearly made him even more excited. He started thrusting deeply and powerfully into me, holding my hips in place as he did so. At this point he was basically breaking my back, but I was more than happy to walk funny for the day.

I watched him in the closet mirror facing the bed and see his face fixated and his body fucking me hard and fast now. He would look up and groan, his muscles quivering with pleasure with every thrust. I moaned louder as he thrusted harder and harder into me.

"Oh God, Rob," I whimpered.

"Ugh, I'm gonna cum."

He ejaculated on my back, as I watched in the mirror, my back still arched and my butt against his upper thigh. Once he was stable, he hopped off the bed and went to the bathroom and brought out a towel. He dried off my back as I lied there just smiling and giggling. He was smiling too.

"I think you realigned my hip," I joked.

Once I was dried off we both plopped onto our backs on the bed and then moved in to snuggle with each other. I laid my head on his chest and he wrapped an arm around me as I let my hand play with his chest hair.

Ten minutes later a knock came to the door. "I'm starving," Megan popped her head in.

"Give us a few minutes, k?" I responded smiling.

She smirked in response.

I rolled back over to Rob as soon as the door shut. "I'm not done having fun yet," I said, going under the covers. I started kissing his dick through his boxer briefs and he laughed as I started to feel him get hard again. *Impressive indeed, Rob.*

He pulled me up and flipped me next to him and reached his hand to my inner thigh pushing it open. He slipped his fingers between my legs and teased me going in and out of me. He then slid them out just far enough and, now very wet, he used that wetness to twirl around my clit, just enough to drive me wild.

"Oh my God, you're driving me nuts," I whispered to him.

I guided his fingers to where I wanted to be touched more and he started fingering me, going back to my clit. He realized this was getting to me and stuck there for a while getting faster and faster with his momentum. My facial expressions started to change whether I wanted them to or not and I started to whimper out, knowing I'm about to climax.

"Oh, don't stop, Rob. Oh don't stop."

With my instruction he kept his same consistency, slipping his fingers over my clit even faster than before. I felt myself start to crack into a thousand pieces. I tried to stay as quiet as possible but I moaned out multiple times, practically panting to get air and nearly biting my own lip off.

I started laughing at the end because I was just a pile of mush and serotonin, grinning ear-to-ear like an idiot. I bit my lip again and looked over to face the man of the hour. The guilty culprit who just watched my screaming O face in all its glory. Yikes. But he was smirking back at me.

"Better?" he asked.

I just laughed and turned my head without answering, clearly giving him the answer he already knew. I rolled over to snuggle with him, putting my head back on his chest, and felt he was hard again. *Was this heaven or what?* I flipped back around putting my butt into him.

"Oh Rob, you just made me so wet. I want you to feel how wet you made me."

I reached behind and started to help him pull his dick back out and slide it into me. He did easily now and I wanted him so bad all over again.

Megan called out to us again, and we both instantly got up.

"Shit," we whispered to each other giggling. Then louder to her, "Yeah uh—coming!"

More like cumming. We both laughed at each other throwing clothes at each other to get dressed quicker. I put on a cotton black formfitting midi dress and skipped the bra and let my nipples poke themselves lightly through my dress because I was feeling sexy. Plus, Rob had already said he loved that, so why not embrace the nip today. *I got motha-fuckin laid, baby.*

We went to a small brunch spot and then headed back to the house, but Rob said he needed to hit the store since he forgot the horseradish for the food he's making for us tonight. I offered to go too, but he said he was fine. He was taking forever and I started to feel bad that maybe he was having trouble finding my turmeric I asked for. Steven came out to crack a beer with me while we waited.

"So you realize Rob is like a dad right?" Steven said, looking at me while cracking his beer.

"Dad?" I said laughing, cracking my beer. I thought of his running shoes, him being on top of all the plans thus far, him being our DD, his dad jokes, his fun facts, and everything else so far from the trip and smiled. "Yeah, I do. He's definitely not like anyone I've dated before, but I kind of like that."

"Ok, just checking," he laughed. "And, just so you know what you're getting into, our friends literally all call him dad."

Rob arrived right after this conversation with the supplies in tow and it made me see him in his even more dad-like light.

Instead of the beach, we decided to hit one more bar, Crabs. It was on the water and we got an outdoor table by the beach and there was live music inside. We grabbed some quick drinks and it started to rain. But it was that perfect kind of warm spring rain where no one really moves inside, they just sit under their umbrellas on the beach and admire it. We decided to head back since Rob was going to cook a seafood feast for us, Florida style.

When we got back to the house, Rob started getting his chef face on and was very focused. Steven and Megan just hung on the couch with each other sipping some wine.

He showed me how to make the cocktail sauce after I insisted on helping and then got to work on the crab claws and the shrimp. Once he finished seasoning the shrimp, he de-tailed one for me and brought it over to me to try before serving it.

"Damn, that's good."

"Right? And so simple to make," he said, flipping his hat back around, which had an interesting emblem on it.

"What's your hat say?"

He flipped it down to show me. "It's the club we hunt pheasant at."

"I've always wanted to go bird hunting, but my family doesn't really do that."

"Well, we have to change that then! I'll take you sometime."

I tried not to swoon over this comment. He pulled out his phone and showed me pictures of him and his mom with their guns at the club.

"My mom isn't used to shooting shotguns so she kept accidentally swinging it past me and I'd be like 'Mom! Watch it!' She grew up shooting handguns."

"That's funny I'm the opposite, we shoot shotguns usually and when I shot my uncle's Colt .45 revolver I was shook by it flying back toward my face and turned around after like 'Woah!' and accidentally flashed our crew with it and they were all like 'Woah, woah!'" I laughed at the memory. "So, yeah, I get it."

I made the cocktail sauce and had Rob taste it to get the seal of approval.

"Yep," he said, smacking his lips.

"Hell yeah! You hear that guys!" I yelled to Megan and Steven on the couch who offered thumbs ups.

"In my house growing up you either cooked or you cleaned, and I'd come home tired after practice and never wanted to do the dishes so I'd just help my mom in the kitchen. I had no idea I was actually a decent cook until I got to college and saw how everyone else cooked for themselves," Rob said.

"Lemme guess—their specialties were chicken and rice? Typical college boy meal. We have the same rule in our house though! Whoever cooks, ain't doing the dishes," I said.

From there we started talking about college and grad school and a car accident Rob had gotten into, and I decided to take the opportunity to get some more girlfriend talk in.

"Is that when you were dating your girlfriend in grad school?"

"Yeah, but she wasn't helpful at all."

"Oh. Is that why you broke up?

"Simply put, she was really selfish and only cared about herself. Plus she had some trust issues. She caught her dad cheating on her mom. So..."

With that, we finished the food and it was time to dig in. Thank God, I had an appetite this night. Now that we were all in a food coma we lied out on the couches for a bit before deciding we wanted to go down to the dock to watch the sunset. We walked down to the end of the dock and it really was a scene. The sky was water coloring from baby oranges and pinks to lavender dipping down closer to the horizon. We all took a couple photos and I joked about us playing truth or dare and jumping in the water. Honestly, it looked like the perfect night to jump in.

Rob pointed out his house and the dock that he grew up on and I asked if I wanted to walk over there with him while Megan and Steven hung back. Rob and I started walking over there, but we had to walk through a couple backyards. I saw a woman on the deck next door to his house watching us and felt awkward.

"Rob, I think this is someone's yard..."

"It's ok! I know everyone here."

"Rob, is that you? Hi hunny!" the voice called out.

We walked over and I introduced myself to this adorable blonde woman with a little tennis skirt and magenta pink top on. She was talking to Rob about how she remembered the last time she saw him and how she was just texting his mom. She told Rob to show me their dock and we were welcome to go out on her dock.

Rob took me to the end of the dock and I was very careful to make sure we weren't touching because the woman made it clear she was friends with his mom. We walked down the dock and Rob showed me the blue heron that had always lived on their dock that was an archnemesis with their dog growing up. We got to the end of the dock and Rob leaned down and kissed me.

"Rob! That woman is friends with your mom and I don't want you to get tattled on or gossiped to."

He laughed. "It's fine my mom already knows I'm here with you."

"Wait, really?"

This totally surprised me.

"Alright let's head back and make sure those two don't kill each other," Rob said, joking about Megan and Steven. We got back and I took a shower. I came out in a towel and Rob was already getting into bed checking his phone. I jokingly said in the towel...

"Clothes on or clothes off?"

"Whatever you want," he said, without looking up from his phone.

Psh! Ok... Not going to take that personally or anything... Naturally, I went into the bathroom and put on a full sweatshirt and sweats. But after cleaning the kitchen and coming back into the room I realized pretty quickly, I would be way too hot in the outfit I picked so I decided to change into a tank and shorts.

"Ok, second chance, clothes on or off... since last time you told me to put clothes on and that you didn't want to have sex with me," I said, laughing, not even being able to keep eye contact, knowing I was being a drama queen.

He sat up. "Wowww, you really just put words in my mouth again that I definitely didn't say."

I started laughing again.

"Well, definitely clothes off now."

"Too bad, I'm putting them on," I said, smirking, pulling on my tank top.

As soon as I hit the lights and popped into bed with him though, he pulled my body next to his and started kissing me. Here we go again! He started getting on top of me and kissing my neck and then I decided I wanted to please him after all the cooking he had done so I flipped him over and got on top and lowered my face to his pelvis.

I started sucking his dick. And choking on it. Like, really good head. Like, Call Her Daddy, Gluck Gluck kind of head. I slobbered all down it, switching up speed, sucking on his balls while I stroked his hard dick in my hand. Kissing his inner thighs and twirling my tongue over the top of his penis in circles and then going down on it all while looking him in the eyes. Of course, his mouth was wide open again over this, but I was getting used to that at this point.

I decided to let myself be gagged by his size a few more times, my saliva dripping down his shaft. Finally I came up for some air and wiped my mouth with the top of my hand and in the most innocent voice I could muster I looked up from gagging and smiled.

"Do you want to have sex with me?" I asked, all doe-eyed and shit, playing games.

He couldn't speak words at first and just muttered inaudible noise staring at me.

"What? YES. Yesyesyesyes," he kept repeating yes as he sat up and grabbed my arms pulling me to him and flipping me over onto my back as I giggled at his stuttering.

"Like, do I want to have sex with you? Is that even a question? Yes, duh duh duh DUH," he said, now maneuvering to slide into me. He tried to put his dick in again and again, but his size and my tightness made us work for it in the best way. Rob started using his fingers again to help get things moving along. I was impatient now though.

"It's ok just jam it in me, Rob. I don't care, I want you in me."

With this he thrusted harder into me and sure enough it jammed right in there. I gasped. Excited to be in me and fully erect after the blow job, he immediately grabbed both my legs at his sides and sent them over my head above my shoulders holding my ankles to the head board. He started thrusting harder and harder, fucking me hard, bent in half facing him, me audibly moaning and him breathing harder and harder.

My moans quickly went from moans to borderline heaves because he was honestly too big for me to fuck me in this position so quickly, but I didn't want to say anything and be a little bitch. I thought I could take it, moaning and then eventually involuntarily my moans and whimpers turned to "ugh... ow... uh... Rob ow."

He finally noticed and immediately slowed up and smiled and kissed me. He smiled and winked at me and got off of me and slipped out of me. I wasn't done with him yet though.

I flipped over and got on top of him and fucked him slowly. I wanted to feel all of him inside me again, but now I was having more control to pull up when he was too much to handle. After going at it for a while on top of him, I rolled over and we both lied there breathing hard and smiling.

"How do you want me?" I asked him.

A mischievous look came over his face. "Flip over."

He bent me down into doggy style again at the end of the bed and started fucking me deep and hard. I was moaning his name because it felt so good and I wanted him to know it was because of him.

"Fuck, I think I'm gonna cum," and all of the sudden, he pulled out so quick and completely belly flopped on my back after cumming and literally lied on top of me breathing hard, all his weight on me. This was a total first for me.

"Well, that was a close call," I finally squeaked out due to his entire body on me, air barely coming into my lungs as I laughed. He then realized he was crushing me.

"Oh, I'm sorry! I usually don't cum that fast ever," he panted out and pushed half of himself off of me. "I'm not even sure my legs are working right now to be honest."

He quickly grabbed a towel and wiped off my back and my butt and gave my butt a little squeeze. I rolled over and smiled and he plopped on the bed and he lied on top of me with his head on my stomach by my belly button. I played with his hair, smiling.

"That was amazing," I breathed out. I didn't orgasm from the sex, but I never do, but that sex was still awesome.

"No. I'm sorry—like I said, I usually don't cum that fast."

"Rob, what are you talking about? We had sex for like fifteen to twenty minutes! That was totally fine and amazing!" I said looking down at my fingers playing with his hair.

"No, seriously—I don't cum that quick I should've lasted longer for you," he said and rolled over and started kissing my stomach and then my inner thighs, working his way up.

Wait... is he really going to go down on me after we just had sex? Most guys get freaked about that after their junk and semen were all up in there. *What a fucking man.*

After he apologized and started kissing my thighs, he slipped his arms between my legs and spread my legs so he could bring his head down to me. He started kissing my bikini line and then slipped his fingers into me which I moaned at. He then pulled his fingers slightly back out of me and slid his finger up toward my clit to separate my lips and just like that, he had access to all of me. He immediately brought his tongue down directly to my clit and started flicking his tongue over it, slipping another finger into me. With two fingers inside of me he reached up to my G-spot and began teasing me by pressing into it and curving his fingers into it, thrusting his fingers into me in sequence with his tongue.

I couldn't help but audibly moan because whatever he was doing with his fingers simultaneously with his tongue was absolutely insane. I had never had anyone do this to me before. It was nearly unbearable. I remember my head falling off the edge of the bed and trying to lift it to watch him and looking to him and barely moaning out, "What are you doing." He had barely been down there for thirty seconds and I could already feel myself starting to unhinge.

There's no way. This quickly? I couldn't. Could I?

Rather than think too much, I just thought of him about to literally feel me cum for him and all of the sudden a thought ran over and over in my head.

He wants you to cum for him.

I looked down to see his face buried between my legs and thought of feeling his fingers inside me. And how when I came he would feel it since he was inside of me. *Feeling me. Tasting me. Wanting me to cum for him.* With that I couldn't help it anymore. I grabbed my own hip and grabbed his free hand on my thigh and held on tight to him, letting him know I was so close. My breathing heightened and I felt all my muscles tense up and I let out a moan and my left leg started quaking next to his head and he steadied it as I arched my back and moaned, curling my toes and feeling every hair on my body stand on end.

HOLY FUCK. OMG. Rob. Rob fucking Bridger. I couldn't even move. He kissed my inner thigh again and scooted up to me.

"There," he said and smiled scooting up to lay on me.

Somehow the only words I could come up with were... "Do you want to know the first line of my book?"

He started laughing hysterically at this. "Sure, tell me."

"It goes something like this—it's fifteen days until my twenty-ninth birthday and I haven't had an orgasm from a guy in two years."

He started dying laughing while I just lied there smiling, looking at the ceiling not giving a fuck what I had just admitted.

"Well, I hope I proved that sentence wrong at least a couple of times this weekend," he said with a wink.

"Let's just say, first sentence shattered."

He laughed. "Well, it was true at the time you wrote it."

"Yep, that's true."

"I think that might have been the best ever," I said, still mind blown about the oral sex and Rob chimed in almost immediately.

"Hah—Well, you obviously already know it was for me. I came so fast."

Oh shit. He just referenced the sex was *the best*. I almost corrected him with what I meant, but I thought better of it. With that we rolled over and were lying next to each other but not touching. We were both sweating and just had our feet touching. This made me laugh.

"I like how we're lying here just our feet touching," I laughed.

"That's so like me." Rob said. "Do you know the five love languages?"

"No?"

"You don't? You know, physical touch, acts of service, words of affirmation—"

"Oh, yeah, yeah. I have heard of them."

"Well, mine are physical touch and acts of service so that's why I'm big on touching."

I laughed knowing I'm the biggest horndog ever and that's why I'm big on touch. Instead I said... "I'm big on physical touch too. So I'm sure mine would be high in that too and, what were the others?"

"Acts of service, so like helping each other out."

"Yep, definitely that one," I responded.

"Words of affirmation."

"Well, writer, so probably yeah."

He smiled. "You should take the test."

I decided to go for it on having *the conversation*. You know, the one where you ask what's next. Except I didn't even know how to start it. And I also didn't want to be cliché doing it right after we had sex, but really, I was out of time. I wasn't looking for a relationship, but I also wouldn't just fly down here and have all this happen for no reason.

"Listen, this isn't just the good sex and the serotonin talking, but like —uh—what do we—*err*—I don't know, what does this mean? I mean, I had a really fun weekend and I like you so..." I trailed off awkwardly looking at the ceiling, not ever giving him eye contact.

He rolled over to face me. "Courtney, I do too. Like a lot. I think we just go with the flow and see where this goes."

"Ok, that's cool. I just—well, I'm just trying to make sure we're on the same page here and you're not going to just ghost me..."

"Oh God, I wouldn't do that," he rolled back over and looked at the ceiling.

A burst of laughter puttered out of me. My turn to roll and face him. "Uh, well you kind of already did, Rob."

"I know. I did. But that was just a really bad time for me and this is different. Now you've come down here. So obviously what's next is I'm coming out to Boston."

"Well damn, after a performance like you just gave I'll put in the effort too," I laughed.

"No, seriously, Courtney. I know how this works. It's my turn to put the effort in. So next up I'm booking a flight to Boston. Actually, can I just come back with you now?"

I giggled at this.

We ended up setting an early alarm and snuggling and going to sleep. Our alarm went off at 4:30 a.m. I rolled around and decided I was not ready for our fun to end just yet, but, then again, I don't want to get gross before my flight either. *Light bulb!*

"I have to rinse off... Want to join me in the shower?" I said, snuggled up under his arm on his chest, now kissing his neck.

"Uh... Yeah."

We stripped in the bathroom and started laughing, just being naked in the mirror next to each other brushing our teeth as the water warmed. I always think that's so funny. We got into the shower and I let my body get wet under the water. Once my hair was wet I dropped down into a squat so my eyes were eye level with his goodies. I took him in my mouth as deep as I could, pulling my head back away from it and close to it. I popped up briefly to take a break to shampoo my hair. While I was doing this he wanted to keep things hot and started fingering me and playing with me. Once I washed my hair out, he flipped me around and bent me over.

Once again, he had trouble getting into me again and really couldn't get it to fit in me. *What am I? The Gates of Mordor?* Also, contrary to popular belief, water doesn't necessarily make things more slippery in this department. He finally gets in and it takes my breath away, per usual. He started rocking back and forth thrusting deeper into me as the water drops poured down my back and down to my head bent over down by my feet. I grabbed his calf as he started fucking me faster. But something's not right... I felt him getting softer. I stood up and turned to him to see what's up, with him still in me.

"I'm so sorry, I'm so nervous!" he said pulling out and now cupping my face.

"What! Why are you nervous?" I asked, now going on my tippy toes to kiss his lips as he held my face.

"No—not like that—like I'm nervous we're going to be late for your flight!"

"Hah! Ok, fine—don't worry about it. We will get out," I said, smirking and giving him a quick peck. "Let me just finish with my hair quickly."

Sure enough, he was right that we were cutting it too close. I would have to go with wet hair, but thankfully I already packed. I finished getting ready and Rob brought my bags to the car. I headed down to the car with Megan to see he already pulled the car up to our staircase for us and was waiting and had the door opened for me. *Cute.*

We listened to music on the way to the airport and he said he had to drive to Birmingham that day for work. He dropped us off at the airport. He gave Megan a hug and then gave me a hug but I leaned up looking at him wanting a kiss so he leaned down and gave me one.

"Have a safe flight!" he said.

"Drive safe to Birmingham," I responded.

Megan made fun of our goodbyes and we both laughed, stealing one more look, and waved goodbye to each other. I watched his tan Silverado drive away with the SMU sticker on the back.

"Bye."

We boarded our flight and I pulled out my phone to look at some of the photos. The photo of Rob and I on the end of the dock in the sunset was really cute. Like really cute. I decided I'd send him some of the photos I got on our trip including that one when we landed in Atlanta.

We landed in Atlanta and I turned my phone off airplane mode and a text came in from Rob.

"Have a safe flight."

There was a tornado warning and severe thunderstorms in Atlanta so we were stuck on the tarmac. I told him the weather was shit in Atlanta and we were delayed and sent him a group of ten or so photos including that one. I smiled out the window after hitting send. I couldn't help feeling sentimental.

I had an interview to become a student professor the next day, and a meeting with an author about my book and advice, and I just had a great weekend with Rob and he wanted to come visit me. I felt stable. My whole life was ahead of me and this is where it all begins…

"Hey guys, looks like we're now cleared for takeoff, but it'll probably be a bumpy one. Flight attendants, prepare for takeoff," our pilot said over the speakers.

Our little plane wobbled up into the sky and we took flight into the middle of a thunderstorm and a tornado. A hell of a combination, but I didn't have a care in the world about that. I giggled out the window at the weather, reminiscing on the weekend like a lust-drunken school girl.

* * *

This is the part where you think we lived happily ever after right? Wrong. Because guess what Rob did? He went full Casper, AGAIN. A-FUCKING-GAIN. I wish I could rename his chapter Casper. *Casper the fucking ghost.* I got back to Boston and did my interviews and he said he was going to give me a call and was so proud of me but then he never called. I sent him another text after one too many martinis, sending him probably the best saying I learned from him.

"I know you said martinis are like boobs—one isn't enough, two is just right, and three you're in trouble, but what about four? Asking for a friend."

Still no response.

Then I asked if he had shipped me the shirt I bought for my dad that I accidentally left in his car.

Still no response. Two weeks went by.

And finally I decided, you know what? Why shouldn't I be allowed to show some feelings or emotions? My friends and mom and everyone really, leading up to this point, was like "You have to act like you don't care," but honestly, why the fuck should I have to act like that when he just conned me for an entire weekend? That fucked me up. This would fuck me up. *I'm going to be fucked up because of this.* What did I do wrong that he felt like he could treat me like I'm a person without feelings or without a care in the world, when I'm not at all that? I have a heart. I have feelings. And I may wear both of them on my sleeve, but I like that about myself. Because I put myself out there and look for love. But this? This would fuck me up a bit. This would fuck up my trust and me wearing my heart and my feelings on my sleeve. And honestly, as much as I hate to admit it, both those were fucking crushed with Rob leaving me with no answers.

So I texted him saying my peace. Still, doing my best to toe the line of "not caring."

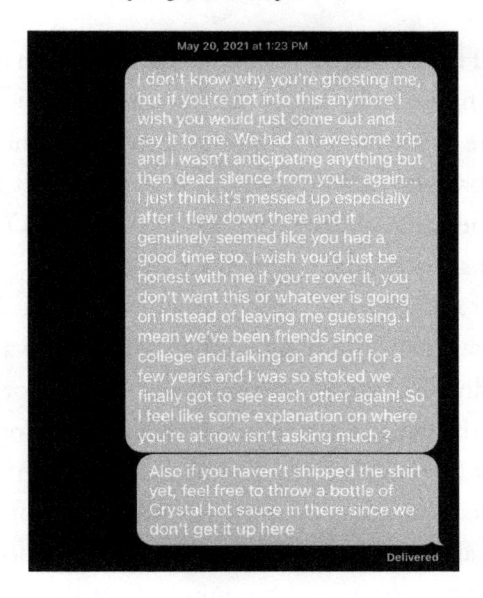

> May 20, 2021 at 1:23 PM
>
> I don't know why you're ghosting me, but if you're not into this anymore I wish you would just come out and say it to me. We had an awesome trip and I wasn't anticipating anything but then dead silence from you... again... I just think it's messed up especially after I flew down there and it genuinely seemed like you had a good time too. I wish you'd just be honest with me if you're over it, you don't want this or whatever is going on instead of leaving me guessing. I mean we've been friends since college and talking on and off for a few years and I was so stoked we finally got to see each other again! So I feel like some explanation on where you're at now isn't asking much?
>
> Also if you haven't shipped the shirt yet, feel free to throw a bottle of Crystal hot sauce in there since we don't get it up here.
>
> Delivered

No response.

How does the saying go?

Fool me one time, shame on you. Fool me twice, can't put the blame on you. But fool me three times? As J. Cole says, "FUCK THE PEACE SIGNS, LOAD THE CHOPPER, LET IT RAIN ON YOU."

To make things even more ironic, Megan and Steven even started seeing each other after our trip. So at least someone got something out of this. Steven even renamed Rob to Voldemort in his phone after he found out what a dick he was being to me. I guess the last time him and Rob hung out Rob noticed too! LOL. *Whatever, serves him right.*

Did I think Rob and I would have a happy ending? I mean, I don't want to be too cliché and admit that my original answer I thought was yes. But like they say, we make plans and God laughs. Honestly, I think the most annoying part is how he got into my head. That's what pisses me off. It's embarrassing that I fell for his shit again. But really, I think I know why I did.

Realistically, when I really think about it, Rob was the first guy I let in and could actually see my life with. *My future.* We went to the same college together. He was smart, well-educated, close with his family, witty, and super hot. And he really knew me. I wanted to believe he was going to come to see me or move to the big city. And maybe he would take me to one of those balls he said he would. Or that we'd sit in a duck blind together or go pheasant hunting together like he said. Or that we'd have a big house with a porch like the ones we talked about that we liked so much. *God, that's so pathetic.*

But after the weekend we had together, what else was I supposed to feel? Why wouldn't he just tell me he wasn't into it or that there was someone else off the bat so I could've had that in my mind going into the weekend? I know I wouldn't be fucked up if I had that at least. But no.

So after weeks had gone by with no response from Rob, I called Kassidy to bitch about it one more time, and we decided I should start talking with someone else to get my mind off of things. Who were the options? A phone memory popped up of Josh and I in the shark outfits but this time I noticed someone else in the photo. I tilted my phone and zoomed in—Daniel, someone who had liked me in college.

"There was this guy Daniel. I think he's a real estate agent or something. Huh... I wonder what he's up to."

Naturally, Kassidy and I stalked him on Instagram to get caught up on his life. He hunted, fished, looked like he had a good job, and was always golfing or traveling.

"Courtney, where the fuck has this guy been?" Kassidy yelled through the phone. "I'm team Daniel."

Kassidy and I schemed a plan on how I could text him.

"Tell him your friend is going to a costume party and you came across the photo," Kassidy said.

I rolled with it. And a solid choice it was. He liked the original text and within a day or two we started talking. I posted a video of me golfing on Instagram and he told me I was "looking damn good," and I told him I could teach him a trick or two. Turns out, he was currently on the golf course and started sending me videos of himself on the course.

"Work is for suckers, am I right, Court?" he said in one golf video. I laughed out loud watching it. He had a great swing, too. We started to text every day practically. One day, I was on the phone with my mom and I decided to tell her about the new whim of a texting conversation I was having. I sent her some screenshots of him and, suddenly, an incoming call from Daniel started beeping in.

"He's calling me..."

"What! Answer it! Answer it!"

"Alright, I will, Mom!"

"And don't be weird, Courtney!"

"Ok, Mom!"

I answered.

"Well if it isn't Courtney Schellin," his voice rang out similar to how I remembered it. Maybe even a little goofy in tone.

"Well hello, Daniel Bronzen."

We talked on the phone for forty-five minutes. FORTY-FIVE MINUTES.

We caught up and reminisced on college times and what we were up to now.

A good golfer who likes to hunt, fish, is conservative, has a good job, a degree, and loves sports... And is tall and handsome and close with his family. A true southern gentleman and sportsman one might even say. Why the hell hadn't I gone for Daniel before?

After our phone call ended, he texted me a few times.

"Btw I had the biggest crush on you in college and you ignored me! Never forget that!!! Lol."

Oh man. Not this again. Why do I somehow end up talking back with the guys who somehow had hidden crushes on me... Every. Damn. Time.

Fuck it.

"If you had such a big crush on me you should've bucked up and asked me to a formal ya ding dong" I responded.

"I would always tell Kenzie to set me up, but you always had another guy or something, and you were a bit outta my league anyway... and still are" he sent with an angel emoji.

"Hahah I don't think I ever had a guy in college but I just loved Beta Beta Beta hahaha" I replied.

I walked downstairs to make a drink. Lynchburg Lemonade was what I was feeling like. I grabbed a lemon off the counter and began to cut it up. My phone lit up, buzzing on the counter.

"Yeah wellllll aware missy," he responded.

This made me laugh out loud as I pulled out the bourbon from the cupboard, which was running low. It reminded me I needed to purchase the new Brother's Bond bourbon that actors Ian Somerhalder and Paul Wesley aka the Salvatore Brothers from *TVD* had created. I picked up my phone to reply to Daniel and to add the bourbon to the grocery list.

"Hahahaha maybe I would've liked Pike... Will never know... Since you didn't ask me to a formal... lol," I responded.

After stirring together the lemonade and adding a shot of bourbon, I squeezed a couple lemon slices on top of the icy liquid and plopped them into my drink. I sank a straw into it and took a sip of the sweet, strong elixir and smiled. *Full of lemons, yet not sour at all.* Well done, Court. I headed back upstairs to continue cleaning my room when another text popped in from Daniel.

"I have some weddings coming up, you a good wedding date???"

I looked up at the pink scrunch dress, which I had just purchased for upcoming weddings and such occasions, hanging on my closet door. I smiled to myself. I sat my drink down and hopped up on my king canopy bed now finally delivered and intact and started jumping on the mattress like a little kid as Morgan Wallen played in the background of my room. Boone flew up on the bed and started jumping on me, likely concerned at my ridiculous behavior. I flopped down on the bed laughing and received a slobbery lick to the face. I opened my phone and replied immediately.

"Do you even have to ask that question?"

Acknowledgements

I want to start by saying this book sprouted from the seed that was just an assignment I submitted to my non-fiction workshop class while in graduate school. Opening up about my dating life was both painful and therapeutic, but I had no idea I would receive the praise I did from that first class and my professor. She was the first person to encourage me, and in our personal review meeting that followed and she told me it was time to take a break from other writing and this was it.

"Write a book?!" I asked.

"Write a book," she insisted.

After that, I set a deadline for myself and began opening Word documents, one for each of the men in my life, and just began writing everything I could think of (memories, moments, texts, anything) until chapters began to form.

Number of tears? Rivers. Number of bottles of wine? I could have opened my own tasting room. Number of times I slammed my computer shut? Only one piece of plastic broke off, so there's that.

I say writing this was like ripping my heart out, smearing the blood on the pages and shoving it back into my chest, and it really does feel like that, but in the most rewarding way. And it all began with that first class.

So, first and foremost, thank you to my Non-Fiction WR 613 class and my professor Megan Marshall. Your critiques, words of encouragement, laughter, and tears are what encouraged me to switch paths and share these stories with the world, and I'm so grateful for that.

My biggest thank you goes to the one who has been through it all with me and never strayed even if I tried to push—God. Although I have audibly cursed the sky after some of these dates and fell asleep crying and talking to you, praying for someone better, I know you've always had my back and still have me on the best path ever. My relationship with you is the most important thing in my life and, although writing a book about my dating life seems odd to some, I know this is the path you had meant for me and that's why there were all the lessons, tears, laughter, and a-ha moments. You never gave me anything I couldn't handle, though you certainly tested my limits. I'm proud to tell my stories in hopes they will help others and encourage online daters that they are not alone in how they feel going through the ups and downs. And that despite all the shit they are worthy of someone who loves them more than they love themselves and someone they feel the same way about. Even though I haven't found that person yet, I know it's going to happen soon and it's all because of you.

To my family who has been with me every step of the way: my mom, my sister, and my dad. Throughout this entire process you've dealt with the ups, downs, mood swings, long periods of me going MIA while writing and editing, and you've always been there to encourage me to keep going, even when I didn't want to. Your patience and encouragement for me to chase my dreams and go back to grad school has meant everything to me, even though I know you weren't thrilled about me moving across the country! Without you, I wouldn't be anything. You remind me that I'm a Schellin and no one works harder or takes more shit than a Schellin, and I'm so proud of that. No one can break me and it's all because of you. I don't know how I could ever repay you for the love and support you've given to me.

To my editor, Rives Kuhar. You are a true wonder. You work through my ADD, keep me on track, and understand my writing through and through and know when it needs to stay authentic or needs to be cleaned up, which I am well aware is no easy feat. I am so thankful you were assigned to me on chance with this project originally in its first draft manuscript stages. After initially working together, I knew there was no one else I'd rather take on the job of editing it prior to the book's big launch. The book has come full circle and reads exactly as it should because of you.

To my author mentor, Suzie Webster, thank you for being with me every step of the way with this process! You were connected to me through a random bar acquaintance, while I was traveling in Charleston, SC, who read a few of my first pages and knew she had to connect me to her "author friend." That said, you didn't have to take me under your wing and help me through this process every step of the way, but you have. I honestly don't think I could have done it without you.

To my best friends, Kassidy and Briana, thank you for being there for me during the darkest times and the brightest times. I wouldn't be sane without the endless hours of phone calls we had with each other, despite being across the country in all different states. We've been friends for over twenty-five years now, and I wouldn't trade those years for anything. Kass, I especially thank you for being such a highlight within these pages. It's been said multiple times by readers that "Everyone should have a Kassidy in their life," and I couldn't agree more.

To my best friend, trusty partner in crime, and German Shepherd, Boone. You can't read because you're a dog, but you've done more than any human could have done for me throughout this process, just by being present. Whether it was sitting at my feet, jumping on me to get me to stop crying, sending me judgey looks when necessary, and even enticing men out of our house during the dating process, you're the realest and my No. 1 protector.

To the first professors to choose my manuscript for their Emerson classes to work on for an entire semester... Thank you Michael Campbell and Nancy Mahoney for selecting my manuscript. When I first submitted a couple chapters to my non-fiction workshop class, I was encouraged I had something. But when not one, but two classes at Emerson College were interested in using my manuscript for their classes, it was solidification that I really was going to have to go through with this. Thank you for giving me that confidence. And especially thank you to Michael, for the countless emails and helping me throughout this process of publishing a book.

To my original editors aka my grad school colleagues turned friends: Nolan and Kirby. Thank you for tackling this piece together and giving it the first major cutdown that it so desperately needed. Five-hundred pages! Yikes!

To Mary Grace and Katherine, thank you for giving me my first incredibly thorough developmental edits and copyediting the book in your class with Michael, and for talking through edits with me on our Zoom calls.

To Nancy's publishing plan class, thank you for the intricate plan you created for me and for really allowing me to see what a publishing plan should look like. Thanks to your help, I was able to head down the path of self-publishing!

To my original ghost readers, Sidney and Emily. Allowing people I actually knew personally to read this manuscript was terrifying. Thank you for understanding me for me, and for giving me the first feedback from a true reader's perspective and telling me when I needed to dig deeper or lay off the ADD.

To my extended family, cousins, aunties and all. Thank you for your support and sharing about the book and all my endeavors online. Thank you especially to my Aunt Michele who stayed up for hours one night in November to help me lay out my plan and dream to go back to grad school. Thank you also to my Aunt Suzy who requested every single assignment I wrote in grad school so she had weekly writing from me to read.

To my Grandma aka my G, thank you for always keeping my spirits up no matter how many terrible dates I went on. Thank you for always keeping me motivated in school and my writing as well and being one of my rocks I could always call when I lived alone in Boston during a pandemic. But mostly, thank you for keeping me in your prayers. I know you've been putting in a good word for me to the big guy upstairs and I love you for that.

To my graduate chair, Steve Yarbrough: As soon as orientation on Zoom at Emerson when you spoke about the importance of reading in your life and your background, I knew I had to get a class with you. Thankfully, I was lucky enough to have two, and have you act as my graduate Thesis chair. Thank you for always believing in me and my work and giving me some incredible words of encouragement in our final chair meeting.

To my fiction professors, Indira Ganesan, Julie Glass, and Jabari Asim. Thank you for pushing me out of my comfort zone and encouraging me to dig deep into my characters. When I came to Emerson I told you I was quite familiar in non-fiction writing based on my journalism career, but what I really wanted to improve on was my fiction writing and storytelling. Thank you for allowing my fiction writing to blossom while still graduating with a fiction emphasis despite taking on this dating memoir project. Especially thank you to Julie, for multiple phone calls and Zoom calls discussing my future in writing and my timeline of publishing and getting this story out there.

To my designer, Alison. Thank you for also taking on my ADD head and working with me on such tight deadlines and helping me navigate the waters of self-publishing. After I had created my own book cover, I wasn't sure what other touches I would need from you, but you really did enhance my cover and the chapters to be exactly what I was hoping for and more.

To all the side characters in this book, thank you for so many memories and the role you've played in my life, whether it was for a night or over years. There are so many of you who have impacted my life in such a positive way, especially my college friends, and I'm happy to have all our memories together.

To the professor who told me I was a "terrible" writer and that my writing was "trash" and that I "shouldn't even be in grad school," thanks for fueling my fire to push even further. I'm sorry you were wrong.

LASTLY, I'D LIKE TO THANK ALL YOU LEMONS.

Crazy as it may be, you are the reason this piece was possible, so thank you. Though many of you have given me some of my most painful memories to relive, all of those moments have helped me grow into the person I am today. I am stronger because of you.

And one final thank you in advance, I suppose. To "the one" who I know is still out there. Thank you in advance for loving me for me, and choosing me even after I air all my dirty laundry to the world. I can't wait to meet you.

ABOUT THE AUTHOR

Courtney Schellin has a boisterous and recognizable voice in both her non-fiction and fiction writing that readers find addictive. From stories of her actual dating life to her fictional characters, Schellin never fails to give readers a good laugh and a hell of a ride in her works.

Schellin formerly worked at ESPN as a writer, where her personality began to attract attention online. She is now best known as "Court Does Sports" where she is considered "the queen of babes, booze and ball games."

Schellin earned a Master of Fine Arts in Creative Writing from Emerson College and Bachelor's degrees in both Journalism and Sport Management from SMU. Schellin was born and raised in Laguna Niguel, California. She loves the outdoors, football, traveling with family, days spent on the water, a good Walla Walla, Washington wine or a cooler of cheap beer. Schellin currently resides in Charleston, South Carolina with her German Shepherd, Boone.

Let's Connect

IF YOU WOULD LIKE TO CONNECT, OR LEARN ABOUT MY NEW BOOK RELEASES – HERE ARE A COUPLE OF WAYS:

Social Media

Courtney Schellin : @courtdoessports
When Love Gives You Lemons : @datinglemons
Instagram – Facebook – Twitter – TikTok

Website & Newsletter

www.whenlovegivesyoulemons.co

CPSIA information can be obtained
at www.ICGtesting.com
Printed in the USA
LVHW021742240423
745193LV00012B/802

9 798987 680926